CONVERSATIONS WITH JESUS?

The Incredible True Story of Mike Phillips—

Alcoholic, Anorexic, Sex Abuse Survivor & Champion of the Poor

GEORGE PHILLIPS

Conversations with Jesus?
The Incredible True Story of Mike Phillips—Alcoholic, Anorexic, Sex Abuse Survivor & Champion of the Poor

For more about this author please visit www.HisGraceisEnough.org

Paperback ISBN: 978-1-966283-18-8
Hardcover ISBN: 978-1-966283-19-5

1. Main category—Books › Religion & Spirituality › Spirituality › Faith
2. Other category—Books › Nonfiction › Self-Help › Abuse
3. Other category—Books › Nonfiction › Biographies & Memoirs › Survival

Published by: AR PRESS
Roger L. Brooks, Publisher
roger@americanrealpublishing.com
americanrealpublishing.com

EXPLANATION OF THE BOOK'S COVER

I chose this photo at Niagara Falls for the cover of the book because it says so much about how I saw Mike and his life. Mike—my much older brother—was larger than life for me when I was a child. In adulthood, he continued to be larger than life—a spiritual giant. The background of Niagara Falls represents power, awe, and mystery of God and life. Enter into the mystery of Mike's life—his suffering, his life of charity and prayer, and his great love for Jesus Christ—his Lord and Savior.

This book is dedicated to Mike Phillips's family, the Irregulars—his friends for life from high school—as well as the clients he served as a social worker and the "hungry people" in the world he sought to assist.

May they all continue to feel Mike's great love, and may we all know God's great love for us.

TABLE OF CONTENTS

FOREWORD

I AM GREATLY HONORED TO HAVE been asked to introduce you to Mike Phillips through the publication of this work. I knew Mike through my pastorship at a St. Paul's Church in Binghamton, New York—the poorest parish in the city.

When I first met Mike, he was seen as eccentric by all. He wore old, worn-out clothing and was known to look in the garbage for cans. He could be seen outside our church with homeless people, the poor, and prostitutes who lived near our parish.

I suspected Mike suffered with serious ailments—which I came to know were alcoholism (which he conquered), anorexia, and sexual abuse.

But as my relationship with Mike grew, it led me to understand that, although he indeed suffered in many ways, he also possessed a deep spirituality and concern for others and practiced an extremely pious prayer life.

The old clothes he wore were part of his devotion to a simple lifestyle. The cans he looked for in the garbage would be recycled—one a time—to gain another five, ten, fifteen. or twenty cents to give to Catholic Relief Services—the charity he donated so much for to help the poor in the world. He knew one dollar could feed a hungry person he would never meet but could help.

The homeless, poor, and prostitutes I associated him with outside our church were people he saw Jesus in and ministered to.

Mike was proof that two contrary things—a life of heroic prayer and virtue contrasted by the torment and severe mental anguish of an eating disorder—can exist at the same time in the same person.

What was necessary in Mike—and in all of us—was that he needed to have experience of conversion to transcend his afflictions into his real self with Christ at his center. At some point—I don't know where or when—his spiritual and pious life took over and led him to a life of sanctity.

Mike's great, steady conversion overshadowed the self-centered practices harming him—especially his eating disorder—and empowered him as a minister of Christ among us.

From wearing his jacket with the large homemade cross on his back—through which he proclaimed who he was dedicated to—to his outreach to street people, his daily devotion to the Eucharist, and his frequent confessions, Mike transformed his own life practices and many of those who met him.

Mike's conversion was not sudden, like a bolt of lightning, but instead, it was like the fanning of a deep ember of coal deep inside him. That ember, fanned by a loving grace of a loving God, grew to a raging fire of compassion, mercy, and piety that touched so many needing hope, charity and love, and their own conversion.

Mike's life-and-faith story is told here in the following pages and hopefully will continue to transform all of us in our need of constant conversion. Young and old need to hear this story of Mike's prayer that the Lord will not only reward him for his openness and deep commitment to Jesus and His grace, but will attain the same results in all of us.

I count my meeting and the honor of knowing and ministering to this holy servant as one of Jesus's greatest gifts to me as a priest. Now, on with our own conversions, with Mike's intercession at God's Holy Throne!

Father Corey Van Kuren is a retired priest of the Roman Catholic Diocese of Syracuse, New York.

I.

WHY A BOOK ON MIKE PHILLIPS?

Why would I write a book about my brother, Mike Phillips, who passed away from an eating disorder fourteen years ago?

Mike was a remarkable person deeply devoted to God, family, and the clients he served as a substance abuse counselor.

A few months after he died in 2010, a remarkable front-page article was written about him in the *Catholic Sun*—a publication from the Diocese of Syracuse—entitled, "His Life is a Lesson."

It detailed Mike's extraordinary life of holiness and the remarkable devotion he had to the world's poorest people. On a social worker's salary in which he never made more than $35,000 a year, he quietly gave an estimated quarter of a million dollars to Catholic Relief Services for its efforts to help hungry people in the world.

Readers of the article were amazed by Mike's life of faith and charity.

Several years after his death, our dad, Deacon George Phillips, found Mike's journal from the 1990s to the early 2000s. As our family read Mike's journal, we entered into the mind, heart, and soul of our loved one's intense struggle with an eating disorder. We saw how he continually called on his Lord and Savior for support and came to know God's incredible love in the face of an intense battle.

But this was not just a journal. As Mike's struggle progressed, the entries begin with God speaking to Mike—or at least how he felt God was speaking to him. The profound words of God lift Mike up in the midst of anxiety, sorrow, and suffering. God continually affirms his unconditional love for Mike.

After a period of deep discernment and prayers—and several incredible experiences at Mike's grave—Dad felt Mike was encouraging him to have these profound writings published.

Dad labored for months, typing with his painfully slow two-finger style, 150 pages of Mike's conversations with Jesus.

In May of 2018, our family published *Conversations with Jesus: How an Alcoholic and Anorexic Found Deep Joy in Christ*, by Michael Phillips.

Dad bought several hundred copies and distributed the books to everyone he knew. It touched many lives.

In 2001—nearly a decade before his death—Mike himself spent hours at an old-fashioned typewriter writing reflections on Mark's Gospel, which he printed and shared with every family member and friend he possibly could. These writings show a man who had tremendous insights into the life, suffering, passion, death, and love of Jesus Christ and made the case that we should all seek to help the poor, as he did through donations to Catholic Relief Services.

Later in 2018 we published these writings as *The Passionate Love of Jesus as Experienced by a Sinner.*

After these two books were published, I felt that there was still something more to do. I really felt we needed a biography on my brother's life that told the story of this remarkable, saintly, spiritual man.

Mike had an incredible impact on my life—greater than anyone besides my wife and parents and now our children—and we had so many personal conversations in which I learned so much from him.

I wrote the book because I wanted to tell the incredible story of Mike's high school friends, known as the "Irregulars," who would go on to have a profound impact on his life for the next thirty years.

I wanted to tell the story of a man who struggled with severe alcoholism but overcame it, and a man who heroically battled a severe eating disorder.

Sexual abuse was Mike's dark, deep, hidden secret that he almost never, ever talked about but was at the heart of his struggles with drinking and his eating disorder.

I wrote this book for the many victims of sexual abuse, for those suffering from eating disorders and substance abuse problems, and for those in jail or prison. These precious souls are all connected with Mike in some way.

I wrote this for my wife, Diana, and our three sons, George, Michael, and Martin, so they could know their remarkable uncle better, and for the rest of our family, which includes many, many cousins.

I wrote this for all of my current and former students to inspire them and share with them the life lessons Mike taught me.

I wrote to raise awareness and support for the cause that Mike believed in so deeply—feeding the world's poor through supporting Catholic Relief Services.

I wanted to tell the story of the most remarkable person I have ever met—the greatest friend and devoted family member you could ever imagine, a tremendously gifted counselor, and a relentless fighter and advocate for the poor and downtrodden who at his core was an incredible spiritual warrior and saintly man.

And I wanted to write this amazing story to give you—the reader—hope. This is the hope that Mike found in Jesus that he shared with me and so many others.

Did an alcoholic, anorexic, sex abuse survivor and champion of the poor really have conversations with Jesus?

I hope you will read the incredible life story of Mike Phillips and see for yourself.

PREFACE—BY MIKE PHILLIPS ON SUFFERING

MIKE WROTE THE FOLLOWING BEAUTIFUL piece on faith and suffering. It very much sets the tone for his remarkable life:

> Suffering is too big a mystery for me to explain, but I can share my experiences. Suffering is a teacher. If I let it, it can cleanse and purify me to see that only love gives meaning to life, only love transcends pain, and only love endures. Pain can make me either more loving or more hateful—it's my choice.
>
> Evil and suffering do exist. God created us in His image, and we have free will: We can choose to love or to hate. Love brings about healing and happiness, and hate brings about evil and suffering. But because we're all connected, any evil affects all of us, and nature too. It's like dropping a single pebble in a pond. The ripples spread across the whole. In the same way, love brings healing and happiness to all of us.
>
> God is always with us. He does not want us to suffer. He sent His Son, Jesus, to show us how to live, to suffer, to love, and to overcome the evil that results from our poor choices. Jesus was crucified and experienced our brokenness and abandonment. He too was an innocent victim, but He never stopped giving, forgiving, and loving. His love overpowered hate, evil, sin and suffering, and He is present with us in our own suffering to show us the mystery of life and suffering and to let us taste God's love and save us from our brokenness.

Many people suffer horrendously, even though they are innocent. I can't claim to have suffered as intensely as many people have, but again, I can share my experiences. Some bad things happened to me as a child. At times my life was a nightmare, and I felt like garbage. As I grew up, I sought relief in alcohol, and in the long run it made the nightmare worse. And when, one day, I was too sick to go on, I broke down, devastated, and my heart became open to God and His healing love.

It wasn't until I was in my twenties that I was able to talk about my experiences. I was blessed to have a loving family and a priest to listen and support me. I'm wounded and scarred now, but it's ok. I have found that suffering helps me let go of my unhealthy attachments and open myself to what is perfect and meaningful: God, His love, and the love of others, especially when that love isn't easy. My suffering and that of others breaks my heart open to meet my God. Only through His grace am I not destroyed by evil, and I am thankful for the hard times that have led me to be more loving and loved. In my brokenness, God can fill me with Himself. I'm truly happy and blessed by Him. May He bless us all.

II.

HORNELL: WHERE THE ERIE NEVER SLEPT

MICHAEL JOSEPH PHILLIPS WAS BORN at 8:27 p.m. on January 9, 1962, to George and Mary Lou Phillips at St. James Mercy Hospital in Hornell, New York—a small town in Upstate New York south of Rochester.

Mike—as he would be called by everyone except his mother, who always called him Michael—weighed only five pounds and fifteen ounces and was nineteen inches long. At the time of his birth, he was listed as having brown hair and blue eyes.

As an adult he had incredible hazel green eyes that had a unique sparkle of brightness and shine. His amazing eyes were more green than brown. Those who were blessed to see Mike's eyes will never forget them.

Mike was baptized into the Christian faith that would become the center of his life on February 11, 1962, at St. Ann's Roman Catholic Church on Elm Street in Hornell, about four blocks west of the house where our dad grew up in, and four blocks east of the house our mom grew up in.

When Mike was born, Dad was finishing his master's degree in ceramic engineering from Alfred University, which was about ten miles from Hornell. In December of 1963, Dad would take a job at IBM in Endicott, 114 miles from Hornell, near Binghamton.

Even though Mike only lived in Hornell a short time, the town and the many relatives he had there would be a major part of his life. In a given year he would visit Hornell for Thanksgiving, Christmas, and Easter, and throughout the year for family gatherings.

Hornell was a train town that centered around the Erie Railroad. Much of our family worked on the railroad; a slogan for the town was "Where the Erie never slept."

Dad always claimed that pie à la mode was invented in Hornell. I heard him tell the story a hundred times: "A guy was at a restaurant in Hornell and the waitress asked him if he wanted pie or ice cream for dessert. He said that he was running late for a train and wondered if she could throw the ice cream on top of the pie."

For Mike, Hornell was a quaint, beautiful, small town full of extended family who were extremely important him. He often remarked that Hornell was Bedford Falls from the famous Christmas movie *It's a Wonderful Life.* The spirit of Hornell and our family there were Mike's roots and at the heart of who he was on so many levels.

Our dad—George Charles Phillips Jr.—was born to George Charles Phillips Sr. and Bernadine Phillips in Hornell in 1937. Dad was the fifth of nine children, the only member of his family who was left-handed and the only one with curly hair. He used to say he didn't know why he was left-handed, but he thought he had curly hair because his mother had a permanent that didn't take on the night before he was born.

Mike was the only sibling in our family who was left-handed and had at least wavy hair with some curls that fit well with the long hair styles in the 1970s, when he was a teenager.

Our Grandpa Phillips was born in 1899 on our family farm between Franklinville and Farmersville, about an hour south of Buffalo, to a family of Irish ancestry. A family mystery remains if we also have the blood of Seneca Indians in the region. Grandpa's father died when he was an infant, and he didn't get along with his stepfather. His Mother ended up running a boarding house to make ends meet.

Somewhere between the age of twelve and fourteen, Grandpa Phillips left home and went to work on his own, working odd jobs in the region. Unfortunately, he cut part of his thumb off working on a roof and survived a flu epidemic, but his hair turned white.

At the age of thirty, while working on the Erie Railroad, he met and married Bernadine Green, who was a decade younger than he was. In the early 1940s, they saved enough to buy a beautiful, old Victorian red brick house on Elm Street.

This house would be the center of so many family gatherings for Mike throughout his childhood and young adulthood.

Grandpa Phillips died in 1968, so Mike's relationship with him was limited, but he made his mark on this world.

During World War II there were only four or five days that Grandpa didn't work in the railroad yard—including Christmas, Thanksgiving, and Easter.

Grandpa was a leader in his labor union, the Brotherhood of Railroad Trainmen. During the Korean War, Grandpa and his union were planning a strike to get Saturdays off, but President Harry Truman seized the railroads to stop them. Grandpa never forgave President Truman.

Railroad workers and their families were allowed to ride passenger trains for free. A major treat for the family occurred once a year when the entire family would hope on a train in the middle of night and arrive in the morning in New York City, where they would spend the day.

Can you imagine nine children from small-town Hornell running around New York City for a day? One year they apparently lost Uncle Jimmy on the subway—but thankfully they found him at the next stop.

When our dad's youngest sister, Margie, was born, Grandpa was fifty years old. In the hospital, he knelt down by her crib and prayed that God would help him live long enough to see her grow up.

God answered his prayer. He lived to see Margie make it to college.

Grandpa's major vice was drinking. He was a binge drinker who would go months without drinking but then fall off the wagon and get incredibly drunk for days. If Grandpa didn't show up as expected, they had to go find him in bars.

There is a genetic component to alcoholism, and unfortunately Grandpa Phillips, as well as both grandparents on our mom's side of the family, passed this trait on to Mike.

Near the end of his life Grandpa finally quit drinking for good. He loved reading about the lives of the saints of the Catholic Church.

After Grandpa Phillips died in 1968, Mike—then only six years old—asked our parents if he could go stay with Grandma Phillips so she wouldn't feel lonely.

What a life my Grandma Bernadine Phillips lived, raising nine children and having thirty-two grandchildren.

Grandma Bernadine's family was German, and I have my Great-Great-Grandfather Jacob Brill's footlocker from the German army. We believe Jacob Brill was Jewish.

Grandma Bernadine's immediate family were devout Roman Catholics, and she had two close cousins who were priests—Father Jack Brill and Father Jack Klentjes.

Grandma Bernadine was short—barely five feet tall, it seemed—and plump, soft-spoken, kind, and loving. She had a beautiful portrait of Jesus in the center of her living room, and her faith was the center of her life. She did an incredible job raising nine children.

The family would pray a nightly rosary—especially in May and October, when Catholics honored Mary. Our Aunts Ann and Mary said that when they were teenagers and boys or friends would call, they would not be allowed to answer the phone during the rosary. There were no answer machines or caller ID. When boys called and they couldn't answer, it was a major sacrifice.

My brother Mike was very close to Grandma, who lived until 1993. She died on April 23—ironically on the feast of St. George.

There was one tragic, deep, dark, horrible secret to Dad's family. An uncle to Dad and his siblings was a serial sex abuser who abused many children in the family over the course of many years.

The remarkable thing about Dad and each of his siblings—whether they were abused or not—was that they each held on to their faith.

I mention this terrible story, as it was known to Mike and shaped him as an adult when he had to confront his own sexual abuse.

Our mom's family story was a mix of hardship and love, as well. She was born on November 17, 1936, to Francis and Ann Gaffney in Wayland, New York, a few miles north of Hornell. Her sister Ellen had been born in 1935, and her sister Caroline had been born in 1933.

Wayland was my mom's mother's family's hometown. Her grandfather worked for the famous Gunlocke furniture company in Wayland and was an extremely talented artist.

Francis and Ann moved to Queens for Grandpa Gaffney's job with the New York State Highway Department.

At one point they lived in Jackson Heights and attended Saint Teresa the Little Flower Church—a saint my wife Diana and I would become very fond of.

Mom had a very turbulent home life that she almost never talked about. Most stories I heard were from others. Unfortunately, her father had a terrible drinking problem and was physically abusive to her mother, Ann.

Ann would run away from home when my mom was only five years old. For a long time Mom went to the mailbox with hope that her mother might have written her a note—but no note ever came. Mom wouldn't hear from her mother for more than fifteen years.

Her father's drinking problem continued, and Mom and her sisters were sent to live and be raised by Grandpa Gaffney's sister Gertrude —or Aunt Gert, as Mom called her—in Hornell. Aunt Gert would essentially become our mother's mom and the person who raised her.

Aunt Gert lived with her sister and brother-in-law, Eldeana and Roy DeVinney, in a beautiful house on Union Street, right next to Hornell High School. Eldeana and Roy had two children, Joe and John. They were a few years older than our mom's oldest sister Caroline, and they were like older brothers to Mom and her sisters. They both served in World War II and landed jobs with the State Highway Department after the war.

Aunt Gert ran a beauty shop out of her home. She worked extremely hard. Her feet hurt from her long hours of cutting hair, and Mom actually gave her foot massages. Aunt Gert died in 1979, when Mike was about seventeen years old. Mike grew up seeing our mom's tremendous love for and loyalty to Aunt Gert.

I found a beautiful note a few years ago that a friend wrote to Aunt Gert. The friend commended Gert for doing a tremendous job raising three girls who were not her own. It brought tears to my eyes to think of this woman's great love for my mom and her sisters.

Grandpa Francis Gaffney retired to Hornell to be with family and passed away in 1976. Grandma Ann Gaffney, who also had a major drinking problem, married again in Philadelphia. My mom never gave up on her mother and helped get her into a nursing home when her mental and physical health deteriorated, but they were never close. Grandma Gaffney died in 1986.

Our mom stayed in touch with her mother's sister, Minion Robinson of Wayland, and her daughter, Marsha, through the years.

Dad attended St. Ann's school and met our mom in third grade when she moved to Hornell to live with Aunt Gert.

In eighth grade a big school dance was coming up. Mom had a crush on my dad's best friend, Tommy Glenn, but he was going with another girl to the dance. Mom invited my dad in hope of making Tom jealous.

Thankfully, Mom and Dad ended up hitting it off at the dance. They went to dances, dated throughout high school, and married in 1960 when they were both twenty-three years old.

A key decision for Dad came when he was nineteen. Grandpa Phillips set him up with a good job on the Erie Railroad as a fireman. Dad had a solid wage he could use to raise a family.

After she graduated high school with Dad, Mom took a job in the night shift for the Erie Railroad, typing inventory on trains.

One night during a long train ride, Dad saw an older worker dozing off to sleep across from him in the railroad car. Dad thought if he stayed with Erie Railroad, he'd have a pretty good job, but twenty years later he'd still be doing the same job as the man across from him.

Encouraged by Mom, Dad took a risk and left his job to go to nearby Alfred University to study ceramic engineering—a state-funded portion of this private university that was practically free in those days.

Mom and Dad were married on August 20, 1960, at St. Ann's Church, with Grandma Bernadine's cousins, Father Brill and Father Kleintjeis, officiating. Mom and Dad got to ride around town in her cousin Joe DeVinney's 1960 Mercury Parkland convertible—still owned by the family today.

On their honeymoon they would travel to Canada and New England. They got to see Dad's favorite baseball player, Boston Red Sox legend Ted Williams, play in his last season and hit a home run in one of his final games.

When Mike was born in January of 1962. Mom would quit her job on the Erie while Dad was in graduate school.

They lived in an apartment on Collier Street next door to Dad's uncle Bobby Green and his wife Doris.

Doris and Bobby had only one daughter, Patty, who had a heart defect. Despite the best medical care possible at the time and tremendous love and care from her parents, Patty died in a hospital, in an oxygen box, with her father Bobby watching her when she was only seven years old.

Aunt Doris became one of my mom's best friends and would care for Mike and our family, like another grandmother. Throughout the year she would hand-knit sweaters to give to Mike and our brothers and then eventually to me every year at Christmas.

Bobby died in the 1970s, leaving Doris a widow at a young age who had also lost her only child.

Mike and Doris had a very special relationship through the years. I have very fond memories of them together. They loved to talk and joke and smoke cigarettes—one of Mike's only vices—when Mike was older.

Doris had so much wit and humor. She was a tough but loving New Jersey girl whose family moved to Hornell when she was a child. Unfortunately, Doris developed lung cancer and passed away in 2003.

Grandma Bernadine, Aunt Gert, and Aunt Doris were three very important figures in Mike's life. In these three courageous women he would see faith, suffering, hope, and great love.

In July of 1963, our brother Rob was born. Mom and Dad moved the family to Endicott, New York, for my dad's job at IBM in December of 1963. In September of 1965 our brother Chris was born.

Trips to Hornell would center around visits to Grandma Bernadine's house, where Dad's side of the family would converge.

Mike loved our aunts, uncles, and cousins. They were very special to him.

Dad's oldest brother, Uncle Tommy, and his wife, Aunt Sally, had eight children—Gennie, John, Mimi, Martha, Patty, Eileen, Danny, and Brian. They lived in Syracuse.

The oldest girl was Aunt Ann who married Tommy Rohan and had five children—Mark, Timmy, Ed, Michelle, and Tommy. They lived in Hornell.

The second oldest girl was Aunt Mary, who married Buddy Kelleher had six children—Mary Margaret, Elizabeth, Katie, Billy, and twins Pat and Pam. They lived around the corner from Grandma in Hornell.

The second oldest boy was Uncle Jimmy, who married Carolyn Moran—one of Mom's closest friends—and had two children, Sara and Greg. They lived in Rochester. Carolyn died young of a liver issue. Jimmy eventually married a devout Christian woman named Nancy whom he would share many years with.

Next came Mom and Dad with their four boys.

Dad's third oldest sister, Sara, moved to California and had a girl, Maria, and four boys—twins Jimmy and Tommy Brosseau—and David and Norman.

Dad's next sister, Sue, was a Catholic nun who served as a schoolteacher for years. She eventually left the religious life to marry Darwin Anderson and live in California before returning to Hornell. Sue has been instrumental in keeping the family together through family reunions and sharing the family history. She is a leader at Hornell's old St. Ann's

Church—now Our Lady of the Valley Parish—where our family grew up.

Dad's youngest brother, my Uncle Mike, who would be my brother's namesake and godfather, lived much of his life in California and worked on the Mars Rover for the Space Program before returning to Hornell.

Dad's baby sister was Aunt Margie. She and her husband Kirby Noye had two children—Chris and Kimberly. They lived in Rochester.

Grandma's sister Madeleine and her husband Harry Kohler, along with their children—Barbara and her husband John, Roberta and her husband Don, and Billy—and their grandchildren have always been a big part of our family.

Uncle Harry was an amazingly talented photographer who served as a guard in the United States Army in the famous Nuremberg Trials of Nazi War Criminals.

My grandma had two other sisters who we visited while in Hornell. Mary Elizabeth—or Aunt Meb, as she was called—was single and a huge Buffalo Bills fan. Margie married a kind widower named Ray in her later years.

So many of these cousins were around Mike's age, so imagine the fun they had at gatherings at Grandma Bernadine's house.

Mike had a very a special connection to Uncle Tommy's daughter, Patty Phillips, who was born on the very same day as Mike—January 9, 1962.

When Mike got older—probably around the age of thirty—he began a great long-distance friendship with our cousin Jimmy Brosseau in California.

Jimmy was a Los Angeles police officer for many years until a motorcycle accident led to horrible back problems and disability.

Mike and Jimmy would talk about once a month on the phone. Like Mike, Jimmy was passionate about his faith and loved being connected with family on the East Coast.

Family visits to Hornell also focused on visits with Mom's family and the beautiful house of Uncle Roy, Aunt Eldeana, and Aunt Gert on Union Street. Unfortunately, their house was torn down to make way for a highway into town. The loss of the house was just devastating, and they moved around the corner to Adsit Street.

Mom's cousin Joe married and moved to his wife Helen Marie's family home in nearby Canaserega, where they raised two children, David and Michelle. John continued to live with his parents, Roy and Eldeana, Aunt Gert, and eventually Gert's other sister, Aunt Edna.

The Gaffney family was full of Irish wit and humor. Aunt Gert never did get over the heartbreak of having my mom leave Hornell. She would always say to my dad, "George, do you ever think you will move back to Hornell?"

Mike also had a great relationship with Mom's sister Caroline and her husband Bob Burdette, who lived in North Hornell with their daughter Karen. Their family grew to include Karen's husband Bill and their son Brian. They had a beautiful house that personified Bob's love for hunting, fishing, and the outdoors, where we spent many great times.

We have been very close to Aunt Ellen's family—Mike's godmother. Aunt Ellen became a nurse and married Hank Ragiel, an architect. They settled in Chester, New Jersey, and had three children—Dana, who was Mike's age, Steve, who was Rob's age, and Sean, who is closer in age to me. Mike enjoyed many family visits to New Jersey to see the Ragiels, the Ragiel family visits to our town, and joint visits with our family and the Ragiels to Hornell.

Hornell and extended family would be a huge part of Mike's life and upbringing, but his life would continue in a valley of opportunity to the east.

III.

A VALLEY OF OPPORTUNITY AND THE BIRTHPLACE OF IBM

MIKE'S FIRST HOME IN ENDICOTT would be an apartment near downtown West Endicott. The family would live there for two years before moving to 311 Norton Avenue in Endwell.

A great description of the area Mike would grow up in came on September 12, 1984, in a speech my mom took me and my best friend Tom Koch to by President Ronald Reagan at Union-Endicott High School in front of an estimated 30,000 people.

Locals call it his "Which Way E.J.? Speech."

President Reagan laid out the story of how immigrants came to a "Valley of Opportunity" to work at the Endicott Johnson—or EJ—shoe company. The only English they knew when they reached America's shores was "Which Way E.J.?"

The success of EJ—which at one point was the largest manufacturer of shoes in the world—paved the way for Thomas Watson to found IBM in Endicott, which brought the world into the computer age.

Reagan's speech was written by Peter Robinson, who graduated from nearby Vestal High School and went on to write Reagan's famous "Tear Down that Wall" speech.

This "Valley of Opportunity" is where Mike grew up. He lived fairly close to Highland Park, where he would swim as a child and ride the carousel that George F. Johnson—the rags-to-riches EJ owner—had donated. Many of his friends and classmates would live in so-called EJ homes that Johnson had built at cost for his employees.

Mike's dad and so many of his friends and classmates' parents were IBMers. Mike would enjoy swimming and basketball at the nearby IBM Country Club, where our father would be in bowling and golf leagues.

The move from Hornell for Mom and Dad was very difficult, and they missed their family immensely. They poured their lives into the Church—Christ the King in Endwell, a few blocks from their new home.

Christ the King Church would become a central part of their lives—and Mike's life—for many years. Mike would attend Christ the King School and be an altar server at Christ the King Church, where Mom and Dad would serve as Sunday schoolteachers, lectors, Eucharistic ministers, on the Parish Council, on the Lenten Fish Dinner Committee, and on virtually every other organization in this small but dynamic church.

Father Fries, the priest during most of Mike's time at Christ the King, was a saintly man. As a young priest he served as a military chaplain who was on the beach on D-Day.

Father Fries was a model of humility and holiness, and he was critical in Mike's spiritual development.

From the age of thirty onward Dad began praying the rosary every day, eventually getting to the point where he prayed all four sets of mysteries—the Joyful, Sorrowful, and Glorious Mysteries, and eventually the Luminous Mysteries when they were added by Pope John Paul II.

After surgery for a leg aneurysm at the age of forty, Dad quit smoking. He also began walking a great distance each day—a mile to Christ the King for daily Mass, then two miles to his job at IBM, and finally two miles home after work.

Dad would work for twenty-nine years at IBM, where he was a quintessential company man. He was the only ceramic engineer in the plant, taught many classes in ceramics to co-workers, and even wrote a book titled *A Concise Introduction to Ceramics* in 1992.

Dad traveled about every month or so for conferences and to meet with IBM vendors—most frequently to Boulder, Colorado, with the Coors brewing company, which supplied IBM ceramics. Dad took an early retirement from IBM at age 55 and became a Catholic deacon a few years later, as well as a physics teacher at Seton Catholic Central.

Dad coached all his kids, including Mike, in youth baseball and basketball. In a setting where parents and coaches could get way out of hand, he was always a calming, positive influence who tried to make sure every kid played and had a positive experience.

Besides the many church activities Mom shared with Dad, she also was heavily involved with the Ladies Guild, the Church Choir, and funeral luncheons. Mom loved Christ the King Church and her many friends there.

Besides church, Mom's major volunteer project for years was with the Ladies of Charities nearly-new shop. People would donate old clothes and the shop would prepare them for families in need in the area.

Mom loved going to our games. I was so much younger than my brothers, so I wasn't around for or don't remember many of their games, but I never remember Mom or Dad missing one.

Mom loved cooking, and she was a great cook. Her chocolate chip cookies are still legendary for the Norton Avenue crowd. She loved gardening and always had beautiful flower beds planted around the yard. And she loved her friends. "The Morning Mass Group" was a group of a half dozen friends who went to Mass together every morning and then out to breakfast.

Mom suffered so much with health ailments throughout her life. In 1969, at the age of thirty-two, when Mike was only seven years old, she contracted breast cancer.

An expected minor surgery turned into a major eight-hour fight for her life when a massive tumor was uncovered and her breast and lymph node were moved.

The cancer never returned, but she developed heart disease at the age of fifty and osteoporosis at the age of sixty—most likely from the side effects of cancer treatments.

Mom and Dad were remarkable Christian people and tremendous role models for Mike. I remember them avoiding the sin of gossip. Mom would mention how harmful this could be. They really treated everyone they met like gold. They had sensitive hearts for those in need and had great wit and senses of humor. Their faith, their character, and their charisma all wore off on Mike.

Everyone I've ever met who knew Mom and Dad loved them and their warm personalities, and everyone loved Mike.

Mike said the most important thing he ever learned in life was from Mom. She said, "Michael, the purpose of life is to know, love, and serve God, and to experience some happiness in this life but eternal happiness in the next."

The phrase was the foundation of the Baltimore Catechism, which she had learned as a girl at St. Ann's Catholic school.

Mom came to know God through her own suffering and perseverance, and to share God with everyone she knew through a life of love and charity for others.

She never complained about her childhood, her health, or the tremendous suffering she endured.

Mike would be the same. They were both happy warriors as they battled debilitating ailments—Mom's osteoporosis and heart disease, and eventually Mike's eating disorder.

The closest brother in age to Mike was Rob, who was born less than a year and half after Mike. Mike and Rob would do everything together and have the same friends.

They were extremely close growing up, but thy had different personalities, likes, and interests. Rob loved sports, followed his favorite college, and would go on to be a high school sports star.

Mike would play sports throughout his youth with his brothers and their friends, but he was not as talented athletically.

Rob would marry his high school sweetheart Kathy Kiluk, and they would have five children—Heather, Jessica, Robbie, Kevin and Rachel. He began work at the local GE plant in manufacturing and impressively worked his way up to be an executive at GE and several other companies, including M&T Bank, where he is today.

Mike would be close with Rob's oldest children, Heather and Jessica, as the Phillips and Kiluk families gathered together for barbecues and birthday parties throughout the year for many years.

Kathy's family was a part of our family for many years. Her parents were Ed and Florence Kiluk—very personable, easygoing folks who loved to joke and tell stories.

Kathy's oldest brother Ed was one year older than Mike and played football with him. Ed had a fine career as a trooper with the New York State Police before passing away from cancer caused by working with toxins when he'd volunteered to help clean up debris from the World Trade Center.

Kathy's second oldest brother Mike was one year younger than our brother Chris and played football with him. He and his wife, Jennifer Brown Kiluk, were fixtures at our family events.

Kathy also had a sister, Debbie, and twin siblings Brian and Jenny, who were two years behind me in school. We played hours of hide and seek, tag, and other kids' games at family gatherings, along with Heather and Jessica, who were only a few years younger than we were.

Mike was Jessica's godfather. He was my godfather, and he was the godfather for all four of his best friend Jim Flint's children.

Mike always made every effort to be present at these many great family events with Rob's family and the Kiluks through the years. When his eating disorder progressed, it was always a little awkward for him, because he didn't each much but he loved being around family.

Rob and Kathy moved to North Carolina in 1994, a short time after their sons Robbie and Kevin were born. Eventually the family moved to Sandy Hook, Connecticut, where their youngest child Rachel was born.

Rob's family knew many of the victims of the Sandy Hook school shooting, which happened two years after Mike passed away.

After Rob moved from our town, Mike's time to be with Rob and his family was more limited to holidays and trips a few times a year, but he always remained extremely devoted to his brother and his brother's family.

Mike was very joyful and excited whenever Rob and his family were coming to town. He'd say, "I can't wait to see them," and he'd even do a countdown. "Only a few more days until they come" was a favorite phrase.

Family meant so incredibly much to Mike. It is hard to put into words how much he loved Mom, Dad, and each of his brothers. When I was older and moved away from home for college and work in Washington, he had the same attitude about my homecomings.

Chris was four years behind Mike but tagged along with him and Rob throughout his childhood. In many ways Chris was very much like Rob in childhood—passionate about sports and a high school sports star.

Chris's career developed in similar fashion to Mike's. He became a counselor for troubled youth at Catholic Charities in the Binghamton area before becoming a counselor for at-risk youth at Johnson City High School. He eventually moved out West to serve impoverished children in Native American schools.

Mike and Chris shared their passion for serving suffering people for many years, and they became extremely close. In later years, Chris was the family member Mike saw the most and spoke to on a daily basis, in addition to our mom and dad.

I was born fourteen years after Mike. Most of the stories I will recount about him until he was in his twenties were told to me by him, our family, and his friends.

I have only a few memories of Mike in high school and barely remember living in the same house with him. In so many ways Mike was more like an uncle or father figure than a brother to me because our age gap was so great.

As a child Mike was always so kind and thoughtful toward me. From my teenage years on, Mike would have an extraordinary impact on my life.

In Mike's obituary it states that he is survived by his best friends Julie McWright, Jim Flint, and Vinnie Palmeri. His friendships with each were truly amazing and inspiring, along with his friendship with Wayne Tremark. Mike would not meet Jim and Wayne until high school.

Vinnie grew up a few houses up the street from Mike but was in Rob's class. Throughout his adult life, Mike would frequently say, "Vinnie is like a brother." Vinnie remained in town most of his life, working as an insurance adjuster. He and Mike would remain great friends and see each other frequently on weekends during Mike's visits to my parents' house.

Mike's friendship with Julie, whose maiden name was Trasolini and who lived two houses down the street from us, and his friendship with Jim Flint, whom Mike would meet during his junior year in high school, were just remarkable and will be major focuses of this book.

When I think of friendship, I think of a college graduation speech I saw on C-Span by the great historian Stephen F. Ambrose in which he focused on the amazing friendship between Merriweather Lewis and William Clark—explorers who risked their lives to explore the American West.

Ambrose said that while family is extremely important, you don't choose your family—you are born into it. Even in marriage, after spouses choose each other, they are sworn to be together.

Friends are people you choose freely. Many people have great friendships in their early childhood years and in high school that fade with time.

This was not the case with Mike and his friendships with Julie, Jim, Vinnie, and Wayne. These amazing friendships were always at the center of his heart.

Mike continually chose to be their friends, no matter at what point they were in the journey of life, and they chose to be his.

I have given a great deal of information on Mike's roots in Hornell and Endwell. Now it is time to tell the rest of his story.

IV.

NORTON AVENUE AND CHRIST THE KING

NO MATTER WHERE HIS LIFE took him, Mom and Dad's house at 311 Norton Avenue would always be home for Mike, and in so many ways his friends.

Mom and Dad made the most of a modest-sized house—turning the garage into a second living room and building a third bedroom upstairs. There was a tiny room downstairs with a small bathroom attached that had been a beauty parlor—ironically just like the house Mom grew up in with Aunt Gert.

They also built a large two-car garage in the backyard with a nice basketball court that first my brothers and then I enjoyed with our friends for many years.

It was a beautiful place for Mike to grow up in.

Norton Avenue was a special place—a booming neighborhood with young families in a booming IBM town that represented the promise of America in the 1960s and 70s.

Next door were the Serkos, who had four children. Two houses up from them were the Kochs, who had nine children. Across the street and slightly up from the Kochs were the Palmeris—Vinnie's family—with four children.

Directly across the street were the Fertigs, who had four older children. Florence Fertig, their mother, was our mom's best friend. Mike would have a special relationship with Mrs. Fertig when she was a widow later in life.

Two houses up from the Fertigs were the Walkers, with their six children.

And, as mentioned, two houses down the street were the Trasolinis, with four children, including Julie, Mike's best friend.

Henry and Mary Trasolini, Julie's parents, were high school sweethearts who moved from the Italian section of Binghamton to Endwell.

Looking at old pictures and growing up years after my brothers, the other thing I find odd about the 1960s and 1970s, besides the long hair styles, was the color of the houses. Our next-door neighbors, the Boardmans, had a pink house and were eventually replaced by our long-time neighbors, the Perricones. The Dundas, four houses down, had a burgundy-colored house. At one point our house was bright green, with bright yellow and brown houses surrounding us.

The Grahams, the Laughlands, the Boczulaks, the Kings, the McCoys, the Nelsons, the Hromeks, the Flukes, the Nortons and the Saddlemires are other great families who still occupy homes in our neighborhood from when Mike grew up. Families we lost in recent years include the Olfields, the Burkles, and Mrs. Mildred Scheider.

My brother Rob said that living on Norton Avenue was like an ideal, storybook childhood. There were tons of kids playing everywhere, running in and out of each other's houses with the insatiable desire to play, play, and play.

Mike's close group of friends who spent hours and hours playing at our house were Rob, Vinnie, and Karl Martin Koch III—the Kochs' seventh child, who had five older sisters.

It was often said that Chip and Vinnie—who were in the same grade as Rob and one year behind Mike—grew up at our house.

Chip was very quiet, but very smart. The group would be sitting around looking at baseball cards, and Chip was able to remember the exact statistics from the card. A few minutes after looking at cards, he would be able to say, "George Brett batted .308 in 1975."

The group gave Chip an additional paradoxical nickname, "The Dummy." He claimed he only ate peanut butter and jelly sandwiches for lunch.

The 1960s and 1970s were noted for men having long hair. Vinnie had a ton of dark, thick hair and got the paradoxical nickname "Skinhead," which later morphed into "Skirny."

Chris—three years behind Rob, Chip, and Vinnie in school and four years behind Mike—was also part of the tight-knit group, always trying to keep up with the older boys. The tough, scrappy younger brother was an incredible athlete but also very thin, causing him to get the nickname "Stix."

Also mainstays at our house were Julie Trasolini and her other best friend, Marge Walker, from across the street. As a child Julie transformed from a tomboy in the middle of all those boys at our house into a prom queen in high school.

Since she didn't have daughters, Mom had a special connection with Julie and liked having her around.

At some point Mike and Julie both gave each other the nickname "Dude." "Hey Dude, what's up?" Mike would say. Julie could respond, "Not much. How about you, Dude?"

Mike and Julie shared so much, spent so much time together, and did so much together that they were like a brother and sister.

Mike said that he will never forget when he and Julie were very young and innocent, Julie's older brother Nick told them about the birds and the bees. Mike and Julie thought Nick had made the story up and they laughed hysterically.

Mike, Rob, Chip, Skinhead, and Stix, with Julie and Marge tagging along and mixing it up with the boys, was the scene that played out day after day on Norton Avenue.

Julie's sister Mary Jo was just a few years younger. She wound up living on Norton Avenue and raising two great children—Gabe and Julie Ann Slavik, with her husband Gabe Slavik. She is also a great family friend and is always a constant reminder of Julie for our family.

There were many trips to S&M—Sam and Mary's—the little corner store on Norton and Watson—to buy ice cream and snacks. It is still run today by Sam and Mary's incredible son, Robbie Scarapicchia.

Hundreds of Mom's legendary chocolate chip cookies were eaten by the group at our house.

The gang played basketball and Wiffle ball in our backyard and threw the football around in the street when cars were not coming. They went swimming at Highland Park and the IBM Country Club in the summer and sleigh riding at great nearby hills in Highland Park and Maine Endwell High School.

One day during a water fight, Rob was trying to drop a bucket of water on Julie and Marge from our second-story bathroom into the backyard and accidentally knocked the window out of the bathroom.

The glass window and metal frame landed on Marge's head, hitting her so hard that Julie thought she was dead.

Thankfully, a few seconds later, Marge managed to get up. She was a little woozy, but she walked away—alive.

Christ the King parish school did not have kindergarten, so Mike attended the Hooper School on the George F. Johnson Highway, less than a mile from his house. Mom said he was very timid and it was a rough time.

In first grade, Mike began his long tenure at Christ the King School, but his Norton Avenue friends actually went to different schools, so his only friend would be his brother Rob in the class behind him. Mike was shy and would be a frequent target of bullying for years.

Mike liked learning and obtained solid grades. Mom said as he got older Mike would read each volume of the encyclopedias we had in our home—always wanting to learn more.

While at Christ the King School, Mike would be frequently called out of class with Rob to serve funerals at the church.

When Mike was five or six years old, Dad took him to pray the Stations of the Cross at Christ the King—a frequent devotion during Friday's Lent for Catholics—and asked Mike what station he liked best.

Mike picked the fourth station, when Jesus met his Mother. He said it must have been very sad for Jesus and his Mother at that moment.

Dad coached Mike and my brothers in sports and helped to found EYO, the Endwell Youth Organization, as an alternative to Little League.

Little League was very competitive. Kids were cut, and some who made teams wound up sitting on the bench. Mike was timid and not a great baseball player. EYO was a better league for him.

Dad said Mike had a kind heart for his teammates. There was a chubby kid on their team who wasn't very good and had trouble paying attention. Mike looked out for him and tried to keep him occupied by giving him candies and treats in the dugout between innings.

When my brothers became teenagers, they actually invented their own game called "Slap Ball."

In those days wooden bats were used. My brothers would take bats that broke and shave them off, so they had one flat side. "Slap Ball" was like baseball with these flat bats, where they hit tennis balls instead of baseballs.

Their field was the parking lot of Endwell Intermediate Elementary School, at the end of Norton Avenue on Country Club Road.

Mike, Rob, Chip, Vinnie, and Chris called their team the Royals, and they played against a group of public-school kids who called themselves the Yankees.

Even though he wasn't a great player for traditional baseball, Mike really enjoyed and excelled at these "Slap Ball" games. He was really fast, so he could slap the ball and run out hits.

Mike had a paper route job in his teenage years, covering an apartment complex on Watson Boulevard. In those days, paper boys would have to go door-to-door collecting from their customers and only made money when they collected all the bills.

People often got behind on their bills and then moved out of their apartments—sticking Mike for the bill. Mike was often barely breaking even or even losing money on the route.

Eighth grade would be an important year for Mike and a time of change.

Mike thought he would finish his elementary school years at Christ the King, but the Sisters of Saint Joseph were cutting back and would no longer offer eighth grade.

Mike would have to attend St. Ambrose School in downtown Endicott for eighth grade.

It was at St. Ambrose that Mike would meet Sister Michelle Bennett, a religion teacher who would dramatically change his life.

Sister Michelle was teaching Mike's class shortly after she was in a car accident. Recovery from the accident was exhausting, and she didn't have the energy to run a traditional lecture style class.

She decided to teach students to meditate in class. Students would reflect upon the life of Jesus and then meditate as if they were actually with Jesus and Jesus was talking to them directly.

These meditations had a profound impact on Mike.

On the last day of school, Mike—then just fourteen years old—came up to Sister Michelle after class. He thanked her for doing the meditations and said they had a profound impact on his relationship with Jesus.

One more special event happened for our family during Mike's eighth grade year: I was born.

It was unclear if my mom would ever be able to have children again after her bout with breast cancer. I was a miracle baby. Mike became my godfather, and my cousin Dana my godmother.

Julie wanted to be the first one to hold me when I got home from the hospital. Mike was so proud and so happy to arrange this for her at our house.

Mike prepared for high school in what would be an extremely difficult year for him and the Catholic school community.

A decision had been made to merge Seton Catholic High School in Endicott—which Mike was scheduled to attend—with Catholic Central High School in Binghamton.

They two schools and their sports teams—the Seton Royals and the Catholic Central Crusaders—were archrivals.

The new merged school would be on the Catholic Central campus in Binghamton.

Mike would spend his next four years of high school on the west side of Binghamton on 70 Seminary Avenue—the home of the new Seton Catholic Central Saints.

V.

THE IRREGULARS

MIKE'S FIRST TWO YEARS AT Seton Catholic Central High School—also called SCC and SCCHS—were extremely difficult.

Early on in his freshmen year he wore a Seton Royals shirt to gym class. An older student—a former Catholic Central Crusader who was bitter about the merger—punched him in the stomach.

Mike played freshmen football and basketball but did not do very well in either.

Mike would later tell me that he hated high school the first two years. He had no friends and was picked on. He couldn't wait for the school day to finish and get home to be with his friends on Norton Avenue.

During lunch he would actually leave the school—something he was not allowed to do—and walk around the block praying the Angelus, a beautiful Catholic prayer that celebrates the incarnation of Jesus.

It is sad that he didn't have someone he could eat lunch with. It is also amazing to think that a fourteen- or fifteen-year-old kid would spend time walking around the block praying the Angelus.

Mike and Julie remained close. However, she was a grade behind him, so not in high school Mike's freshmen year.

Julie continued to have a strong spirit. She said when she needed to talk to Michael, she'd cut right through the Boardmans' backyard—the neighbors who lived between our house and the Trasolinis' house.

The elderly Boardmans—often resting on their back porch in the line of view where Julie was walking—were often a little taken back by Julie cutting through their lawn. But Julie didn't care. She needed to see my brother.

Julie would ring the doorbell once and then just walk right in.

Our mom would say, "Hi, Julie" before Julie sat down at the kitchen table to talk to Mike. The conversations were often long and often included eating too many of Mom's famous chocolate chip cookies.

After a bleak freshmen year there was actually some joy for Mike in junior varsity football in his sophomore year. The team was terrible and lost in blowout after blowout. But Mike had become really fast. The quarterback, Pat Larabee, would throw the ball up in the air to Mike for long bombs.

Dad estimates the two connected for about ten touchdown passes. The scores of the games might be 60-to-7 blowouts, but the touchdown catches gave Mike great joy and hope for the future—that he could be a varsity football star.

Mike practiced and practiced and practiced for basketball, hoping to improve and make the junior varsity basketball team. But he told me he just couldn't seem to get any better and bowed out gracefully—not even trying out for the team, rather than getting cut.

In the beginning of his junior year Mike became part of an excellent varsity football team. The early days of the Saints' 1978 fall football season would mark an important turning point in his life.

On one of the first days of school, after roughly two weeks of practice, the team got a transfer from Union-Endicott High School named Jim Flint.

Flint was beginning his junior year at U-E. On the first day of school some kids were blowing cigarette smoke in his face. He told them to stop. When they refused, Jim got into a fight.

Jim's father sent him to the Catholic high school for reform. All Flint cared about was football, and he heard the Seton Saints had a good football team.

Jim had no cleats the first practice and an orange-and-black practice jersey from U-E. He joined the Saints team wearing green and white—his new school's colors. His new teammates really roughed him up without cleats to maintain balance, and they made fun of him for the orange-and-black jersey. He got knocked on his back the whole practice.

After practice, Mike came up and introduced himself to Jim. They became best friends from that day forward. Mike would almost always refer to Jim by his last name—"Flint," or often even "Flints"—and I will do the same from this point onward.

From the beginning they were an odd couple. Even though Mike was trying to make it in football, a rough and tough sport, he was a graceful wide receiver and, in his heart, a peaceful, kind soul.

Flint was a fighter—in every sense of the word. He was big, rough, and tumble—a lineman or linebacker who played football like a high school version of Chicago Bears great Dick Butkus or Pittsburgh Steelers great Jack Lambert.

Mike and Flint developed a remarkable friendship and intense loyalty to each other. They would be there for each other during many good and bad times through the years, and they had two memorable years together at Seton.

Seton Saints football in 1978 had a larger-than-life atmosphere, led by head coach Brian Smith. From the stories I have heard about him, the image that comes to mind is a hard-nosed, rugged football coach known for yelling and intense discipline.

On Friday nights before a Saturday game, the team would have a spaghetti dinner together in the school gymnasium. They would then go to Coach Smith's house to watch game film.

Smith tried to keep the players with him as late as he could, so they wouldn't be out partying and drinking before the game.

After film sessions got out, Smith would actually call players at their homes up until 11 p.m., to make sure they weren't out.

The rough and tumble Flint quickly became a rising star in the Saints football program.

Mike hardly played at all, but this was not unusual for a junior. At that time, you had a lot of kids playing sports. Unless you were a really outstanding junior, the coaches would usually defer to a senior and give him a chance to start and play in his last season.

The Saints, led by quarterback Chick Muscatello, had a great season. Flint recalls that they were 6-2-1 and could have had a championship year had it not been for a tie to Norwich in the last game of the season and losing their star wide receiver—Dave Benedict—to injury during a preseason camp in Pennsylvania.

The Norwich-Seton game was a knock-down, drag-out slugfest in the mud. Saints kicker Mike Farrell (a future OBGYN whose four daughters I taught) missed a field goal that would have won the game, and they had to settle for a 6-6 tie.

Flint and Mike's friendship and plans for a great senior football season were cemented. But there was an even more exciting development: They formed a new group of friends called the Irregulars.

The Irregulars were each misfit in some way—eccentric personalities and heavy-set kids who were picked on or bullied throughout their lives.

As the leader of the group, Mike was always finding new people to invite in. They forged amazing friendships that would endure for a lifetime.

The Irregulars were as follows:

Mike and Flint, who would be part of the Seton Catholic Central graduating class of 1980.

Andy Chambers—nicknamed the "Bear"—and his best friend, John Legge, who were also in Mike and Flint's class.

Andy had a large frame and thick beard that made him look thirty years old, rather than the teenager he actually was.

"Legge" was a solid, humble, fairly quiet guy who personified the loyalty and friendship the group had for each other.

The rest of the group were a year younger than Mike—from the class of 1981, Rob's class.

They included our brother Rob and his best friend Chip Koch from the old Norton Avenue crew. Besides "Robbie," Rob also took on an additional nickname—"Kermit," because of the frog noise he would make while snoring.

A tremendous, lifelong friend of Mike's was Wayne Tremark. After high school Wayne went on to serve in the military in Iraq, run a small business and work in an important position in a New Jersey state penitentiary. He is in great shape and is a great family man.

In high school Wayne personified the shy, round kid Mike brought into the Irregulars. Kids could be rough to each other in those days, and he was called "Wayne the Train."

Wayne made a lot of great decisions in life and worked very hard to achieve success, but I like to think Mike's friendship and mentoring of Wayne had a really positive impact on this fine man. Several people I interviewed for the book recounted how special Mike was to Wayne.

As I wrote this book, I wished I could have included more stories about Wayne. Many times when it was a smaller group of Irregulars it was only Mike, Flint, and Wayne hanging out together.

Mike and Wayne were extremely close and maintained an incredible bond, even though they lived far apart from each other throughout most of adulthood.

Wayne also sometimes called Mike "Michael," something only my mom did. I think this gesture underscored how much Mike meant to Wayne and Wayne meant to Mike. Mike also had a nickname for Wayne—"Wayners."

Wayne would later tell me that he always considered Mike his best friend.

The next Irregular was Danny Cucci, who went on to become a local singing legend. Danny was also heavyset, but not shy. He was a real talker and gabber. Apparently, a few times his talking got the Irregulars into fights with rival groups.

The Irregulars like to joke that Cucci got his start singing at Irregular parties. Years later I saw him singing at a political fundraiser for my good friend Don Castellucci. Cucci sang Sinatra so well and so powerfully, if you closed your eyes, you would swear Sinatra himself was there performing in magnificent fashion.

Cucci also sang at church and was so proud to make it to the Vatican on three different occasions for audiences with Pope John Paul II.

Mike's other best friend—Julie Trasolini—was a year younger than Mike and also part of the Irregulars. Julie had gone from a tomboy on Norton Avenue to being a popular teenage beauty queen in the "in" crowd.

Julie said that she had to put on a façade of being Miss Popular at school, but when she was with the Irregulars, she could just relax and be herself.

Julie said the best way to describe the Irregulars to someone who didn't know them personally was the 1985 movie *The Breakfast Club*, about a group of students who are misfits. They are all from different walks of life, but they become enduring friends.

And what a great personality Julie had to fit into this group. Mike always said one of Julie's greatest attributes was that she would tell you exactly what was on her mind.

Julie's boldness made her a fun instigator with all of those boys—mixing it up as they busted each other's chops.

Even though he went to a public high school, Mike's great lifelong friend Vinnie Palmeri—a.k.a Skinhead—was invited to be in the Irregulars and would hang out with the group regularly.

Another Irregular in Rob and Julie's class was Bob Guyton. He was a tough, working-class kid with a solid frame who looked like a prototypical defensive end or tight end on a high school football team.

The next year, in December of 1979—Mike's senior year, which will be detailed in the next chapter, and Rob's junior year—Julie set Rob up at the junior prom with Kathy Kiluk. Rob and Kathy began a high school romance that would result in their marriage. Kathy would be part of the Irregulars, giving Julie the chance to have another girl in the group.

Two other friends from high school who hung with the Irregulars at times and were in Rob and Julie's class were Mark Prosinski and Tom Gallagher—"Pro" and "Gals."

"Pro" grew up with Mike and Rob at Christ the King Church and grade school. He was a solid guy and great athlete from a great family. He was one of the best high school golfers in the area.

"Gals" was from a large Irish Catholic family on the West Side of Binghamton who have lived and breathed Saints sports to this day through their family grandchildren. His father, William "Pete" Gallagher, was the superintendent of Broome County Catholic Schools and an amazing man of character and faith who passed away in 2014. The Seton Catholic Central gym was recently named "The William 'Pete' Gallagher Gymnasium" in his honor.

Jim Greene (known as "Greenie") loved to hang out with the Irregulars, but Flint said he lived in the boonies and couldn't always get rides into town to be with the gang.

Sean Keegan—known as Keegan—was always the life of the party and would crash Irregular events from time to time.

What a crew this was: Mike, Flint, Bear, Legge, Robbie also known as Kermit, Chip also known as Dummie, Wayne, Cucci, Skinhead, Guyton, and, of course, the two girls, Julie and Kathy, with Pro, Gals, Greene, and Keegan sometimes in the mix laughing, joking around, engaging in pranks around town, feeling at ease with each other and—unfortunately, in this crazy era—partying and drinking way too much.

Our brother Chris was four grades below Mike and unable to hang out with high school kids at this time. But as the Irregulars graduated high school and maintained their great friendships, Chris—or "Stix," as he was called—would be a full-fledged member of the post-high school Irregulars and develop great friendships from the group.

Chris's best friend, Gary Cooper, also tagged around the Irregulars.

Flint mentioned one time when Chris and Gary—or "Coop," as he was called—showed extreme courage during a tense moment when it appeared the Irregulars might be heading into a fight. Flint was just out of high school. The two younger guys were ready to stand by Mike's best friend. The fight never happened, but unfortunately fighting was common in those days.

The story of how Mike gave the group its name is interesting. They would sneak into Endwell Intermediate School, where the Mike, Rob, Chip, Vinnie, and Chris would play those great Royals-Yankees "Slap Ball" games.

The Irregulars would play basketball in the school gym and steal ice cream from the school cafeteria. It's sad to think that a great group of guys who meant so much to each other were starting to make bad decisions.

Flint said the school was having open gyms on weekend nights that the Irregulars attended and had a great time at. They were angry when the school stopped having the open gyms. When they found that the locked door could be easily be popped open, they went in and continued the open gyms on their own.

As they were sneaking around in the school, one of the group members cried out, "Can't we ever do things the regular way?" And Mike said, "No way, always the irregular way—always irregular." The name stuck.

Another event happened on the grounds of Endwell Elementary that the Irregulars still talk about. The school had a concrete staircase in its back parking lot leading to a path that cut through the woods to other neighborhoods.

One night the Irregulars were drinking beer on that staircase and shooting off fireworks—which caught the attention of the police.

A police car came and cornered the group on the stairs. In a daring escape Mike ran toward the police car and hurdled it completely in one amazing jump. The startled officer pursued Mike in his car, but Mike was so fast, he was able to get away. Mike's incredible leap gave the rest of the Irregulars time to climb the fence and also escape.

Drinking was part of the culture for teenagers in the 1970s, and these were wild times compared to today. The drinking age was eighteen. Fifteen and sixteen-year-olds could often go to the supermarket to buy alcohol without getting carded.

Alcohol quickly became a major vice for Mike. Rob said he never saw Mike drink just one or two beers. The first time they were at a party together—down by the Susquehanna River, near Lourdes Hospital, a few blocks from Seton—Mike got really drunk. Mike always drank to get drunk, and he always drank way too much.

This was the first sign of something deeply troubling within Mike's interior life.

The group took tremendous risks drinking and driving. Mike would later say that the person who was the least drunk would drive.

One night Mike clipped the driver's side mirror off my parents' Buick—the unofficial car of the Irregulars—when parking it in our parents' garage, because he had drunk too much.

Parishioners at Christ the King were wondering why the Phillipses were missing their side mirror at Mass the next morning.

Flint said on one of the Saturday nights Mike had way too much to drink he got really, really sick. Flint watched Mike in our backyard on a hammock, throwing up almost the whole night, to make sure he was alright.

The Irregulars always had each other's back, and Flint always, always, always had Mike's back.

After getting a few hours of sleep at his own house, Flint called to see if Mike was alright. Mom answered the phone and was angry, knowing the boys had drunk too much. She said abruptly, "Michael is at church—the same place you should be!"

Things that are completely unacceptable today—teenagers legally drinking at bars or even drinking alcohol in front of their parents at home and then driving—were common then.

The Irregulars also had a rival group at Seton Catholic Central that called themselves the Genesee Bombers. They were Binghamton kids who played pickup basketball and other sports games with the Irregulars.

The Genesee Bombers were named after Genesee Beer—a favorite of many in the Binghamton area at the time. It was also the Irregulars' favorite beer.

I heard a funny story about Genesee Beer during a conversation I had with former House Speaker Paul Ryan through my connection with the Jack Kemp Foundation. Ryan's older brother had come to the Binghamton area in the 1980s to work at IBM.

Speaker Ryan told me he remembered visiting his brother in Johnson City, at his house in a working-class neighborhood. Ryan said everyone seemed to sit on their porches and drink Genesee Beer.

The Irregulars liked to set bonfires on Patterson Creek, near the Country Club Road Bridge at the end of Norton Avenue. One day the bonfire got out of control, and flames were bursting up both sides of the bridge.

The Endwell Fire Department was only a block away and quickly responded to the fire, but a wild scene ensued for the entire neighborhood.

When the fire got out of control, the Irregulars had raced down Patterson Creek and snuck through neighbors' back yards to get back to our home.

Dad went up to see the fire and came back, telling the group, "Some kids started a big fire on the Country Club Road Bridge."

The Irregulars said, "Wow that's crazy," but slyly did not admit involvement.

The Irregulars also loved hitting the drive-in movie theater. They would pile guys into the trunk to avoid paying the movie ticket and then cause trouble throughout the movie.

The Irregulars went to the Broome County Airport at night and snuck out near the runway—getting a rush while watching planes land.

A hangout of the Irregulars—in addition to their unofficial headquarters at our house on Norton Avenue—was a bar named Yondas, in a working-class neighborhood in the First Ward of Binghamton.

The thought of sixteen, seventeen, and eighteen-year-old high school kids hanging out at a bar today would just be unthinkable, but it was common in that day.

The Irregulars would also like to hang out and have card parties—low-level games of gambling with playing cards—at the old Endwell Motel, which was only a few blocks from Christ the King Church. The card parties actually started on Norton Avenue at my parents' house, but they would be extremely intense and go late into the night, so they decided to move to this activity to the very low-dollar Endwell Motel.

At the Endwell Motel one prank the Irregulars pulled was putting a bed by the window in a room they rented, opening the window, and taking turns jumping from the bed through the window. Needless to say, the owners didn't care for that stunt.

One night there was a crazy party at Flint's house that was originally planned to be for football players only. Mrs. Flint had left some laundry on clothes hangers in the back yard. The Flints were not happy when they returned and found over a hundred people at their house, and that someone had burned a hole in Mr. Flint's new white shirt with a cigar.

The party at the Flints' house was not the only time parents had to deal with the Irregulars' bad behavior.

On one occasion, Mrs. Tremark—Wayne's extremely faithful, loving, loyal mother—had the unfortunate duty of driving the Irregulars around after they had had too much to drink, and one of the Irregulars threw up all over the back seat.

Once all the boys were dropped off, Mrs. Tremark took Wayne to the car wash. They rolled down the windows and let the carwash clean the inside of the car from the vomit.

Drinking and driving was the most dangerous activity of the Irregulars. It was taking thousands of innocent lives. Unfortunately in the late 1970s, many people were drinking and driving, and there were often little ramifications.

Irregulars frequently slept in our basement after parties in their unofficial Norton Avenue home.

Drinking too much, getting in fights, breaking into a school and stealing ice cream, leaping a police car, and irresponsibly setting bonfires were simply unacceptable behavior. In many cases they were actual crimes that Mike and the other Irregulars could have gone to jail for.

Our parents suffered tremendously through these misdeeds. They always loved Mike and all of their children unconditionally, but it was not an easy time for them.

In adulthood, as a devout Catholic man, Mike was not proud of this behavior. He expressed true contrition and left a deep impact on me to avoid alcohol and miscreant behavior. And he would be clear with me how unacceptable his behavior had been and that it had been very hurtful to our parents and others.

Mike turned the Irregulars—a shy group of misfits—into overconfident, obnoxious pranksters who at their core were a group of deeply loyal friends who loved and cared for each other tremendously.

Despite the many poor decisions they made, there were also many good decisions that reflected the love, care, and loyalty they had for each other.

And as their leader, Mike also accomplished much good in helping each Irregular feel valuable and special. This was an incredible gift Mike gave to a group of young people trying to find themselves.

The great interpersonal skills Mike had to touch the lives of the Irregulars so deeply would be on display with his work in the future as a counselor for thousands of people in need.

One of my favorite Irregular stories is from a night the group was having a party at Julie's house on Norton Avenue. The group was sitting around drinking and laughing in the Trasolinis' backyard.

The Trasolinis had these green metal chairs with a frame on the bottom that you could rock back and forth on. They were strange, ugly-looking chairs that can only be described as something out of the 1970s.

Bear was rocking back and forth in a chair. This big, heavy young man rocked a bit too much. The frame of the chair snapped, and Bear fell to the ground. The drunk teenagers burst out laughing.

Bear was so embarrassed that he stormed away from the party down Norton Avenue. Mike quickly followed, walking with Bear to comfort him after this embarrassing moment. I can still envision in my mind the sight of Mike and Bear at the end of our street on a hot summer night.

For posterity, it is important to note that the Irregulars were also known by a more official, formal title—"The Irregulars of Norton Avenue."

Great things were happening to Mike in high school with regard to his faith. Yes, he was making some really bad decisions with the Irregulars, but there were a lot of good ones as well. Amid the turbulence of adolescence, Mike continued to search for God and his mission in life.

Dad recounts the West Virginia mission trip as an amazing experience for Mike. Each year a group of Seton students traveled on a mission trip to impoverished communities in West Virginia, to serve the poor in the Appalachian Mountains.

The group gathered in the Seton chapel for a Mass with families before the trip. After the Mass and final blessing, the event closed with the singing of the legendary John Denver song, "Country Roads," which includes the words, "Take me home, country roads, to the place, I belong, West Virginia."

Dad said there wasn't a dry in the chapel by the end of the song. This trip was part of Mike's deep lifelong devotion to the poor, and a life-changing experience.

At some point in Mike's time in high school, the school welcomed guest speaker Franciscan Father Bruce Ritter, the founder of Covenant House in New York City. The mission of Covenant House is to rescue young people from lives of drugs and prostitution on the streets of New York from the pimps and criminals who are using them.

Founded in 1972, Covenant House was rapidly expanding by the time Father Ritter spoke at Seton. Mike was amazed by Father Ritter, his organization and its mission. Father Ritter's talk was a transformational moment in Mike's life. At this moment Mike began discerning a vocation to the Franciscans with a dream of working at Covenant House.

There were two great religious songs I remember Mike playing again and again at our house on an old-fashioned record player, songs that spoke to the deep religious conversion he was going through in the midst of the craziness of his late teenage years.

The first is, "Be Not Afraid," by Father Robert J. Dufford. I believe the lyrics spoke to the great spiritual mission of Mike's life:

> You shall cross the barren desert
>
> But you shall not die of thirst
>
> You shall wander far in safety
>
> Though you do not know the way
>
> You shall speak your words to foreign men
>
> And they will understand
>
> You shall see the face of God and live

The second is, "I Will Not Forget You, My People," by Carey Landry in 1974, based on Isaiah 49. I believe it speaks to the fact that Mike had confidence that God was always with him, no matter what struggles he faced:

> I will never forget you, My people
>
> I have carved you on the palm of My hand
>
> I will never forget you
>
> I will not leave you orphaned
>
> I will never forget My own

Despite his misdeeds, Mike continued to develop into a deeply spiritual young man.

Another real positive for Mike was that he began running on Seton's track team to train for football.

Mike was really fast and excelled at track. This was good for his self-esteem and also brought him into a new group of friends.

Mike's track coach, Rick Matarese, said to me a few years ago, "I had the honor and privilege of being your brother Michael's track coach."

I ran track for my legendary coach, Brian Hyland. Running until it hurts, lungs and legs burning, gasping for air, training and pushing yourself and your teammates further than you ever thought possible—this is all part of the incredible atmosphere Mike was able to experience in track.

On the track Mike was amazing. He became part of a 4 x 800 team that was one of the best in the area. 800 meters is two laps around the track. This was a hard, grueling race that pushed Mike to display both his pure speed and to develop tremendous endurance.

Mike also made some great friendships on the team beyond the Irregulars. One of those friends was Jan DeAngelo, who was two years younger than Mike.

Jan was from a large, boisterous Catholic family that has given so much to our area and Catholic schools. Jan is a colleague of mine at Seton Catholic Central, where he has served as a music and theology teacher for thirty years.

Jan has great memories of Mike and from track practices. During winter track they would train at the old West End Armory and hold meets in the Broome County Veterans Memorial Arena.

One day they were riding to practice at the West End Armory in a school van with a teammate named Chris Mackin, a strong, big kid nicknamed "Orca." The song "We Will Rock You" had just come out and was playing on the radio.

Mike, Jan, and Orcka sang and screamed "We Will Rock You" at the top of their lungs.

In another trip to practice at the West End Armory there was a snowstorm. Jan said the van almost slid off the road and they all thought they were going to die.

Another time the track team was practicing in the school after school let out. When the weather was bad the team could run in the halls or work out in the old dungy wrestling room in the armpit of the school—which today is a fantastic first-class weight room, thanks to the generous donations of the Myers and Fahs families.

Orcka was chasing Mike around the school. Orca was great at throwing shot put and discus—but he wasn't as fast as Mike.

At the top of his lungs Jan and others heard Mike yell, "Orca!!!" and sprint down the hallway. He knew Orca just couldn't catch him.

Jan, Mike, and others also attended a conference in Pennsylvania for the Fellowship of Christian Athletes (FCA) and had an amazing time.

Singing "We Will Rock You," the snowstorm ride, yelling "Orca," and the great FCA trip. These were all part of the joy of being a young person.

For many football players, track was also part of the training for football.

Just like the expression "all roads lead to Rome," at this point in Mike's life all roads led to Mike's senior season in football.

Mike practiced and practiced and practiced with Rob. Mike was the fast, swift, graceful wide receiver developing Rob's arm, as Rob would be the team's quarterback for the next season.

For many hours they practiced right in the middle of the street on Norton Ave. Mike would run the pass pattern—often a deep bomb. Rob would hit him with the long pass. Mike would run pattern after pattern and catch pass after pass on those hot summer nights.

Mike lifted weights and developed a strong physique to prepare him for football season. Other Irregulars—including Bear, Legge, and Wayne—would be going out for football, but for Mike, Flint, and Rob, you might say football was almost as important as life itself.

The one aspect of Mike's life I have not included in high school is his academics, which I will mention here as part of the lead up to senior year in football.

The consensus among family and friends was that Mike was really smart but didn't exert himself too much in school. Julie would joke that she never saw Mike take a book home.

Mike's Seton Catholic Central transcripts show that he ranked seventy-first in a class of 187, with an 87.5 overall GPA.

Mike had finished all of his New York State Regents requirements by the end of junior year. When I looked at his classes for senior year, to say it was a light load would be an understatement.

Mike did not have a single class in English, Math, Science, or Social Studies—the four core classes.

His schedule was as follows:

Two half-year semester classes—moral guidance and mysticism—to fulfill the school's theology requirement.

A semester of health and college prep—both school requirements—as well as a full year of physical education.

The four full-year courses Mike chose were mythology, Latin I—which was good preparation for his life the next year in Catholic seminary with the Franciscans—typing, and drawing and painting.

Mike was talented in art.

We have one beautiful painting from Mike that still hangs in my parents' house. Chris believes it is from the eighth grade at Saint Ambrose, when Sister Michelle was inspiring him so much with those meditations.

Chris offered the following analysis of this painting: The focal point of the work contains an outline of man superimposed by two larger shadows for a total of three images—symbolizing the Trinity. There are eleven stars symbolizing eleven of the twelve Apostles. A large teardrop falling symbolizes Judas's betrayal falling into a puddle of blood. Finally, a beautiful vine tree grows up from the base of the painting—symbolizing our new life in Christ.

This was deep work for a young man who was only thirteen or fourteen years old at the time.

I am sure Mike did amazing work in his drawing and painting class in his senior year as well.

Overall, his senior year schedule was about easy as could possibly be.

It was tailor-made for Mike to have a great time in his senior year, with the Irregulars and focusing on his goal of being a football star.

VI.

SAINTS FOOTBALL: NOW AND FOREVER

THERE HAD BEEN HOURS AND hours of training and great hopes and dreams for Mike's senior-year football season in 1979.

My favorite picture of Mike is from this time. Mike, Julie, and I are in my parents' yard in front of our large, beautiful maple tree when I was only three years old.

Mike is wearing his Saints football jersey and looks in phenomenal shape. He has that classic 1970s hair over his ears. His hair was thick and wavy.

Julie—the friend he loved so much since they met as young children—is in her cheerleader outfit and is a beautiful young woman.

The tree behind us is overflowing and bursting with bright orange leaves.

For me the picture symbolizes the beauty of fall and friendship, the tremendous love Mike always had for both Julie and me, and the hopes Mike put into the glory of football.

When describing the 1978 Saints football season, I laid out the glory of football. There were the team dinners and film sessions with a spirited coach. There were great games, like the famous 6-6 mud game against Norwich.

But as someone who played football, I can attest to the not-so-great parts: violent hits, bodies flying everywhere, and coaches yelling and cursing.

Mike faced these realities. Unlike Flint and many others who relished the physical battles of blocking and tackling, Mike looked to football as a graceful enterprise where he would run, pivot, and skillfully catch footballs and hopefully touchdown passes, as he did two years before on the junior varsity team.

One comment I remember from my brothers that shows how awful some football coaches could be was what a coach told Saints football players about their soccer classmates.

"They are faggots. Don't talk with them. Don't let us catch you sitting by them at lunch."

What a sad, mean comment about young men in the same school playing soccer, the world's most popular sport, which soccer legend Pele called "that beautiful game."

The language used by some football coaches, which too many times filters down to the players, is simply uncalled for.

Mike faced the ire of hotheaded coaches who rode him with criticism. Jan DeAngelo, who also played football, talked about one coach who was just horrible to Mike and a few other players.

As I mention Mike's football coaches and Julie's new boyfriend in this section, for the first time I begin to talk about people who were a nemesis to Mike in some way.

In the spirit of Mike's own kindness, I will use an alias for these and other nemeses or not mention them by name.

Coach Brian Smith left after the 1978 season for Florida, and there was a new group of coaches for the 1979 season. Assistant coach and gym teacher John Allen was elevated to head coach.

Jan said he absolutely hated how that one coach was constantly on Mike.

Jan didn't get into the details, but with all the problems Mike was having interiorly, the coach's riding him could have taken its toll.

There was a continual flood of bad news for Mike and the team.

In the first game, their starting running back broke his leg and was taken away in an ambulance. In the second game, their second-string running back—who was now the starter—broke his collar bone. The third-string running back had what you might say was "shell shock" from seeing those brutal injuries and played tentatively.

The team lost game after game after game. Most games were close—often 6-0 or 13-0—but the team had a weak offensive line and no running game.

To make matters worse, despite all his tremendous efforts, hours upon hours of training, and the tremendous aspirations in his heart to be a star, Mike hardly played at all.

This was heartbreaking for Mike and our family.

Various reasons were given for Mike not playing.

Early in the season against Johnson City, Mike caught a magnificent fifty-yard pass from Rob. The pass was a little bit off and it caused Mike to break stride and lose his balance after he caught it. He fell down and couldn't go all the way for a touchdown.

Did the coaches get angry with Mike for blowing this play?

There was also the theory that the football coaches also coached wrestling and favored wrestlers. None of the Irregulars were wrestlers.

There was the theory that the coaches just didn't like the Irregulars. Apparently one time they were late for practice when they carpooled from Endwell and Endicott, because Bear had to stop to get cat food on the way.

Looking back all these years and having played high football myself, I wanted to float yet another theory: It has been and remains difficult for teams on the high school level to pass.

This situation for Mike was just devastating for the entire season.

To make matters worse, he had fallen in love with Julie, but she had a new boyfriend on the football team.

Male-female friendships are simply fascinating. Can a man and a woman be extremely close friends, talk about and share everything, and then really just remain friends without becoming attracted to each other?

As a young girl Julie had been a tomboy, always mixing it up with the boys.

By her freshman year in high school, she had developed into a bold, confident, and physically beautiful young woman who probably half the school had a crush on.

Julie won Freshman Prom Queen and Junior Prom Queen at a time when Mike was growing into his identity as a young man and started to be attracted to girls.

Julie didn't know that Mike had fallen in love with her. She still thought of their relationship as a brother-sister one, and they continued to be extremely close.

The Irregulars were aware that Mike loved Julie and would let her boyfriend—who was on their football team—have it.

We will give Julie's boyfriend an alias—Joey DiLoro.

Flint tells the story of Joey DiLoro from an Irregular perspective. He said the Irregulars were just a bunch of common kids from working class families, while Joey was a rich kid who drove a fancy blue sports car.

Joey would be at Julie's house, frequently parking his fancy car on Norton Avenue essentially right in front of our house for Mike to see and lament.

The Irregulars felt this guy Joey was on our turf with our friend and fearless leader's girl. This was just unacceptable.

The beautiful, innocent friendship between Mike and Julie turned into jealousy and pain for Mike. The reality of the birds-and-bees story Julie's brother Nick told them developed in these two great friends now on dramatically different paths with respect to their romantic interests.

The Irregulars knew what Mike was going through and wanted to support him. Unfortunately, their idea of support was to constantly target Joe DiLoro with blistering hard hits at football practice.

Julie said the situation was absolutely outrageous. Joey was subjected to continual torment from Flint and the other Irregulars. They beat the tar out of him due to their misguided loyalty to Mike.

In their forty-five years of friendship, Julie and Mike only had two fights—both over her boyfriend Joey DiLoro. But their friendship would still endure.

Amazingly, Flint said that he and Mike never had a disagreement in over thirty years of friendship.

Another bittersweet part of the 1979 Saints football team for Mike and our family was the success of Rob, an amazing athlete who played every single play and was the best player on the team.

On offense as quarterback Rob actually didn't do too well, as the running backs were injured and the offensive line just couldn't protect him. Rob and the entire offense were just constantly overwhelmed by the opposing defenses.

Rob was knocked out in a game against Susquehanna Valley - by one of the Kimmel brothers who played in the NFL - with a concussion long before concussion protocols. He threw up all night and just went to practice on Monday.

Even though the team struggled on offense, on defense Rob was simply a phenomenal cornerback. He was quick and aggressive and made tackle after tackle after tackle.

Rob was so good that he actually received a recruitment letter from the legendary Iowa football coach Hayden Frey.

The other bright spot of the team was Flint, who was amazing at middle linebacker.

In the Ithaca game—against a large powerhouse school the size of U-E—Flint got an interception and fell out of bounds on the Ithaca sideline. Ithaca's players started kicking and punching him as a fight broke out. High school sports were heated in those days.

Besides the heartbreak of Mike not playing, the situation with Julie and her boyfriend, and the team having a miserable season, there was also the contrast of Rob and Mike.

Mike had worked so tirelessly to help develop Rob as quarterback, running all those pass patterns on Norton Avenue, but he ended up never playing himself.

My parents wanted to be supportive and proud of Rob, but they couldn't talk about games too much for fear of hurting Mike more than he already was.

For his part, Mike was not jealous of Rob; he was happy for both his brother and he best friend Flint's success. But he was crushed by his own failure.

Rob made first-team all STAC (Southern Tier Athletic Conference) on defense for the league local teams competed in—an impressive feat for a Junior. Flint made second-team all STAC.

One other bright spot on the team was its new equipment manager—a close friend of Dad's named Tom Cheevers. "Cheeves" was an IBM employee who put nine children through Catholic schools. He loved football and the team—staying with the program for almost 20 years. He told Coach Allen that he wanted to be buried on the practice field when he died.

Cheeves would try to follow Coach Allen around and keep him calm. Coach Allen kept throwing his arms in the air; one time he actually knocked someone over. Cheeves said, "Coach, you just knocked over Father Hobbes, the team chaplain."

Underscoring just how bad the 1979 season was, one of the most memorable parts was a rock fight. The football practice field next to the school's parking lot was always in terrible condition.

Younger players on the JV team started throwing rocks at the Varsity, and the Varsity responded. A massive rock fight broke out. The team spent the entire rest of the practice running hills behind the school cafeteria as punishment.

The 1979 Saints finished a dismal season with only a single win against Sidney—a school from a small rural town.

Despite all the disappointments, Flint and Mike continued their inseparable bond. They were the last two players out of the locker room every single game, and they walked onto the field together every single game.

Flint said that even though Mike hardly played at all his senior year, he still hoped they could go to college together and play football. At some point in their senior year, Mike told Flint he had decided to enter Franciscan Seminary.

Flint was disappointed, but at the same time he was happy for Mike.

Through all the ups and downs of high school and the inner struggles Mike had, he clung to his tremendous faith. To think of an eighteen-year-old entering seminary is really special.

The beautiful picture of Mike, Julie, and me under the tree in our front yard still gives me so much joy, because I know Mike eventually overcame the bitter disappointments of football and it made him a better man. But when I think of that picture, I remember and see the pain as well.

There were plenty of good times to be had for Mike, Flint, and the Irregulars in the rest of their senior year in high school. But there also were setbacks.

That winter was the Junior Prom. As mentioned, Julie set Rob up with Kathy Kiluk—who would become his wife. Flint said that of all the Irregulars, the last two guys you would expect to have a girlfriend were him and Rob. They were both so serious about football and sports and didn't have time for girls.

As winter arrived, the big attraction for the Irregulars and the entire school was now Saints basketball—a great program playing in a tough league with many intense rivals.

The only Irregular to play on the basketball team was Rob. As a tremendous athlete, he was one of the team's stars. Tough and scrappy at 5'10", he had to guard the other team's big men, who were often considerably taller than him.

The ritual from Saints basketball in the 1970s and early 80s continues today. The crowd starts to fill the gym during the JV game.

When the JV game finishes, the Seton Stage Band begins revving up the crowd by playing class tunes. For 40 years, the Stage Band was led by legendary music teacher James Wheeler, who retired from Seton in 2016 and sadly passed away the next year.

The varsity team would sprint out to the court to the tune "When the Saints Go Marching In."

The song was an unofficial theme song for the Irregulars, who liked to sing it at parties and get- togethers.

The team wore green checkered warm up pants—1970s style—with white tops. The stage band continued playing great tunes. Today their line-up includes "Sweat Caroline," "Living on a Prayer," and "Don't Stop Believing."

"Don't Stop Believing" was not released by Journey until 1981—the year after Mike graduated from high school—but would be a favorite of the Irregulars in their post-high school years. The lyrics—referring to the journey of young people in the city, "street lights," and "living just to find emotion"—would remind me of Mike's future work with young people in New York City.

With the crowd—in those days nicknamed the "Zoo"—and players revved up, the gym was rocking. Next it was time to introduce the players—with the crowd going wild.

Next was the singing of the national anthem—in which the crowd closed the song shouting, "the home of the Saints!" instead of "the home of the brave."

This was followed by the school's alma mater—again played by the Stage Band—with cheerleaders, players, and the Zoo singing their hearts out.

Now lift your voice and raise a song,
For beauty and for truth.
For our dear Alma Mater,
the honor of our youth.
Oh, stand beside her colors,
Find courage at her side,
For green and white
For honor bright,
For loyalty and pride.
Here's to our own dear SCC,

Steadfast and true she stands.

Here's to our faithful green and white,

Leading loyal SAINTS to glory.

Proudly we raise her banner high,

Bravely defend her name.

Praise to our Alma Mater

To our own dear S C C H S.

With the game finally ready to begin, the Zoo, the Irregulars, and Mike were ready to go wild.

Unfortunately, in a time where the drinking age was eighteen, they were almost all drinking and almost all drunk.

A typical scene would be Mike and others on the shoulders of other Irregulars like Flint, Bear, and Legge to make things even crazier.

In this wild, crazy, larger-than-life atmosphere, if you were a boy, to be a star on the basketball team was much coveted.

If you were a girl, the coveted place was the cheerleading squad.

As mentioned, Julie was one of most beautiful and popular girls in the school. She had made the cheerleading squad in previous years and thought she was a shoo-in for the upcoming season.

Then the devastating news came: The roster of the cheerleading squad was posted in the girls' locker room connected to the gym, and Julie did not make the squad.

She ran out into the hallway in tears and went into the telephone booth between the boys' and girls' bathrooms across from the gym.

Mike just happened to be walking by and saw Julie. He went into the phone booth with her and embraced her. What a scene this was—two amazing friends holding each other and crying during this moment of bitter disappointment for a teenaged girl.

The basketball season went on with larger-than-life school rivalries in those days.

Union-Endicott had a great team that sent three players to play Big East Division I basketball: Sean Kerins and Sonny Spera, both of whom went to Syracuse University, and Mike Sinicki, who went on to play for Boston College.

But before going to the Big East to play with and against legends Patrick Ewing of Georgetown, Dwayne "The Pearl" Washington of Syracuse, and Chris Mullin of St. John's, these great U-E stars had to first survive the Zoo at Seton Catholic Central.

Flint said the scene was so crazy that opposing players would start sweating and shaking when they had to dribble the ball near the Zoo.

Besides Seton Catholic Central, Binghamton had two public high schools—Central and North High Schools—which combined to become Binghamton High School a few years after Mike graduated from Seton.

Central High School was located only a few blocks from Seton, and the two schools had just an incredible rivalry. Mark Ward, a Central High School star who years later would go on to become my basketball coach at Seton, told us stories of the intensity.

Ward lived directly across from Seton Catholic Central on Seminary Avenue. Given that he was six-feet, seven-inches and had a soft touch, Saints Coach Joe Stoner tried to convince him to come to Seton, but was not successful.

The day before the game at Seton, someone threw a green rock through Mark Ward's bedroom window. The next day in the game, with the Zoo going wild, Ward threw a big dunk down against the Saints on his team's way to victory.

After the game he went to the Seton locker room to pay his respects to Coach Stoner, who was just beside himself with emotion after losing a game against such a big rival.

It was if Stoner and his team had just lost a game that would have taken them to the NCAA Final Four or the NBA Championship. That's how big Saints basketball was in those days.

Coach Stoner was protective of his star players—including Rob—during this wild and crazy time for teens with much underage drinking.

Stoner would cringe when he saw Rob getting into my parents' old Buick packed with Irregulars. These guys were wild, and he didn't want Rob to get in trouble.

Stoner had other reasons to be skeptical of the Irregulars. One time, when the team was returning from a road game in a traditional yellow school bus, an intense snowball fight broke out between the basketball players and the Irregulars waiting in the parking lot for Rob.

Needless to say, Coach Stoner was not pleased.

After basketball season, it was on to spring sports. Mike had made a name for himself on the track team, but unfortunately, in addition to drinking, he had picked up another vice that would remain with him for the rest of his life: smoking.

Even smoking moderately made it too difficult to run track, so Mike quit the team in his senior year.

Mike's drinking and antics with Jim Flint and the other Irregulars continued into a dangerous spiral.

In the 1970s it was also more common for kids in white, middle-class culture to fight. The Irregulars would fight with the Rats, a rival group who went to public schools.

One night there was a standoff between the groups behind what was Fays and is currently Rite Aid in Endwell on Hooper Road, about two blocks from our house on Norton Avenue.

The Rats picked Mike to fight one of their toughest guys.

Mike took a few hard shots and was knocked down. He returned a few hard blows and held his own before the fight was broken up.

For those who knew him later in life as his religious transformation had come to fruition, it is nearly impossible to imagine Mike in a fight. He was such a gentle and kind man—a St. Francis figure who was kind to everyone. I tell this story and others just to show how profound Mike's redemption and deeper conversion to the Lord was.

A frequent activity of the Irregulars was to go to all-night diners in the area to eat and sober up after drinking.

Mike and Flint had way too much to drink once and decided to stop at a diner in Endicott in the middle of the night. Both seemed to think the other guy had money to pay and forgot they didn't have any money.

In a split second Mike and Flint made a horrible decision to skip the bill. They dashed toward my parents' car, hopped in, and drove safely away—or so they thought.

A short time later at our house, Mike answered a phone call from the Endicott Police. The owner of the diner had written down the license plate number on the getaway vehicle and reported him.

Mike was asked to come to the police station. He found some money and simply thought he would have to pay the bill. To his surprise when he arrived, he was arrested and told he would be spending the night in jail.

Inmates could make a phone call, so Mike called his parents' house, and Rob answered. Rob called Flint to tell him what happened.

Flint was a loyal friend who would give his life for Mike. He wasn't going to sit by and let Mike be in jail while he got off, so Flint turned himself in.

Our dad heard the news from Rob and made his way down to the jail to bail Mike and Flint out.

To this day, Jim Flint gives thanks for this and other times when my Dad came to his assistance. Unfortunately, more drinking-related problems would be coming Mike's way.

Rob was also a star on a baseball team that featured future Chicago White Sox pitcher John Pawlowski. The Saints reached the championship game in baseball but were big underdogs against Union-Endicott.

Near the end of the game, with U-E ahead 2-0, Seton managed to get two runners on base with a strong power hitter named John Yesensky coming to the plate. Yesensky blasted a really hard ground ball that went between two of the outfielders. With no fence, the ball just kept rolling and rolling, and Yesensky managed a game-winning home run for an incredible upset.

Mike watched the game with Kathy, his future sister-in law. I mention this story because it was an amazing moment for Rob and the school at the end of Mike's senior year.

A side note, but something that would be important to Mike a few years later, was our brother Chris's amazing success as an athlete. Like Rob, Chris excelled in football, basketball, and baseball and was part of Seton Catholic Central's class of 1984.

"Stix" was All-State in football, set records as a wide receiver, and helped lead his team to a 10-0 record. In basketball his team lost to future North Carolina star King Rice in the championship game.

In baseball Stix's team upset Union-Endicott in another dramatic championship game. Star pitcher Danny Smith threatened JV Coach Jim Clarke on the mound in the middle of the game when the coaches talked about replacing him (it was a heat-of-the-moment threat, not a serious one). Smitty recovered and struck out the side to win the game in front of a capacity crowd at Recreation Park.

Mike was extremely proud of Chris, but I believe he was in New York City working at Covenant House during many of Chris's games.

Back in 1980, as Mike completed his senior year of high school, he was struggling with drinking and internal insecurities, but he had come a long way from being a shy, bullied freshman.

There was one more major event to discuss for Mike before he completed his time at Seton Catholic Central as part of the class of 1980. It was the Senior Prom.

Julie, a junior, was still dating the same boy the Irregulars were so hard on during football practice, but she agreed to go to Mike's Senior Prom with him as a friend.

Mike was just thrilled to be going to prom with Julie, his best friend from childhood whom he was now wildly and still secretly in love with. The two had a great time that night, but Julie's emotions for Mike would never go beyond an extremely strong brother-sister love.

As the years went by, Mike's romantic emotions for Julie would eventually subside, and a tremendously close friendship endured.

Julie always said that she and Mike knew secrets and stories about each other that they would take to the grave. Some of those stories and conversations are from that night at the prom.

After his senior year, Mike's internal problems would implode, and he would snap.

He was heavily drinking alone one summer night and stumbled by the liquor store on Hooper Road, a few blocks from our house. In a drunken rage he kicked in the glass door of the liquor store, went inside, and stole several bottles of alcohol.

Mike stumbled home and called Flint, explaining to him what had happened. Flint, who was hanging out with Wayne at the time, rushed over to Norton Avenue to check on Mike.

Mike was so drunk that he couldn't even remember where he put the bottles in our house. Flint finally found them in some cabinets in our kitchen.

Then Flint and Wayne started driving around town, trying to find the liquor store Mike broke into. Finally, they realized it was the one right by our house on Hooper Road.

They retraced Mike's steps and realized he had dropped a few bottles during his drunken walk home. Flint and Wayne worked hard to clean up the evidence so the police couldn't trace the trail.

They realized there was a witness in the vicinity who either lived around the corner or was visiting a friend. Flint and Wayne talked to the witness, threatening that if he did not remain silent about Mike's crime, they would beat the tar out of him.

Covering up evidence and threatening witnesses? These were certainly not the right actions directed by Flint that night following Mike's disastrous decision.

But I mention these actions to underscore how deeply loyal Flint was to Mike, how much he loved him, and how he would do anything for him. He had gone to jail with Mike. He would take a bullet for Mike if he had to. Wayne accompanied Flint that fateful night and was also dedicated to Mike with his whole heart.

When Mike sobered up the next day and realized what he had done, he was absolutely devastated. He took full responsibility for his actions, and with help of family attorney Salvatore Fauci, he was able to rectify the situation with the liquor store owner.

The question was—what caused Mike to snap so badly? Yes, he was devastated by his failure in football. And yes, the situation with Julie and her boyfriend was extremely difficult.

But there was something deeper tormenting Mike deep down inside. It is something that would remain almost a total secret for many years.

The liquor store incident and his other sins from this time period would give Mike great humility. They also helped him develop incredible compassion and understanding for the many troubled people he worked with through his years as a social worker.

When Mike was working with young women who had been prostitutes on the streets of New York and with young boys in group homes who had been in trouble with the law, and when visiting clients in jail as a drug abuse counselor, he would have an extremely nonjudgmental view and empathetic connection with those he served.

The harsh reality was that at eighteen years old, Mike had a serious drinking problem that would torment him for years.

But Mike also had many, many good things going for him as well. His deep family roots from Hornell, his extremely loving family, and his friends and his faith would sustain him.

I titled this chapter, "Saints Football: Now and Forever." This was actually the slogan for my Saints football team many years later, but I felt it fit well for Mike, Flint, and the Irregulars for what they started together in the fall of 1978, their junior year.

The Saints played their last football game in the fall of 2017. I attended the game, and we beat Cooperstown before the school became too small to field a team. But Saints football remains alive in Flint's heart and in the hearts of many others.

Flint loved football more than anyone I had ever met, and he would play in college, the Army, and in a semi-pro league. Years later, I spent many hours with him and Mike listening to stories of those two unforgettable seasons of friendship, hardship, and endurance.

Mike would rise about the ashes of the disappointments of high school, the liquor store incident, and eventually his drinking problem to go on a mission to be a different type of Saint—not the star athlete with the Prom Queen girlfriend he had dreamed of, but a saint knowing, loving, and serving God with all of his heart.

Mike was on to Saint Hyacinth's College Seminary in Granby, a small town in western Massachusetts near Holyoke, to study with the Franciscans.

VII.

THE FRANCISCANS AND COVENANT HOUSE: "I CAN LOVE THEM"

MY MEMORIES OF MIKE DURING his high school and college days are very limited, because I was so very young. I have vague memories of football, track, and the Irregulars.

I do have one lasting memory of Mike at Seton that actually came from the summers after he graduated: He had a summer job at his alma mater as a janitor helping the full-time staff.

The janitor's office is off the side door to the school near the school gymnasium. There is a long table in the front of a room that expands into the boiler room.

I loved visiting Mike at the school while he was working as a janitor. He was so kind to the full-time janitors, including a heavyset, soft-spoken guy everyone loved—Kenny Greer. I thought the janitor's office and the boiler room were so cool when I was a little kid. And it was nice spending time with Mike in a school that had meant so much to him.

Another memory I have from this time is visiting Mike at Saint Hyacinth's Seminary and the incredible car ride. I remember looking out the window and seeing the brightest, most beautifully colored orange fall trees you could possibly imagine. It seemed like an endless sea of colors.

This Franciscan Seminary had the beautiful mission following in the footsteps of Saint Francis, one of the greatest saints in Christendom.

Mike was predisposed to these Franciscan virtues of humbleness, poverty, and focus on helping the poor. It seemed like a great fit for him.

He would meet one of the greatest influences in his life there: his spiritual advisor, Father Sixtus. Mike referred to him informally as Sixtus and talked about him to me for years after his time in seminary.

Sixtus came to visit us one time when I was child; it was exciting but also strange to have a priest staying in your house.

I thought of Sixtus as Mike's Obi-Wan Kenobi. I was really into *Star Wars,* and the image of the Jedi trainer in the movie was analogous to what Sixtus was trying to do with Mike in the spiritual life.

Sixtus joked that the first time they met he was in a bathing suit on the beach. It showed that priests are actually regular people. I like to think their beach meeting was analogous to Jesus meeting his disciples, the fishermen on a beach.

Sixtus mentored Mike during a very turbulent time in his life. Mike continued to struggle tremendously with drinking and was rapidly developing a new illness: anorexia.

Mike—who was about five-foot-nine or five-foot-ten—had been a healthy 155 pounds in high school, with a solid build from football workouts.

A beautiful sketch of Mike by Franciscan Brother Bernard, which we used for the cover of our other two books of Mike's journals and spiritual writings, shows that he had dropped considerable weight, and his face looked gaunt.

Sixtus saw the tremendous good and tremendous gifts Mike possessed. He told my parents that God had a very special plan for Mike. I imagine he knew full well of Mike's drinking, eating disorder, and sexual abuse.

As a seminarian Mike experienced the Franciscan life of prayer as part of his training. He would have daily Mass and prayer with the seminarians. There was also outreach to the community. Mike later wrote in a job application about the deep impression working with poor children in Holyoke had left on him.

Mike took some great courses in Seminary. They included Elementary Latin I; Intro to Group: Theory and Practice; Fundamentals of Catholic Teaching; Introduction to the Old Testament; Introduction to Franciscan Studies; General Psychology; Patristic Theology; Introduction to the New Testament; Philosophy of Man, Thinker and Doer; Counseling Psychology; Sociology of the Family; Liturgy and the Sacraments; and Acts of the Apostles.

Mike told me that his Old Testament course was taught by a rabbi and that it was just fantastic.

These courses would be a solid part of Mike's continued spiritual formation and preparation for his eventual work as a counselor. He managed a 3.36 GPA.

Mike was preparing to be a Franciscan brother—not a priest. For Catholics a brother is like a religious sister. They take vows and live lives of prayer, holiness, and service. Unlike priests, they cannot celebrate Mass or other Catholic sacraments.

I often wondered why Mike chose to follow the path of being a brother instead of priest. When I asked him about it years later, I believe he said he didn't feel worthy to be a priest.

In later years Mike almost never talked about the seminarians he was living and studying with. I know the seminarians went out on the town drinking—something that was not a positive for Mike, given his problems.

I remember him telling me the group he was with was small—certainly less than a dozen seminarians—and that the majority of them were gay.

When I was an adult years later, Mike told me there were unwanted sexual advances from others, but did not get into details.

Jimmy Brosseau, the cousin from California who Mike loved talking to so much, told me years after Mike's death that there was actually a violent sexual assault.

Details remain murky, but apparently the perpetrator was a much older seminarian who had left another career. Dad said they filed a complaint with the seminary, but nothing seemed to happen.

After two years of study, Mike took a year off from seminary and returned home. I was never fully clear on what caused Mike to take this leave, but he was struggling a great deal with his drinking and his eating disorder.

Mike did talk to Flint about the sexual assault. He and Flint were drinking way too much in town one night and they decided they were going to drive to St. Hyacinth to "get this guy."

Thankfully, Mrs. Flint heard about the plan and took her son's car keys. The extremely loyal Flint's judgment wasn't the always best, but his heart was always with Mike a thousand percent.

Flint told me that there was a five-year period, starting in high school and spilling into the first few years after, when the two were home on breaks—Mike from seminary and Jim from college and then the Army—that anytime someone saw Flint alone, they would say, "Where's Mike?" And anytime Mike was out alone, they would say, "Where's Flint?"

Flint said neither of them cared what people thought of them. They were just great, great friends.

As Mike's drinking remained disastrous, Flint was always his great protector. Unhinged when drunk in a time when bar fights were frequent, time and time again Flint had to protect Mike and keep him from getting into a fight or getting beat up in a bar.

Flint said sometimes they would stay up drinking and talking all night at a special location near the train tracks. There even were times when they slept the whole night drunk on park benches.

My parents were relieved by Flint's presence in protecting Mike as his guardian, but they were greatly troubled by Mike's overall struggles. They had dealt their own alcoholic parents and were now witnessing their son's suffering from this wretched disease.

Mike took the dramatic step of attending inpatient alcohol rehab programs on several occasions during this period. He learned the Twelve Steps of Alcoholics Anonymous, but nothing seemed to work long term.

Mike did some part-time work—including at Kmart—and kept discerning a return to the Franciscans.

The Franciscans negotiated a plan that would allow Mike to work at Covenant House in New York City—the job he had dreamed of since hearing Father Bruce Ritter speak at Seton. Mike would live with the Franciscans and work with young people brought off the street in their under-21 shelter.

Unfortunately, as he prepared to go to New York City, Mike made another horrible decision.

Danny Cucci was at our house, and he and Mike had had way too much to drink one night. Mike told Cucci he could sleep in the basement.

But Cucci said he hadn't told his mother he was staying at our house. His father had died, and his mother would be so worried about him if he didn't return home. He begged Mike to drive him to Binghamton.

The two got in the car and rode down Norton Avenue. At the end of Norton Avenue, Mike rolled the stop sign and turned left onto Watson Boulevard.

Mike didn't see the nearby police car and officer, who immediately pulled him over and arrested him for DWI.

From what I have been told, DWI arrests were rather new during this time in the early '80s. They would be used as a powerful tool to help save thousands of lives from drunk driving accidents.

Mike was trying to do the right thing for Cucci and Cucci's mother, but he risked his life, Cucci's life, and the lives of other drivers on the road with this awful decision.

By pulling Mike over, the police officer may have prevented an even greater tragedy.

Flint vigorously maintains that both the liquor store incident at the end of high school and the DWI never, ever would have happened had he been with Mike those nights.

My grandparents' lives were torn apart by alcoholism, leaving much emotional carnage in the paths of their children and others. Mike's life was torn apart for a time, and I know stories of too many other lives ravaged by the destruction of alcoholism.

One theory is that the risk of alcoholism and addiction to other vices like drugs is much greater if you use them in your teenage years and early twenties, when your brain is still developing.

If young people can avoid alcohol, or at least the abuse of alcohol, until they pass their early twenties, they have a much better chance to avoid developing a drinking problem.

The other huge risk factor is genetics. Three of Mike's grandparents were alcoholics, and this obviously left him susceptible to addiction.

What causes people to drink too much—which in Mike's case was his deep hidden secret of sexual abuse—and dealing with the root cause or causes is also critical.

I never had a problem with drinking, but I was very hesitant to drink until I was twenty-one or ever drink too much because of my disastrous family history.

With my wife and me raising three boys, I decided to quit drinking completely several years ago. I was never a big drinker, but I wanted to be able to tell our boys that this has been a poison for our family and to avoid it at all costs.

When I talk to my students, I say to them, "Explain to me why you can't have a great time without drinking." No one has ever been able to give me a good response.

I follow up by saying, "I see you coming to this class every day, happy, smiling, laughing, and joking around. You seem to be having a great time without alcohol."

For Mike, the DWI was devastating. He again worked with our family attorney, Salvatore Fauci, to deal with the legal side of his decision in as forthright a manner as possible.

Even though Mike would still drink, he would never drink and drive again. He also felt unworthy to return to the Franciscans.

But after prayer and discernment and realization of redemption in Christ for sinners, Mike made the journey to New York City to live in a Franciscan community and begin his work at Covenant House.

It is hard to imagine more vulnerable young people than those at Covenant House. The Franciscans rescued these children from life on the streets of New York, where they were used as prostitutes and drug dealers and were often homeless.

The broken family background of each Covenant House resident is hard to comprehend. Many of them had been physically and sexually abused and abandoned by their parents.

As mentioned, when I think about Mike's work with street kids in New York, I always think of the Seton Stage Band song, "Don't Stop Believin'" by Journey.

More importantly I think of Jesus, who ministered to the woman caught in the act of adultery and was to be stoned. He said, "Let those among you who have not sinned cast the first stone."

When the men who were about to stone the woman slowly walked away one by one, He said, "Do none of them condemn you? Neither then do I condemn you. Go and sin no more."

The Franciscans at Covenant House brought this loving message of Christ to the young men and women they sought to serve.

Mike would write about Father Ritter and Covenant House years later in glowing terms for a job application for a social work job in Binghamton:

"Father Bruce Ritter is a person who has vitally affected my thinking. He is a Franciscan priest who has worked to provide shelter for homeless and runaway youth. He is an advocate for these young people and has made the public aware of the injustices they suffer. His work and ideals are an inspiration to me. He made me aware of my responsibility to help change what is wrong in our society.

"I heard Father Bruce speak when I was in high school. Listening to him and reading about him stirred up in me a desire to become involved with serving the homeless youth. I am from a good, loving, middle class family. It haunted me to know that many young people suffered so much. It did not seem right to turn my back and walk away.

"After graduating, I entered the seminary of the Franciscan Order to which Father Ritter belongs. My dream was to one day work with homeless youth. The seminary was in a tough inner-city neighborhood. Living there, I became involved with some of the local people. They were often victims of poverty, drug addiction, lack of education, lack of opportunity, and broken homes. The more time I spent with them, the more their suffering bothered me. Despite their sometimes-rough exteriors, I found them to be good caring people. I was fortunate to get to know them.

"I left the seminary after two years and returned to my family. A year later I joined the Franciscan affiliate program and went to New York City. There I worked as a full-time volunteer, and later as a paid staff at Covenant House/Under 21, a shelter for homeless youth that Father Ritter founded.

"Living in the city and working at Covenant House was an awesome experience. I worked with girls that were pregnant and/or had children. They taught me much. Despite their pain, they had so much hope and love for their children. They taught me about the dignity and sanctity of life. It was a privilege to learn from them.

"On one occasion, Father Bruce spoke with the staff regarding the Covenant House's mission. His talk had a lasting impact on me. He challenged us to have absolute respect and unconditional love for the youth and each other. To have absolute respect for and to love anyone unconditionally seemed impossible. It was and is an ideal I strive for. Father Bruce made the impossible seem possible by pointing out that God loves us unconditionally. We do not deserve it. He simply loves us in a special and profound way. Experiencing unconditional love is what allows us to reach our potentials. With God's love this is possible."

Mike saved a copy of the Covenant House Mission Statement, which reads:

> We who recognize God's providence and fidelity to
> His people are dedicated to living out his covenant
> among ourselves and those children we serve, with
> absolute respect and unconditional love. That commitment
> calls us to serve suffering children of the
> street, and to protect and safeguard all children.

> Just as Christ in his humanity is the visible sign
> of God's presence among his people, so our efforts
> together in the covenant community are a visible
> sign that effects the presence of God, working
> through the Holy Spirit among ourselves and our kids.

Mike absolutely loved his work with these young people, who were so troubled yet so precious in the eyes of God.

When he returned home for his first visit after beginning his work at Covenant House, he told Dad he had found what he wanted to do with the rest of his life.

Mike explained to Dad that he didn't have the education or the training to work with these young people, but he said, "I can love them."

What an incredible, profound yet simple mission. This would be Mike's mission with thousands of other people he would work with through the years. He would love them.

Visiting Mike in New York City—the Big Apple—was so exciting for our family.

Dad remembers his first visit to New York while Mike was working at Covenant House.

They were walking near Covenant House when Mike was off duty, and some of the girls were there outside with their babies in strollers they had had as teenage mothers.

They lit up when they saw Mike, waved, and called for him.

Mike quickly and politely waved back, but he had to keep going. A critical part of his work as a social worker was the confidentiality of his clients. He couldn't stop and talk to the girls with Mom and Dad present; it would break the confidentiality of the girls.

For the next twenty-five years, Mike would constantly talk about how much he loved his job as a social worker and his clients, but he would never talk specifically about them, strictly respecting their privacy.

We will never know on this side of heaven the amazing stories about Mike's interactions, relationships, and healing messages he shared with thousands of people through the years. But Mike's tremendous love for the people he served became a central part of the heart of who he was as a person.

Father Juniper was the Franciscan priest who headed the Manhattan house Mike resided in. Mike spoke glowingly of Juniper, who, like Sixtus, had an extremely positive impact on him. But after a year of living in community with the Franciscans, Mike concluded that he did not have vocation to be a Franciscan.

He left Franciscan religious life for good, but he would continue working at Covenant House as a regular staffer.

I remember two visits with Mom and Dad to see Mike in New York.

On the first one we took a Greyhound bus from Binghamton to Port Authority Bus Terminal. From there we went to a park where we would meet Mike for a tour. I remember pigeons everywhere and asking my parents, "Where's the Empire State Building?"

When Mike arrived a few minutes later, I said again, "Where is the Empire State Building?"

Mike said, "Look up, you are standing right in front of it." I stretched my head as much as I possibly could to see that amazing structure.

Mike felt that the World Trade Center had an even better view than the Empire State Building and took us there.

It was amazing as a young boy to be at the top of the World Trade Center, and I remember the brochure that read, "The closest some of us will ever get to heaven."

Ever since the September 11 terrorist attacks that killed thousands, I have thought about that phrase from the brochure, and it brings tears to my eyes.

The second trip started at Mike's apartment in Staten Island, where he had moved after leaving the Franciscan house in Manhattan.

Mike rented a tiny room from a woman in the upstairs portion of her house. It was barely big enough to fit a single bed and an end table. He shared the bathroom and kitchen with the woman he rented from.

We followed the path Mike took to work. First, he took a bus, then the Staten Island Ferry, and then the subway to get to work. It was a long but exciting trip.

Our brother Chris visited Mike in Staten Island as well and toured New York City. He said it was the greatest weekend of his life.

Flint visited Mike in that little apartment too. He slept on the floor next to the bed. Looking back, it's hard to image that tiny room fitting middle linebacker Jim Flint on the floor, but it did.

Mike just loved New York City. He loved the people, the energy, and the excitement of the city that never slept.

Several things linked to New York City in the 1980s always remind me of Mike, including the Broadway musical *Cats* and the song "Arthur's Theme (Best That You Can Do)," which includes the famous line, "When you get caught between the moon and New York City."

Mayor Ed Koch reminded me of Mike's time in New York City as well. Mike loved Koch's wit, energy, and love for New York.

Despite all the joy and excitement Mike was experiencing in New York, there also were continued struggles with drinking and his growing eating disorder.

Mike also missed our family and the support they provided. He was homesick and decided to leave Covenant House—the place he loved so much—to return home for support amid his great internal struggles.

VIII.

THE BINGHAMTON SOCIAL WORKER: LISTEN, LOVE, AND LEARN

MIKE WOULD RETURN TO THE Binghamton area and settle into his work as a social worker, where he would touch the lives of thousands of people he would see not as outcasts but as precious children of God.

Before talking about his work and life, I wanted to share some of my memories of Mike from this time period, when I was a child. Some of the stories would have occurred when Mike was home visiting from seminary, and then New York City, and some occurred after.

I absolutely loved my little Star Wars figurines when I was a kid. I played and played and played with them for hours and hours, alone and with my friends—Tom Koch, Andy Parsons, Ed Woiccak, Dan Cartie, Nate Slavik, the Hranek twins—Chris and Chuck—and the Curtin brothers—Jon and Brendan.

Mike actually took the time, patience, and love to play Star Wars with me. He watched me set up all the figures and listened to my make-believe action stories.

Mike even took me to the movie *Star Wars: The Empire Strikes Back.* I can still picture him sitting there in the theater with me.

Mike's interest in my passion for Star Wars meant so much to me.

Since Mike was so much older, I only remember one family vacation with him—to Niagara Falls and Toronto. The vacation was so special, and I have already explained the significance of the photo of Mike and me at the Falls.

Here are a few other thoughts on the cover photo:

Those who have had near-death experiences or seen visions of heaven have said when we go to heaven and are restored we will look like we are 24 years old—at our peak physically. Mike is not quite 24 in this picture, but he looks at his peak. I like to think this is what Mike looks like in heaven today.

I also like Mike's style—with the beard and long hair. You might say he has the Jesus look a bit.

As mentioned, the mighty waterfalls behind us invite the reader to enter into the deep beauty and mystery of Mike's life of friendship, suffering, joy, redemption, and hope in Jesus Christ.

I also remember a visit to Our Lady of Fatima Shrine in Lewistown, near Niagara Falls, which features an enormous dome with a statue of Mary and over 100 life-size marble statues of saints.

I remember taking great joy walking among the saints with Mike at the shrine.

One time our parents went away on a trip to Boston for Dad's work with IBM. Since my brothers were much older, I grew up like an only child and didn't handle it well.

Mike watched me during the trip and accompanied me so kindly that night as I cried my eyes out and cried myself to sleep. I'll always remember his kindness.

When Mike returned to the Binghamton area, he would live most of his time in a tiny apartment on Cary Street on the north side of the city, about a fifteen-minute drive from Mom and Dad's house.

Cary Street would be his longtime base of operations for his remarkable prayer and spiritual life.

Mike would come to our house to visit on weekends and holidays. Holidays were always so special with Mike, and he relished being with family.

I started to learn in my early years that something was not right with his eating. He wouldn't eat Mom's delicious meals. Instead, he brought his own food, with meager portions due to his eating disorder.

Mike loved our parents so much and his brothers and his nieces and nephews. He always looked forward to spending time with all of us.

But the times I was able to share with Mike while he was with Flint and Julie also stand out in my mind.

After one year of college at St. Mary's of the Plains on a football scholarship, Flint spent six years in the US Army before eventually settling down as a truck driver and family man in Endicott.

I loved being with Mike and Flint, because I could see how much they loved each other and how much they loved me. I was their little side and they were my larger-than-life heroes. They were cool, funny, and just great to be around.

Even then, I was amused by their odd-couple appearance. Flint was the rough-and-tumble middle linebacker, and Mike was the kindhearted peacemaker.

One of my best memories with Flint and Mike was watching them play video arcade games on those large clunky machines.

I loved being around Flint's family with Mike. Flint's siblings, Patty, Bobbi Jo, and Mark, all loved Mike and were amused by the dynamic of the Mike-Flint friendship.

One time I got invited to the Flints' house with Mike for Mrs. Flint's specialty lasagna dinner. Mike kept saying Mrs. Flint's lasagna was simply out of this world.

Flint later told me later that the lasagna dinners were a very special ritual. The Flint children could each invite one friend for Mrs. Flint's delicious lasagna dinner on special occasions.

I can still picture myself sitting at the Flints' table in eager anticipation. It lived up to the hype. I loved Mrs. Flint's lasagna, but I loved hanging out with Flint and Mike at Flint's house even more.

Mike and Flint also helped me celebrate a milestone in life: eating my first Whopper (although today I'm a staunch Wendy's man). I felt so important being at Burger King—across from our church, Christ the King—with Mike and Flint. They joked that I ate only half the Whopper—the rest was all over my face and shirt.

Julie graduated from high school one year after Mike and then attended college for nursing at the State University of New York at Plattsburgh. She lived in Philadelphia, working as a nurse for a number of years, before eventually settling down in Baltimore.

I already mentioned how Julie was the first one to hold me when I got home from the hospital as a baby. She would be like a big sister to me.

A very special memory was getting to go to the Pepper Mill restaurant with Mike and Julie—their regular hangout. I felt cool being out to eat with grown-ups.

Like with Mike and Flint—I loved being around the Mike and Julie, because they loved each other so much.

I loved how they called each other "Dude," how they joked around and seemed to be able to talk about anything.

I wasn't sick much as child, but remember one time I had a terrible earache that put me in excruciating pain. Julie was home on break from nursing school and accompanied Mom and me to the doctor's appointment.

For me, it was like she was representing Mike and was there on his behalf. She was great at giving medical advice and comforting me until the doctor's diagnosis came through and the anti-biotic was able to kick in.

The moments between Mike and Julie might not have been as dramatic as some of his times with Flint and the other Irregulars, but all those hours together shaped an extraordinary friendship.

These were the days Mike would make his mark on the world in Binghamton, where he loved living, working, and going to church.

Most of all, Mike loved people.

He loved saying, "People are special."

Mike's jobs in Binghamton may not seem as dramatic as working with kids who were prostitutes, drug dealers, and homeless on the streets of

New York City, but there were plenty of broken lives and needy people for Mike to serve and minister to in Binghamton.

His first job when he returned home from Covenant House and New York City in 1985 was as a childcare worker at the Family and Children's Society Group Home for adolescents separated from their families.

One funny story I remember from the group home is that Mike had to cook for the residents. Picturing Mike cooking meals for a bunch of teenagers was really funny for me, but he managed.

Mike also started part-time work around the same time at the Salvation Army Open Door Youth Shelter, again serving youth displaced from their families.

The Salvation Army—or "Sally," as it was nicknamed—soon became Mike's full-time job.

Most people are familiar with the Salvation Army's bell ringers outside supermarkets during the Christmas season, looking for donations in their little red kettles.

In addition to being a charitable organization, the Salvation Army is a Protestant church whose members are soldiers for the Lord, trying to bring salvation to the poor and destitute by meeting their physical, emotional, and spiritual needs.

Since Mike was Catholic and not a member of the Salvation Army faith, he was considered a lay worker. Mike loved and respected the Salvation Army organization, religion, and staff he served.

While working for the "Sally," Mike provided counseling and helped prepare the youth of the program for discharge from their shelter to independent living. He also visited young people in their apartments, the jail, and at local psychiatric programs.

Mike wrote about his work at the Salvation Army in an application for another job:

> "After almost two years in the city, I returned to my family due to being homesick. In Binghamton, I was fortunate to get a job at the Salvation Army Open Door Youth Shelter, a shelter for homeless young men who are from 16 to 21 years old. These

> youth are often viewed as tough, uncaring people. I found this to be untrue. They act tough to survive and are often victims of our self-centered society. Working there, I have gotten to know many young men who have really been hurt in life. They want to be cared about and cared for. Getting to know them has been a privilege. They have challenged me to reach my potential. I received more than I gave. Working with them has enriched my life."

As intelligent as Mike was, he didn't have a college degree. He had two years of college in seminary, but he was so busy working with young people after he left that he hadn't managed to go back to school.

He decided to further his career and help the people he was serving more by getting a college degree. He started by taking classes part-time at Broome Community College while continuing to work in 1987.

Unfortunately, Broome accepted almost none of his credits from Saint Hyacinth's. His many theology and ministry-type courses didn't meet the requirements for a broad two-year degree.

When he transferred his credits to Binghamton University (The State University of New York at Binghamton, as it was referred to in those days), they accepted almost all of his credits from Saint Hyacinth's as electives, and he was quickly able to obtain a BS in applied social science.

The professor who changed his life at SUNY Binghamton was George Yonemura, who had been forced into the Japanese internment camps during World War II. Mike loved professor Yonemura's kind and gentle manner, and the counseling style he promoted focused on the Carl Rogers person-centered therapy.

Rogers broke from the Freudians, who focused on uncovering past experiences in the subconscious mind, and the Behaviorists, who focused on how human behavior had been conditioned.

The most important part of therapy, the Rogerians held, was simply to listen to another person and to hear and affirm them. Healing and growth would occur just by having another person listen to you.

Mike absolutely loved this approach to counseling and made it his own. His personal motto and mission statement became, "Listen, Love, and Learn," and he was absolutely phenomenal at doing this with everyone he met.

Family and friends could attest to this. Mike was always so focused on us and our needs and at listening, affirming us, and building us up.

His great background in social work and his SUNY Binghamton degree would help him obtain a job he would love so much—working at the Broome County Mental Health Department's Chemical Dependency Unit as a drug abuse counselor, a job that would take him to the Broome County Jail.

At first, Mike was nervous about his work. He had been accustomed to working with young people. How could he counsel these older people, who were often hardened criminals?

Mike remained steadfast with his mission of "Listen, Love, and Learn" and always remembered a central tenet of his Judeo-Christian faith: that each person is made in the image and likeness of God and has infinite value.

Given that he was working for a government organization, he could not share his faith unless the client brought up faith first.

Mike always strove to see the infinite, extraordinary value in each client he served. Mike would say that whether a person was a doctor, a lawyer, a janitor, a drug addict, or a gang member, those titles were not the most important title: being a person. Simply by being a person you have infinite value in the eyes of God.

The clients he worked with at the Broome County Jail would often be forced to see Mike by a court order.

I asked Mike how he was able to get them to talk. He said that he learned from studying Carl Rogers that if you remain silent long enough in a meeting, the other person will eventually start to talk.

For these clients from tough backgrounds who had made many mistakes in their lives, Mike may have been the first person who truly listened to them.

Having made his fair share of mistakes during his days with the Irregulars, Mike could also relate to his clients. The disastrous nights at the liquor store and with the DWI could have landed him in jail for long periods of time.

Mike never had to look at those he served in jail and say, "I can't believe you did this," because he had made some really bad decisions.

Mike was keenly aware of the tremendous blessings he had during his own legal problems—incredibly supportive family and friends as well as his deep faith. Most of the people he was working with in the jail were not as fortunate.

In the early 1990s he was beginning to do great things as a drug abuse counselor. He would continually attend training sessions and courses to improve in his field and become qualified as a Credentialed Alcoholism and Substance Abuse Counselor (C.A.S.A.C.) in the State of New York.

Even though he never had a problem with illegal drugs, the fact that he was an alcoholic enabled Mike to relate to his clients as they battled addiction.

In the early 1990s, when he started to work at the jail, Mike had serious health problems due to his anorexia. He was very, very thin.

I think Mike's frail appearance actually worked in his favor with clients in jail. The clients had all sorts of problems that had landed them in jail. When they first saw and met Mike, they realized he had problems too. Mike would offer a positive, non-judgmental approach to these inmates who had been judged by so many others in society.

Mike Prosinksi was an officer at the Broome County Jail and the older brother of Mark, who was a grade behind Mike at Christ the King and was involved with the Irregulars during Mike's high school days. Unfortunately, Mark died in a car accident in college.

Mike Prosinski could attest to my brother Mike's great presence at the jail for many years. The guys at the jail loved and respected Mike and really looked forward to seeing him.

Father Stan Gerlock, who passed away several years ago, was a wonderful priest who served for many years as the Broome County Jail's chaplain. He said that when Mike visited the jail, a buzz arose among the inmates to see him. Mike always had a sense of knowing who needed to see him the most.

Carl Giammichael, a founding member of Christ the King Church who led the rosary every Sunday before Mass and served our church along with my parents in almost every way imaginable, was a model of holiness. He also volunteered at the Broome County Jail.

Mr. Giammichael told my parents that they had raised an incredible young man who was doing amazing work. One inmate told Carl, "No one in the world cares about me. No one loves me. The only person that loves and cares for me is my counselor, Mike Phillips."

Another person who saw Mike's dedication to his clients was Paul Battisti, a local attorney who now serves as the Broome County district attorney and often did cases as a public defender for Mike's clients at the jail. Both appreciated each other's dedication to helping people in need who had made bad decisions.

Like many others, Paul would pull up his car by Mike and offer him a ride. Mike always politely declined, because he loved to walk.

Like his clients, Mike loved his co-workers. His two closest friends were Colleen Sullivan and a guy named Bob.

I can't remember Bob's last name, but I went out to breakfast with him and Mike many times. He was spirited and opinionated. He loved Mike.

Bob, Colleen, and Mike worked together for many years and had many great times together.

Mike had tremendous respect and admiration for Art Johnson, the longtime head of the Department of Social Services.

Art O'Neil, whose children I taught; Julie Perlick, whose brother Matt went to high school with me; and Jim Golden, whose son plays baseball with my son, are other co-workers of Mike's I have met through the years.

One time Dad was picking Mike up at the hospital when he was visiting a client. Dad made the mistake of finding Mike in the client's room—

which was a break in the client's confidentiality but gave Dad an unexpected glimpse of Mike's relationship with a client.

Dad saw a really large man lying in a hospital bed. The man pointed at Mike and said to the woman next to him, "See this little guy over there? He is going to save my life!"

The bottom line was the guys at the jail loved Mike, and Mike loved them. Ironically, despite the fact that his weight was around 100 pounds or less, they called him "Big Mike."

Mike was slender in size, but his big heart brought healing and hope to these downtrodden but precious children of God.

Although Mike would not talk about his clients, Rob confronted him about a brutal, horrific murder in Binghamton and two men he would be counseling.

High on drugs, the two men killed a police officer and then ran over his body numerous times with their truck.

The community was sickened and outraged. Most wanted the harshest sentencing for the men who had committed this heinous crime.

Rob said to Mike, "You are going to be counseling them. How can you do this after what they did?"

Mike admitted that what the men did was absolutely horrible, but he repeated his core belief, saying, "There's still a piece of Jesus in them. I'm ready to receive them and try to work with them."

Mike's spirituality continued to grow in what was for him a jail ministry. He was attending daily Mass, reading spiritual works, and entering into a deep, deep life of prayer and relationship with the Lord.

Thankfully, Mike had made much progress in conquering his own drinking. Long gone were the days of Mike getting drunk in bars and wildness.

Unfortunately, he continued to drink once a week, on Friday night in his apartment. He would get drunk alone and have a bad hangover the next day.

In June of 1994, right before I graduated from high school, Mike took his last drink. Through the grace of God, the sessions he had done with AA, his deep spirituality, and love of family, he conquered this terrible addiction once and for all and never drank again.

But unfortunately, his eating disorder was getting worse and worse. By the early 1990s, a strong flu or bout with pneumonia could have killed Mike when he not yet thirty years old.

Mike's great struggle was revealed in his journal, which our family has called "Conversations with Jesus."

IX.

CONVERSATIONS WITH JESUS

YOU HAVE HOPEFULLY GAINED A sense of who Mike was. At the age of twenty-eight in 1990, he was a remarkable man who had deeply touched many lives.

As mentioned, eight years after his death, our family published his spiritual journal, "Conversations with Jesus," which he began writing during this time.

Dad would go to the cemetery to Mike's grave and pray. He felt that he would get signs from Mike, passed on by how the rain covered his name on the tombstone.

Dad said, "Mike, should I publish your journal?" He noticed that one day only the "I" and the "S" were not wet from the name Michael Phillips. "I S" backwards is "Si"—yes in Spanish—so Dad's work was on.

Dad normally wakes up a 6 or 6:30 a.m. When he was typing Mike's journal, he said Mike kept waking him up at 4 or 5 a.m. to type the journal with his slow, two-finger approach and finish the project.

There are several important people Mike mentions in the journal whom I have not mentioned yet. He saw a counselor named Linda to discuss the psychological side of his problem. He also met with Paul Battisti's mother, Helen Battisti, a nutritionist who helped him maintain weight.

I will now reprint excerpts from this journal that show Mike's tremendous interior struggle with anorexia, his faith in God, and how his relationship with Jesus was transformed into a deep personal relationship.

The journal began on October 17, 1990—almost twenty years to the day before his death on October 19, 2010.

MICHAEL'S JOURNALING

Wed Oct 17, 1990

Trust. Today it really hit me on how little I trust. As usual I tried to begin the day with some quiet pray full listening. I try to be open to God. As usual many distractions crept into my mind. I was not open but preoccupied with self-concerns and worry. I wonder what the day will be like and what I should do. Later walking to Mass and feeling cut off it hit me—TRUST. Suddenly I thought about my life—who and what I am and the problems (that I so often worry about) that I have failed during my life. Trust. When I look at my life, I can see God has been and is with me. He calls me to trust in him and his love. He calls me to trust in his goodness. He wants me to be "me" before him and with others. He wants me to trust others—trust in their goodness. And nurture their goodness. He wants me to trust in my goodness—that I am created in his image as we all of us. I must face my selfish self and be I in Him. All he asks is that I trust. He will take care of me.

Thursday Oct 18, 1990

"It is what we are excited about that educates us" Mike Rose's *Lives on the Boundary*.

Today I brought a book, *On Becoming a Person* by Carl Rogers. George Yonemura, my counseling teacher has made me excited about learning. Psychology has often been a dry and impersonal area of study for me. George has enkindled a desire in me to learn about Carl Rogers's philosophy of counseling. It is based on the individual. Each person is a beautiful and precious unique mystery. Counseling is not a matter of diagnosing and curing and acting as a doctor. Counseling is being yourself for and with another in a way that helps and allows another to be themselves and find their own answers, the answer that lie within them, to their own problems. This philosophy calls us to see our common goodness and nurture it within each other. I'm excited to learn. This philosophy of helping is very much supportive of my theology—which I believe God is and who others and myself are in the world. I hope that I can learn so that I can be me for others. (This is the first class I've ever taken where I chose to read an additional book—George gave us 2 books to start off with and told us to read whatever else we desired).

Sat Oct 20, 1990

Today I met with George Yonemura. He is a very powerful, humble and loving teacher, counselor and person. In the short time I have known him he has enriched my experiences of life and being me. A while back I wrote a story about me. The story described my experiences in life of coming to terms with myself and the impact God and others have had on me. I'm happy to say that today I am glad to be me. (I've not always felt this way.) George challenged me today. He sees me as someone good, humble and loving. He expressed great respect for the struggles and pains I've gone through. He respects and honors me. I have some trouble accepting his recognition of this goodness. I kept mentioning that I still have so many faults. I am still selfish; I am still weak and imperfect. He challenged me to accept my weakness and handicaps and failings and to focus on what is good about me. He encouraged me to focus on enjoying being me and not wasting my energy focusing on my limitations.

What is good about me? I am a person who has suffered much, I am "handicapped"—I know pain and loneliness. Pain has taught me compassion. It made me a humble person. I have a reverence fear or awe of God, others, life and myself. Life is an awesome and beautiful mystery. Each person including me is also an awesome and beautiful mystery. My pain forced me to face my selfish self—in doing this I realized how poor and broken I am—in this poverty I expressed my need for God and others. I need to be loved and to love. Love brings about wholeness and unity—my heart begs for it. What a gift—hungry faith. My faith involves quiet waiting—it calls me to listen and be open to others and the other. My faith in God and in man's goodness leads me to be open to love. Through the grace of God and the love He has shown me through others in pain He has healed me. It heals me and makes me grow in love. For this I am thankful. My struggle and pain could have ended in my being bitter. I am thankful it did not, and I am thankful to be me.

Oct 28, 1990

Fr. Brown told me to just be me in confession a few weeks back. I felt good about me after that—that it is O.K. to be me. Today at Mass he said, "Life is a love affair with God". Grace is not a thing but God's love pursuing us. Sin is not a thing but a matter of being unfaithful to our lover. Pondering on my love affair with God I believe I should start treasuring His presence, treasuring who I am and treasuring my experience with others.

Oct 31, 1990

Who am I becoming?

I feel like I am starting, just starting to become me. I'm starting to slow down and relax as to who I am. I'm finding the need to slow down a bit more. Slowly I'm becoming aware of who I am. I am a student, a person who works with the youth, a brother, a son, a friend, an anorexic, a Catholic but I am more than these. I am I and experiencing this being is good. I hope to become more open and aware of who I am, doing this I believe I will be more open and aware to experience the goodness and awesomeness of life—creation, others and God. As I get to know myself more, I feel I'm starting to be a more open and loving person. It's a feeling of joy and awe and wanting to share in the joy of life. It is good to be me. I hope to listen more.

Nov 4, 1990

It has been a long day of study and work. It was long, as well as good. I feel good—I'm starting to accept me and appreciate me. I want to take care of me. It's funny but this is not a selfish taking care of me—it does not close me off from others. Rather this taking care of me opens me to care more about others. It's a good feeling—I can accept me as imperfect and changing.

At work a young man stopped in to talk. He really made me feel good. I listened to him for quite a long time and tried to understand him. He shared that he thought that I was the only person that understood him. This is sad because he is such a good person. I am privileged to be getting to know him; hopefully others can do this also. Relating to different people he talked to, including professionals and psychologists, he said you seem to be the only one that really understands me—you don't use numbers and reasons. I took this as a compliment; I am trying to move away from judging and analyzing, to being more accepting and compassionate. It seems as though this non-direct approach has much more power for insight for another and myself. It was a good experience. I am learning—he taught me. I am grateful.

April 12, 1991

Today, I saw something special—it made me feel good yet sad. It was a rough week at work—lots of hurting kids. I took two of them shopping for groceries in the van and on our way back they caught sight of a kid that used to live with them at the shelter, he was put in the psychiatric ward at the hospital by me and the police because he was suicidal and was walking around downtown with a hospital staff. The two kids in the van went crazy—they were so happy to see him—I let them out of the van and they took off to see him. It really hit me—to everyone else they are misfits—but they have something special—they are united as people—so often we are so divided in our high-class world—they showed me something about what it is really like to be loved. They experienced being brothers—maybe they really aren't the ones that are the misfits. What a privilege it is to be part of their lives and get to know them.

Jesus helps me to be still and come to know the mystery of your love in me. Help me to trust in you loving care.

May 5, 1991

Today, I am overwhelmed, discouraged and depressed by my helplessness and inability to deal with and overcome my sickness, weakness and sinfulness. I try but fail. Life is a struggle. It seems to be more that I can handle. At times I feel like a dog—a reject and misfit, pretty miserable at times. Day to day life is a struggle. I need a Savior; Jesus have mercy on me a sinner. I do not deserve to be loved by you. I am not worthy of your forgiveness. It's hard to believe you love me. How could you who are so good love me a sick, ugly and sinful man? Help me to accept and be open to the mystery and glory of your love. You who are God suffered and died for us all, especially for me, even though none of us deserve such limitless and unconditional sacrificial love. I am sorry for being so closed and untrusting towards you. Grant me the grace to slow down and open up to you and be aware that you are with me, you who are my God and Savior. Thanks

July 27, 1991

"You should not be working for perishable food but for that remains unto life eternal, food which is the Son of Man will give you."

God, thanks for the gift you have given me. Thanks for the gifts of generosity, compassion, faith, understanding, gentleness, the desire for you and love. These are the gifts you have given to me—an unworthy sinner. Help me to see that any good that I have or do comes from you.—Your gifts reflect you. May I see your gift in others too. I offer you what you have given me—me—received me to do what you will. May I use the gifts you have given me to give you glory—to make you known in the world, Thanks, I love you.

June 9, 1993

"I do believe. Help my lack of faith".

The last entry I made in this book was 3 years ago. My life has changed—You have been with me—and I'm still hanging in there. Still after 14 years I'm struggling with my sickness—seems like the past few weeks have been some of the worst. Sickness, worries and stress are wearing me out and I feel kind of lost sometimes, like a failure. Today, due to work responsibilities, I couldn't get to Mass. While taking a quick cigarette break, standing alone and wishing I had made it to Mass, it hit me—you are always with me. Perhaps life has been so difficult lately because I have not been as open, aware and trusting as you call me to be. Lord, help me to believe you are always with me, help me to turn my life over to you, grant me this gift of the Spirit so that I might serve you in a world full of people starving for your love. Help me to trust in your limitless, unconditional and personal love for me—with you I have hope and strength. Thanks

June 15, 1994

"Love your enemies…be made perfect as your heavenly Father is perfect".

Jesus—I fall so short at your gospel call—the challenge to love unconditionally and give of myself limitlessly as you did and still do. I'm weak and sinful. There is so much in me that blocks me from being made perfect. Have mercy on me and grant me the grace I need to overcome the obstacles within me that blocks me from getting to know you.

Nov 18, 1994

"Trust Me, be open to Me and My love. I AM with you, you are sick and broken, you need Me, and I AM here for you."

Thanks for the really good sleep, thanks for touching me thru my brother's compassionate hope—he reflects your love and hope for me—thanks for loving me and for the hope you have given me.

I'm scared of dying but it is a possible consequence of my sickness. Numbness still seems to be shielding me, slowly reality is sinking in and I am sad and afraid. I also feel guilty—somehow my anorexia is my fault and I'm hurting those who love me and I'm hurting myself. Perhaps it is too late to play Monday-morning quarterback pondering what I should have done—the past cannot be undone.

Now, it's becoming obvious that my life is at stake. Fear and anxiety grip my gut, yet hope is dawning. You Lord are my hope, and with the help of your grace I'm slowly beginning to change. Help me to progress little by little. I feel guilty because "I should make big radical changes". This is a nice thought, however as an anorexic, it just doesn't fit—to go too fast, too far, too soon could cause the "binge monster" to come back and I fear him—the viscous binge-purge cycle—almost as much as death. The cycle is living hell. Lord, I hope that making small, consistent changes will be enough to keep me alive. Perhaps the answer is learning to live my problem and me.

Guide me and protect me, oh Most holy Son of God. Help me to listen to you and respond. Thanks, Jesus, have mercy on me a sinner, I trust in you. Love Mike

Dec 6, 1994

"...People. Came to hear Him and be healed—"

"Blest are you poor—the reign of God is yours."

"Come to Me, be in My loving presence. I AM with and in you, I AM healing you and I will give you rest—trust Me."

Dear Lord, Help me tonight to trust in you—I'm a sinful and sick and exhausted man. I'm having trouble sleeping—anxiety—change and growth are good but painful, also will be seeing the doctor Thursday—the last of my health worries will be confronted—I'm either O.K. or having done some/possible severe damage to my body. Receive me tonight Lord—help me to trust in you—you are my salvation—in my poverty and brokenness I'm beginning to know my need for You. Thanks for teaching and healing me. Love, Mike.

Feb 3, 1995

"Mike, I really want you to know Me and how much I love you."

Lord, you prayed Father forgive them. Thanks for the effort, sacrifice, and gift of you. You offered forgiveness, healing, reconciliation, union and peace. Receive my anxiety, worries, scared, sinful and preoccupied with my cares and family—help me to trust in you and be open to the life you have for me. Lord have mercy on us. Thanks

Feb 4, 1995

"Mike I greatly desire to forgive and heal and love you and reveal myself to you."

Lord, forgive me for being so selfish, heal me body, mind and soul. Thanks for today, thanks for my family, thanks today for Bob and Alice. I love you, have mercy on us.

Feb 5, 1995

"Mike be united to me, experience me in communion and love."

Lord, help me to be open to you, Thanks.

Feb 6, 1995

"Mike, I desire to share my life with you—PASSION, DEATH, RESURRECTION—trust, be still open and know that I am your lover, Savior, God"

Lord, I'm sick, tired, scared, anxious, crazy—help me to trust in you receive me in my brokenness, Thanks

Feb 7, 1995

"Mike, I love to have you enter into my love—the Passion mystery—be open to my Spirit."

Lord, Thanks for helping me—continue to reveal yourself to the world and me. Thanks, I love you, Have mercy on us.

Feb 8, 1995

"This is My Body to be given for you. This cup is the new covenant of My Blood which will be given for you."

Mystery—I gave you myself and My life—flesh and blood and I who am true God and man—your Savior—I gave my life for you. I did that that you might share in My life—I love you immensely, thirst for you.

Lord I offer you my life's problems, receive them and heal me. My anger, sadness, depression, worries, sacredness, anxiety, confused, doubtful, guilty,

Receive me in my boredom, sickness and selfishness Thanks, grant me help, I love you, have mercy on us.

Feb 9, 1995

"This is My Body to be given to you. I love you; I am with you and I will take care of you. Trust Me."

Lord, I am sick and scared tonight—my butt—worried, fearful of hospital, sleep, bathroom, eating, health, guilt, embarrassment, family. Receive me tonight, my body, mind and soul and grant me your help. Thanks for the gift of yourself help me to be open to you. I love you. Have mercy on me. Have mercy on us.

"Take this and eat it—this is My Body to be given for you—Do this as a remembrance of Me. they crucified him, Forgive them…

Reach out, despite your pain, do what I did—show who you are—be open to my forgiveness, healing, love and share it with others."

Lord forgive me for being so caught up in me. Grant me the grace to teach out to others even when I am tired. I love you have mercy on us.

Feb 10, 1995

"I greatly desire to give myself to you—My Body and Blood—given for forgiveness, healing and union—be open to receive me—surrender to my love."

Lord, receive me tonight, help to surrender…thanks for loving me so much, I love you have mercy on us.

Feb 11, 1995

"…Do this in remembrance of Me"

Lord make me a channel of your peace. Grant me the grace to reach out, forgive me for my selfishness and caught up in my worries, guilt, using family and self—help me to be better in your will, surrender and be open to be a channel of your love. Thanks, I love you, have mercy on me.

Feb 18, 1995

"This is My Body to be given for you…they crucified him" I am with you and in you—I am your crucified lover, Lord Redeemer, Healer and God. Open up to my healing love. I am healing you—believe. I want to have you know me and my love for you so very much—listen."

Lord receive me tonight. I am sick, scared, helpless, powerless, doubtful, sinful and afraid. I need saving and help. Forgive me for all that I have done, heal my brokenness, help me turn my life around to you—let go—surrender. Have mercy on us Thanks Lord for helping and answering my prayers. I love you.

Tonight, I am wiped out. Third time in three weeks my hemorrhoids are bleeding, anxiety—it's overwhelming—how can I make it. Will I end up in the hospital—it's scary? I need to change and make small steps towards getting better. Perhaps I am too hard on myself maybe I need to slow down, take small steps, be realistic and not get depressed. I need to accept who I am, what I am, a sinner, sick and need help and say that you oh Lord are there for me and with me—slowing healing me to prepare me for yourself. Help to surrender—to learn from the cross, teach me and guide me Lord. Continue to heal me and know how dependent I am on you. Without you I have no hope with you I have it all.

Feb 21, 1995

"Mike, slow down, give thanks in all things, learn to surrender to my loving care for you and others. I call you to a holy relationship with me—loving unity. I call you to enter into the passion/Paschal mystery and be transfigured—I offer you my life."

Lord, thanks, receive me tonight (this A.M.), I am stressed, can't sleep (probably from the juice). It is my own doing catching up with me. I need saving. I am a sinner and am sick physically, emotionally and spiritually. Thanks for opening me to your holy love and help me to become more aware of my dependence on you.

I am worried about my hemorrhoids—help me to be patient, Thanks for helping me. I worry a lot about my brother; he seems so broken. I want to see him get better. Help me to trust you loving care for him. You are with him. Help him much more than me. Help me to let go of what I want and simply pray, love and trust.

I am worried about whether I should go visit tm brother (in Connecticut) during Holy Week. Lots going on during Holy Week, perhaps it will too soon. Maybe I will wait six weeks and take a vacation day. I prefer to save it up and get $ for CRS [Catholic Relief Services]. Help me to let go. I can save a day next year. Holy Week would be too much stress too soon. I need/want to spend a week with you. Help me and guide me.

Sorry about the distraction in my prayer, it's my sickness hurting me. I blame myself and feel guilty—it's my sin—forgive me for beating myself up but I am sick. I need to forgive and love myself—help me to value who I am—made in your image by your Father and a temple of the Holy Spirit. I am awful hard on myself. Help me to be patient and contented. I am sick and broken and sinful and lovable.

Grant me the grace to accept the sickness myself as we are and others and surrender to your loving care. Grant me the grace I need to continue to make small changes and grant me the grace to be thankful in all things. And surrender to you my love, God and Savior. Thanks, I love you, Lord have mercy on us and on me.

"The cup is the new covenant of My Blood which will be shed for you" "I offer you me and my life."

Lord receive me tonight, tired, anxious, angry yet blessed. Yes, I have problems with self, health, hemorrhoids, brother, and I'm sorry for my anger of myself and life forgive me—my problems are myself and my environment. You only want to love me. Help me to trust in you. Thanks, I love you and have mercy on us.

April 14, 1995 Good Friday

"…they crucified Him…. 'Father forgive them'…"

Mike, I died for you—to save you from sin and evil—I died for you because I love you and want you to have a personal relationship with Me. I AM your God, Savior, Lover and Friend."

Lord, I need a friend right now. Sit alone in my sickness, binged last night, missed Mass, purged (Ex-Lax), took pain pills to knock me out because I didn't want to feel bad today. I'm numb, in shock, it has been maybe 3 years since I've gotten sick, yet realistically I am sick even today, filling up on liquids, dependent on juice to keep in regular and interrupted sleep, exhausted, depression, for me that a normal day. I should be meditating on your passion and love. I am too sick and emotionally stressed out and numb to be open to your passion. Forgive me I'm unworthy and can never be worthy or do anything to earn your love—Calvary is a free gift, undeserved for all mankind. Thank you, Lord, in my brokenness you have always been there—thru many years of my ups and downs—you have never abandoned me but always continue to love, forgive and accept me—thanks

Lord, I offer you my life and suffering today—I am not able to make it in this world on my own—Help me Lord to not only "think" I need you but to live and been dependent on you. Thanks, have mercy on me and us all, I love you, Mike

April 15, 1995 Holy Saturday

"Oh, my people I will open your graves and have you rise from the…" Ez 37

"Mike, hope in Me, I will get you thru day of suffering, sickness—depend on Me."

Lord, I got sick on Thursday, binged and purged, knock myself out with pain pills, was sick all Friday, and into Saturday (today). I'm devastated, shocked, numb, angry, sad, disappointed in me. I feel dead, broken, helpless, and unsure of what I should even eat today, overwhelmed and lost. Seems to be the sickest I have ever been. My body aged, considerably from anorexia, cannot take this kind of stress, my insides are messed up, and I am terrified. Weight gain, body problems—Lord—I don't know what to do or how to live and I am scared—I need you—without you I am lost. I long for you Lord, you are my only hope. Help me to hope—help me to hope, to trust, to want, to listen, and be dependent on you. Thanks for hearing and answering my prayers. I love you, have mercy on us.

April 16, 1995 Easter Sunday

"Don't be terrified you are looking for Jesus, who was crucified, He is risen, He is not here…"

"Mike, don't be afraid—I AM your crucified Savior and Lord—I AM risen and I AM with you to share My life with you—believe in Me—be and live in Me."

Alleluia—praise to you risen Lord, receive me today—help me to come to know you as my personal Savior and Lord, save me from my sinfulness and sickness, and help me to share the Good News of your love with my brothers and sisters. Thanks, I love you, have mercy on us all.

Apr 21, 1995

"they crucified Him"

"I AM with you always, I AM in you, I will take care of you and help Me when you call on Me—I love you very much, want to be your Savior and want you to be Mine."

I'm stressed out trying to handle it—help me—angry—why did I have to gain all of this weight 99-106—I've barely been eating much more—it's upsetting—if I gain this much I don't want to eat better—I'd hoped that I could increase my intake and not gain, even continue to lose—guess my metabolism is set to not require much—I'm disappointed and disgusted—can't wear the clothes I want to—too tight—also I've "gained" due to increase liquids and increase fiber—not real gain but shows on scales—I want to lose and get control again—I lost it on vacation, again this week, and now on day #4 I'm finding that you will give me the strength I need to not get sick and I'm feeling better, hopeful and thankful—now need to decrease intake and liquids so my butt can heal and I can sleep—help me to continue to change and eat healthy—I want to cut back and lose and build on that and feel safe and in control—I believe I can do this and feel better by taking it one step at a time, seeing this I'm making it—today, first day this week (in 2 weeks) that I've not had lots of gas and pain—I'm getting better—thanks—I know I messed up a lot but I'm making progress—healthy choice which I hope to build on—help me to hang in there and become more dependent on you—help me to be free and open to develop the relationship with you—thanks, have mercy on me, I love you, love Mike

April 23, 1995 Emmaus

"We were hoping that he would be the one that would set Israel free..."

"Mike, I AM your crucified risen Lord, God, Savior and Lover. I died to set you and all people free from sin and evil. I want you to be free of sins and evil—hope and trust and believe in Me—spend time with Me, listening, as the disciples on the road did—I will reveal Myself to you and in Me you will know freedom, wholeness, and love."

Lord, thanks for dying for me and forgiving me, thanks for giving your life for me—help me to open up and receive you as my Risen Lord, God, Savior and Lover. I want to know you—help me to listen, receive me a broken sinner tonight—hoping to be saved and freed from my sins and brokenness by you oh Holy God—help me.

"Look at My hands and My feet, it is really I, touch Me."

"Rejoice Mike, I AM truly and really with you—I love you and I AM here for you."

Praise to you Holy Savior—Thanks, Mike

April 24, 1995 After Emmaus

"Mike—peace—let go of the thoughts that disturb you turn them over to Me. Look at My wounded hands and feet—I took on and defeated your weakness, sickness and sin and I died and now I

am alive—risen and I offer you Me and My risen life—open up and rejoice and let Me be your Savior and Lover."

Risen Lord—Thanks—receive me tonight and my brokenness—grant me the grace to accept you into my heart as my personal Savior. Thanks, I love You, have mercy on us. Love Mike

"Mike—peace—don't be disturbed—turn your life—your worries over to Me—look at My hands and feet—I defeated sin and evil and died for you and now I AM with you, it is I—trust Me—reach out and touch Me—be still and come to know Me."

Lord, receive me, broken and needy to trust and give you me in love—help me to trust—let go—be still and open to touch and experience to—oh Holy Crucified, Risen Savior. Thanks, I love you.

"Peace. do not be disturbed…look at My hands and feet—it is really Me—touch Me".

Lord, I am so disturbed by worries and cares—it stresses me out—help me to accept my sickness and simple lifestyle and continue to work with the people you have given me to help out—I'm scared yet hopeful—help me to trust and surrender to you—you are my savior and my hope—forgive me for still resisting and not wanting to deal with those you have put in my life to help me—thanks, I love you, love Mike,

April 30, 1995

"Why are you weeping? Who is it you are looking for? I AM ascending to My Father and Your Father, to My God and to your God."

Mike, you like Mary Magdalene weep, mourn, and look, yet fail to see me—you cannot "find Me"—I reveal myself to you—my revelation is pure gift to be accepted in faith—let go and believe and trust—I AM the way to your heavenly Father, God. I AM the bridge; in Me you can find what you need in your brokenness. Continue to worship Me in fear, calling on Me and I will reveal Myself to you."

Lord, tonight I am hurting—stressed out about my eating problem—knowing I have not surrendered my life and will to you—receive me in my brokenness and grant me the grace to surrender to you and your love for me. Thanks for the lifesaving gift of faith, help me to be open to meeting you, love Mike

May 3, 1995

Peace…He showed them His hand and side…as the Father has sent Me, so I send you. …. He breathes on them. Receive the Holy Spirit

"Mike, know that I love you very much and call you to unity to My Father's love. I know you cannot make it without us, be open and receive the Holy Spirit who will empower you."

"Worship Me in fear—I'll protect you—I AM the joy of those who love My Name—call on Me often—I AM with you and I love you."

Lord—thanks for getting me thru a rough and painful day—I called on you and you answered me—my life is out of control—I'm sick and hurting and sinful and offer you me and my worries—help me to let go and to trust and give my life over to your guidance—grant me the grace I need to be a loving servant—thanks for being my Savior—for the awesome gift of your life and yourself—have mercy on me, I love you, love, Mike

May 4, 1995

"Mike, Peace, see My hands and My side—I died for you and I love you—I AM with you—I AM your risen crucified Savior, God and Lover—I send you to love as My Father sent me—you can do nothing on you own—be open to the gift of the Comforter, the Holy Spirit—He will give you the strength you need to face your brokenness and the strength you need to go forth and be a witness."

Lord, receive me tonight, broken, scared with my sickness, sin, anxiety are all too much for me to handle—my life is out of control—thought I lost it last night—sick as a dog last night yet in my brokenness and pain—help me to rely more and more on you.

I am angry, I gained four pounds, no longer at 99 but now at 104—I am so mad—afraid—I lost control—I want to look thin and feel good—I use to be 110 to 115—ten years ago I was 127—really "thin"—I know I am sick—probably be content with feeling good while losing weight—when I am losing weight I am not helping myself and I am exhausted—help me to change—Linda and family pointed out that I need to change. I am a broken person—I have been hurt badly early as a child—as a teen—I am broken, hurt, sick, ugly and sinful yet I am also loveable—I am not totally bad—deep inside is the me—you died for and called me to be—I have to go through a lot of pain to get to the real me. Help me—my life and my family are your gifts—praise and saved—help me to value the gift of me who you died to save. Thank you, I love you, have mercy on me, Love Mike

"Peace be with you, see My hands and side—I love you—I AM with you—worship Me in fear, call on me often, I'll protect and save you—find life and joy in Me—I AM the joy of those that love My Name."

Lord, what a night—anxiety, panic, stress, almost binged—overwhelmed by what I need to do—go back and work on my life—the hurt, humiliation, shame, guilt and "feel" what I never allow myself to feel—I need to get in touch with and experience some frightening stuff—I need to change—change terrifies me—I like my "fish-bowl" life and the security it offers—I am angry and scared—don't want to go thru this yet I believe you want me to do this for me and begin to love myself and others as you love me—Risen Lord—I can't make it without you like the disciples—I am locked behind walls of fear—you came to them to show your Risen life with them. May I be open to your love to me and open to the joy of a new life you offer—Forgive me for my sins, receive me broken yet at peace—I know I am powerless—in my brokenness—I'm beginning to know my need for you—I not only need you but I want you in my life—guide me—thanks for revealing yourself to me and offering me the help I need to grow—receive my worries about change and help me to trust depend on you one moment at a time—thanks for loving me so very much—have mercy on me a sinner, I love you, love, Mike

May 5, 1995

"…they crucified Him…Father forgive them"

"Worship me in fear…"

Lord, forgive me for not making time for you—for being caught up in me and my sickness—forgive me—help me to worship you in fear and get to know you—your forgiveness and limitless love for me, Thanks, I love you, have mercy on us, Love Mike

May 6, 1995

"Mike, open up—listen and trust—I AM you God, Crucified Savior, best Friend and Lover—call on Me --I am with you to help you—I give you myself daily—listen, open up, trust and love.

Receive me tonight Lord—worries and hopes—Lord, Jesus Christ, Son of God have mercy on me a sinner. Thanks, I love you, Mike

May 7, 1995

"See my wounded hands and side—

Do not pursuit in your unbelief but believe—

Blessed are they who have not seen and believe—

Worship me in fear—call on me often --I will protect you."

"Mike, you are blessed with the gift of faith, you must nurture it—praying—calling on Me often and love—learn to trust—I will get you thru week at work—I AM your Savior."

Lord, receive me tonight—thanks for the awesome life-giving gift of faith and for being present to me and speaking to me—help me to rely on you more—I worry about the changes—yet I know I must, give me the grace I need to make it, Thanks, have mercy on me a sinner, I love you, Mike

May 8, 1995

"Don't persist in your unbelief—but believe...."My Lord and My God"

"Mike—I AM your crucified and risen Lord and God and Savior—I AM with you to help you and protect you—trust Me and love Me."

Lord, thanks—feeling good—rested. receive me tonight—stress—indulged in pastry and food—feeling fat because I'm at 104 and not 100—sick, yes—struggling, yes—but hopeful you are giving me what I need—help me to keep focused on what is truly important—i.e. You, My Lord and My God—you are life—my life in you and with you I am blessed and called to be a covenant relationship with you my God—how awesome—thanks for blessing me with faith—the greatest treasure—help me to worship you in fear, call on you often, listen and trust.

May 12, 1995

"Mike, don't let your heart be troubled—have faith in God, have faith in Me—worship me in fear—I will protect you, call on me often—I AM the joy for those who love My Name.—I AM with you Mike and I died for you—I love you and want you to be mine—believe and trust."

My loving Lord receive me tonight—thankful—beautiful day off—thanks for the precious gift of life and faith, thanks for speaking to me, giving yourself to me and being with me, thanks for the peace of mind I am getting and thanks for your gift of self on the cross.

Tonight—stress—food, fat, worry, sleep, up early, bathroom, party, food, relatives—stress and worn out, fear, angry—weight gain—I am sick, broken and sinful but slowing am getting better physically, emotionally and spiritually—help grant me the grace to accept you as my Savior, Lord, God and Lover and call on you often—you are with me. Help me to listen and be an instrument for your loving presence to my brothers and sister. Thank, I love you, have mercy on us, Love Mike.

"I have heard you cry Mike. I have rescued you, call on me—do you love Me? Feed my sheep.

Lord, thanks, I called you in my brokenness and you answered me—stressed food, weight—ordination party—you gave me the grace to make it and to be loved and to those brothers and sisters who shared in my Dad's day. Thanks, I love you have mercy on us, love, Mike

May 14, 1995

"how does this concern you, your business is to follow Me"

Lord, accept me tonight—broken and sinful yet hopeful—I give you my worries, fears, anger, jealousy, vanity—help me to let go to follow you—how scary is your call—thanks—grant me the grace to respond—worshiping you in awe and love—loving as your love—Thanks have mercy on me, I love you, Love Mike

Follow Me, I see your misery—sorrow—let me take your pain in My hands, depend on Me, I AM your helper—I hear and answer your cry for help—call on Me.

Have mercy on me Lord. I thank you, love Mike.

May 15, 1995

"follow Me"

Lord, I am stressed out today—upset—fighting and angry—eating plan didn't pay off as expected to weight loss and gain—frustrated—wanted to lose—really struggling and worn out by thinking—how can I improve nutrition and lose weight—very upsetting—fear losing control and butt's acting up—scared—help me to follow you—seek you and your Father's way first and then address eating issues—trusting that you will guide me—forgive me for losing track of what is really important—I'm sick and looking to get better—help—have mercy on me, thanks again, I love you, love, Mike

May 16, 1995

"Mike, as I love you so must you love your brothers—unconditionally, limitlessly, uniquely, and totally. This is how you intercede for me in the world—this is my call—I call you to love your brothers this is your vocation."

Lord, thanks for speaking and being present to me. Thanks for the hope and glory and your personal call—I am messed up and have anxiety tonight, grant me the gift of your Spirit so that I might love. Thanks, have mercy on me, I love you. Love Mike

"Mike, I know exhausted and in pain—take refuge in Me and My love. I will empower you thru My Spirit to love and be my witness to the world."

Oh Glorious, Savior, God—thanks—all praise to you—in you I have life, hope, security, peace and wholeness—receive me—broken hurting, sinful—forgive me for anger at others and myself for beating up on me. Grant me the gift of faith and thru your Spirit lead me to dwell in you and your Father's love and share that love. Have mercy on me, thanks, I love you. Love Mike

"…they crucified Him."

"Mike, I AM with and in you—I AM your refuge—find peace, strength, and healing in Me.—I died for you—I AM your crucified Savior and I want you.

Lord, thanks forgive me for my selfishness and sinfulness—heal my brokenness and receive me today—sick, anxiety, worried, exhausted. I love you, have mercy on me, thanks, love Mike

May 18, 1995

"Mike, take refuge in Me—I will protect you and I will give you the grace you need to make it—continue working and be gentle with yourself—I love you because you are you and I know you"

Lord, receive me tonight—sick, tired, exhausted—physically. Spiritually and emotionally—forgive me for doing unloving things today and grant healing to any I may have hurt—grant me the grace to be thankful and rejoice in my brokenness in that it offers me an opportunity of increased dependency on you—help—you with my life—have mercy on me, thanks, I love you, love, Mike

Aug 17, 1995

"Master we are lost"…"Where is your faith?"

Mike have faith in Me—trust Me—I AM with you and in you and want to save you for Myself to live in and with you"

Praise you Holy Savior—in many storms you rescued me lately—thanks—thanks for the gift of faith—life—giving and saving—time in and time out you show me how much you are there for me—accept me tonight—2nd thought about seeing Linda and Helen for help—guide me and continue to help me at my work with trust in you—thanks, have mercy on me a sinner, I love you, love Mike

Aug 18, 1995

"they crucified Him…Father forgive them."

"Mike, I forgive you—be sorry for your sins and rejoice in My mercy and love for you—I died to save you."

Lord, "Happy is he whose faults are taken away" thanks for dying to set me free from my selfishness—receive me tonight—sinful, broken and anxious and continue to have mercy on me a sinner, thanks, I love you, love Mike

Aug 19,1995

"...they crucified Him...Father forgive them."

"Mike, I forgive you, I died to free you from your sins—believe in My limitless love for you My precious one."

Lord, accept me tonight—anxious and guilty—forgive me for being selfish, unbelieving, untrusting—Lord have mercy on me a sinner, thanks—Praise to you Holy Savior—I confess my sins to you and you forgive me and take away my guilt—Lord, help me to learn from you and your love—and grow from my sins and sickness—help me to be humble before you and not that I know it all—help me to forgive and love myself—have mercy on me a sinner, thanks, I love you, love, Mike

Aug 21, 1995

"Daughter your faith in Me has cured you—go in peace."

"Mike—reach out and open up to Me so that I can heal you—believe in Me and My plan to save you and how much I love you."

Lord, thanks I got thru the day—"ratted" my boss out—thanks for giving me the courage to move beyond my fears to do what is right and loving—thanks, now receive me stressed—anorexic—want to lose to get to 100-99 got mad—said "hospitalization"—no way I hit 99—I don't want to deal with and face my problems—forgive me—thanks for the need of you and others—I'm so guilty and ashamed—have mercy on me and on us and forgive me Lord—help me to continue to grow in my need for you—I love you, have mercy on me a sinner, I love you, love Mike

Aug 25 (28), 1995

"they crucified Him…Father forgive them."

"Mike, I am with you, I died for you—I forgive you and love you very much—let me save you, moment by moment to live in love with Me."

Lord receive me tonight—thanks for getting me up for Mass—no bleeding and good sleep—I'm a little tired and anxious—seeing Fr. T today—I don't know when I am going and I'm scared, Lord—I'm sick, sinful, anorexic, selfish, resistant to TX (therapy)—I don't want to change—is this a sin?—wanting to call TX, give $ away, have more time lost weight 99 goal—Helen said hospital—save me yet I don't want to maintain or gain weight, just lose—complicated—right now reduce juice and food—"control"—guilty am I running out on you?—killing myself—Lord, have mercy on me—Past two weeks lots of anxiety and guilt, crazy, yet you have shown me your powerful and saving love for me—gotten me through crisis after crisis—Lord I'm so fragile and broken—feeling bitter, yet I know how weak I am in my sinfulness and brokenness—I am coming more and more to know how much I need you—thanks Lord—at the bottom of all this I just want to be loved and have peace—only in you and in love with you can I find this—help me to open up and let your love in—Forgive me, help me and save me with your Holy Crucified Savior—open me to your guidance and grant me the grace to love—forgive me for being proud, selfish and resistant and help me to be open to come to know you. Thanks, have mercy on me a sinner, I love you, love, Mike

Aug 29, 1995

"Mike—let me love you, love Me, others and you and pray as I did not My will but yours be done, Father"

Lord—thanks—you answered me today—anxious—wanting to know you—will—seeking guidance—thanks—you help me to listen and trust in you and you answered me—WOW—also I'm growing in love with you and love for me—thanks—accept me tonight—broken, worried, anxious, sinful in love with you—have mercy on me a sinner, thanks, I love you, love Mike

Aug 30, 1995

"Father, not My will but Your will be done."

"Mike, I forgive you for your sinning, lying and failing to love yourself—look to become more like Me moment by moment surrendering to our Father in love—trust Him—He and I love you greatly."

Lord, forgive me for lying—trying to cover up my anorexia and cheating at work—signing up on time when I am 5 to 10 minutes late—it's wrong I've sinned and need to change and face the anorexia that leads to a life of lying—Lord, receive tonight broken and longing to become in need of you—grant me the grace to depend on you—thanks for teaching me and revealing you to me—have mercy on me a sinner, thanks, I love you, love Mike

Dec 14, 1995

"Let Me be your Savior Mike—I love you and want you"

Lord, Thanks, have mercy on me a sinner, I love you, love, Mike

Dec 15, 1995

"…they crucified Him"

"I died for you because I love you—I want you to be Mine"

Lord, Thanks, have mercy on me a sinner, I love you, love, Mike

Dec 16, 1995

"I love you—let Me save you—give yourself to Me in love"

Lord, Thanks, have mercy on me a sinner, I love you, love, Mike

Dec 17, 1995

"I AM with you—don't be afraid—"trust Me."

Lord, Thanks, have mercy on me a sinner, I love you, love, Mike

Dec 18, 1995

"It is I—don't be afraid—I'll save you"

Lord, Thanks, have mercy on me a sinner, I love you, love, Mike

Dec 19, 1995

"I AM God, and I AM saving you from your sins—Rejoice"

Lord, Thanks, have mercy on me a sinner, I love you, love, Mike

Dec 20, 1995

"Rejoice—I will save you My beloved one"

Lord, Thanks, have mercy on me a sinner, I love you, love, Mike

Dec 21, 1995

"Rejoice—I AM your Savior"

Lord, Thanks, have mercy on me a sinner, I love you, love, Mike

Dec 22, 1995

"...they crucified Him"

"I died for you—I love you—I AM with you now to save you—surrender in trust to let Me love you and thru you"

Lord, Thanks, have mercy on me a sinner, I love you, love, Mike

Dec 23, 1995

"Rejoice—I AM your Crucified Savior God and Lover—My beloved one"

Lord, Thanks, have mercy on me a sinner, I love you, love, Mike

Dec 24, 1995

"I AM God—I AM with you—I AM your Savior"

Lord, Thanks, have mercy on me a sinner, I love you, love, Mike

Dec 25, 1995

"Rejoice, I AM with you and among you with love—My beloved"

Lord, Thanks, have mercy on me a sinner, I love you, love, Mike

Dec 26, 1995

"I AM with you"

Lord, Thanks, have mercy on me a sinner, I love you, love, Mike

Dec 27, 1995

"I love you—I AM with you always"

Lord, Thanks, have mercy on me a sinner, I love you, love, Mike

Dec 28, 1995

"I AM in you and in love with you"

Lord, Thanks, have mercy on me a sinner, I love you, love, Mike

Dec 29, 1995

"Father forgive them"

"I forgive you—believe—rejoice"

Lord, Thanks, have mercy on me a sinner, I love you, love, Mike

Dec 30, 1995

"I love you—let Me love you and thru you"

Lord, Thanks, have mercy on me a sinner, I love you, love, Mike

Dec 31, 1995

"I AM with you now and always and I love you"

Lord, Thanks, have mercy on me a sinner, I love you, love, Mike

Sep 9, 1996

Dear Lord, I come to you today, sick, weak, and sinful—pleurisy—lots of pain, gas pain—breathing pain—my diet is not working—milk is causing so much gas and pain, I'm broken.—Called in sick to work—feel guilty—anorexic and health problems—hurting my job performance—also don't want to go into staff party—not ready to even try to eat something normal—help—forgive me—my varying isn't working—been angry and depressed and disgusted in losing weight—left comfort zone—gained, depressed, now lost a little but nowhere near enough—want to get under 100 to feel good—sick and insane. Lord, I want to try something new—tuna fish instead of milk but I'm scared—I believe if this works, I can feel better about myself and my life—it should really improve my time with you—so often broken up by gas pain also work and my personal life—should benefit—living in continue pain has happen too much—I'm really hurting and need and want to change—my job, spiritual, emotional and physical health is dependent on it—help—help—help—I can't make it on my own—have mercy on me a sinner, thanks, I love you, love, Mike

Nov 27, 1996 (Thanksgiving)

"Jesus have mercy on me a sinner"

"Your faith has been your salvation"

Lord, it's 2:30 AM and up anxious and awake—slept good—nervous—been feeling better, sleeping good, less pain, bleeding stopped, prayer is deeper—thanks for blessing me with faith—life-giving and saving—in you oh Holy One—Thanks for family, health and work. I'm sick still—anxious—losing weight—want to keep changing diet for better and lose, not gain, get to my comfort zone and mandate—so scared tonight—last year I got to it—blew it—and was depressed for over 3/4 of the year—Lord have mercy on me—I'm sick and sinful and I offer you me tonight. Help me to call on you and rely on you and you alone—on my own I'm stuck in a cycle of insanity. Thanks, thanks, thanks Lord, for loving, forgiving and dying for me and for all of us. Love, Mike

Dec 21, 1996

Lord, thanks—its 2 AM—slept well—anxious—help me to get some more good rest—what a day—thanks for getting me thru it and home safe and alive!—Went to nutrition counselor on Friday—she was out—started bleeding—thought it was hemorrhoids—went to doctor without appointment—they took me in because I was bleeding—made me lie down—couldn't move—called ambulance—internal bleeding—fear hemorrhaging—I was terrified—was I dying or going to have to be hospitalized—almost broke down—ER visit—Doctor seem to think I had a bleeding ulcer from taking so many Advil (14 plus) per night to ease stomach, chest and back pain caused by my muscle weakness, gas, coughing—anorexic—I'm destroying my body—Lord, thanks for getting me home—I can't make it without you and I don't want to either—help me to trust in you—help me to stay out of the hospital and be one who serves you with my whole heart and love—thanks for having mercy on me a sinner, love, Mike

Jul 30, 1997

"Courage it is I, do not be afraid, there are no limits to my power to save "

"Mike, trust me—I AM with you—I can and will save you if you let Me—I AM the Savior of all—trust Me and My love and power to save"--

Lord, its 3:30 AM—thanks for helping me sleep and being awake now—feel sad—like crying—yesterday I turned my boss in to her boss for what I believe was unfair treatment of my co-worker—people were getting hurt and it looked like—I am not happy to have to turn her in—I like her a lot but I couldn't sit there and watch others get hurt—I tried speaking to her but it didn't seem to do much good—I didn't want to hurt her and I didn't want her to be hurt but maybe some "hurt" and help will be an opportunity for her to grow—I know many of my "hurts" in life have helped me to grow—I feel badly because she'll be in a lot of pain and I know she cares a lot about me—I'd like to cry—I'd like to tell her I'm sorry that I can do this—I'm scared because I don't know where this will go—in a selfish way, I'm scared of losing my job—financially care to worry about and I really like working with people—I'm scared and afraid of having to go back to work and face the bosses—scared too I may not have done the right thing or handled it right—scared too because she can hurt me too because she is my boss and knows that I am anorexic—something I hope she doesn't choose to use against me—I'm vulnerable—I know that when I told her it was a risk and I told her that—however, I felt it was worth talking and still do because getting help saved my life—and I hope she would get help also—given it's kind of funny—looking back it's true—there are no limits to your power to save—you get me and us through things—help me to trust that you know what's best and rely on your grace to love—have mercy on her and my adolescence and my family and on us all—help me to deal with my fears, sadness in healthy ways—help me to grow more dependent on you—thanks for loving me and being with me and dying to save me—have mercy on me a sinner, thanks, I love you, love, Mike

Jan 4, 1998

"Jesus, have pity on me…your faith has saved you"

"Mike, continue to call on Me thru your suffering and I'll continue to save you—know that I love you very much—I died for you"

Jan 7, 1998

"Jesus Son of David, have mercy on me"

"Your faith has and will save you—trust Me"

Good morning Lord, thanks for a new day and some sleep last night—offer you my tiredness and suffering today and hope to sleep better tonight—really I'm overwhelmed—unsure of what's causing sleeping problems—probably anxiety and depression plus not spending a good hour with you daily plus smoking too much—help me to make small changes and offer all my worries and cares to you—I'm upset because I don't want to take Rx for sleep or anxiety and depression because I feel my mental state for prayers will be diminished and that is so meaningful for me—Rx would be a block between you and me and the thought makes me feel like a failure—my anorexia has caused me much hurt, my family, job and relationship with you—now I'm scared and nervous because I don't know what to do—guide me Lord—help me to give in to your will—thanks, I love you, love Mike

Lord—I'll try to work on dealing with stress and feelings this week and stick with Rx 1 + 1 and be open to being in therapy (TX) for depression and anxiety if that is what it takes what I need—guide me Lord—I offer you my sickness and suffering and hope for your help.

Jan 11, 1998

"Mike, I AM your God, personal Lord and Savior and I love you and want you to be Mine—I want to heal you and live with and thru you"

Lord, thanks and praise to you—I love you and want to give you myself—thanks for healing me and continue to heal me as you chose to—help me to open to your way and your will for me—teach me to be more loving and more like you—I offer you my anxiety and fears about my health, anorexic, sleeping, family, and work and trust that you will be with me to help me—thanks, I love you, have mercy on me a sinner, love, Mike

Nov 11, 1998

"Mike, call on My Name and I will save you—I want to save, heal, forgive, live and be with and love you—please let Me"

Lord, thanks for calling me—I'm so sinful, selfish, proud, vain, jealous, untrusting, and unworthy of You and Your love—Its overwhelming to think that You could and do really love and want me to be Yours. Tonight, I'm having trouble sleeping—all stressed out—new doctor will keep me on Rx for my problems—told her about me today—I'm a pretty sick person—my doctor saw me today—I could see her—she looked at me as one very sick and dying person—my family's worried—it hurt to see my dad's face and hear his voice—Lord, forgive me—so many people care and love me and I'm wasting away—sometimes I feel it would be better to be dead if I could be with you and not have to suffer and be so sick anymore. Lord, teach me how to suffer and love I offer you the insanity of my anorexia—Help me Lord, forgive and save me Lord, love and heal me Lord—accept me to be yours. Thanks, I love you, Mike

Dec 20, 1998

"Mike, I love you, I washed away your sins with My own Blood."

"I AM your God—your Lover—Savior—I forgive and love you and want you to be Mine"

Lord, thanks for forgiving me, loving me as I am—uniquely me and dying for me—help me to accept and experience your love and forgiveness—personally and unique to me and to see this uniqueness of your love and goodness me and others and help me to love like you and let go of my fears, jealousy and resentment, accepting and loving me and others as you do. I'm stressed with holidays, cold weather, new year coming, fearing job change or loss—help me to trust in you and rely on you, I love you, love, Mike

Feb 11, 1999

"They crucified Me for you and each person"

Mike Attends an AA Meeting

Aug 31, 1997

Felt very nervous going to meeting—it's been 13 years and I am a recovering person who has been very blessed by God with the grace to live sober. I fear seeing clients and self-disclosure—want to keep working totally separate from personal living and was relieved to see no clients at the meeting—felt nervous going in and sitting down yet welcomed—feeling I belonged. Early in the meeting was easily distracted—member reading and talking—lots of echoes—one member commented how he was glad to go to another room for small group discussion because of the poor acoustics of the old classroom we were in—I was glad to get to stay in the room and was able to get focused—persons began encircling the discussion table and I felt, however as I sat down I felt welcomed and safe over again and then enviousness kicked in scared to go take a place—what should I say when it was my turn to speak?

Being attentive and listening and being open to the person speaking gave me peace—persons shared the 3rd step "We made a decision to turn our lives and our wills over to the care of God…" It was powerful, listening after all these years—no I am not drinking but in a lot of ways I am a dry drunk—plagued by the problems that led into my drinking but just not drinking—life is good but hard because the inner me is still very hurting and broken and looking for peace and healing in the wrong places all too often—my life is still very insane and unmanageable at times—listening and pardoning gave me a feeling of hope and happiness—I feel far short of the daily process of turning my myself over to God's care and will and often get discouraged—many worries and care I seek to control—listening gave me peace because 3 members shared how it's helped them greatly to experience the "care" part of the step—(i.e. God cares very much about me) and peace came in this—turning self over to the care of a loving and caring God—this won't shield us from pain and suffering but trusting is the answer—I don't have to worry because God's will for me is to trust Him to give me the help I need and with that we can make it thru all the things I see as overwhelming.

Aug 31, 1997 Sunday Speaker Meeting Binghamton Phelps Hall 7:00 PM

Sep 1, 1997

Going to 2nd meeting in a day after years of not was good—much more relaxed—turning my worries over to God's care helped me immensely—generally I am a very nervous and self-conscious when going someplace new but again giving in I felt welcomed, like I belong and relived because I wouldn't have to speak. After the meeting started, former clients sporadically stopped to say hi and it's great to see you and shook my hand—no longer was I counselor but another human working on recovery—felt connected and safe. The speaker, a man I'm familiar with, really surprised me—after years of recovery he went back out and is now back on track again (he compared himself to a train) and reinforced the importance of the "rooms" i.e. AA fellowship—as the meeting closed we made a large circle and I was glad and humbled to be part of something bigger then myself as we prayed the Lord's prayer, afterwards a former client came up and shared his growth and hope with me—I need that because I've been in a rut lately. Exiting the room I felt nervous and in awe of the fellowship—persons gathering outside to smoke and be together—slowly I moved beyond and began my journey home—privileged to feel the power of fellowship and yet not an active member of it—left feeling hopeful—recovery works and so too does fellowship, driving home, I couldn't help wonder if it might be good to be involved, however, where I am at today I don't know if it would be the right thing to do, but maybe someday.

Sitting here now 4 PM Labor Day preparing to go back to 11 days without a break—I'm thankful to go back having received something to share—not that I'll speak at length of this experience but hope that is in the memories I take back to the DAC with me and hope to be able to pass it on.

Sep 5, 1997

"Lord, I do believe—help my unbelief"

Day one of training class—thanks for getting me thru Lord, and accept me tonight—learning about alcoholism a disease—obsession—compulsion—sickness—right I feel hope because I admit I have a sickness and you have gifted me with faith in you and your power to save me—help me to believe and trust and surrender more—

I'm so sick, enslaved by anorexia—fatigue, poor sleep, mental exhaustion, chronic pain, guilt, shame, sadness, bleeding, gas pain—I offer me to you tonight, Lord, you who suffered and died on the cross in my place (and for all) to defeat evil, sin, sickness and death—you and your love conquered all—have mercy on me a sinner, thanks, I love you, love, Mike

Sep 12, 1997

Went to Al-Anon on Wednesday—powerful—3rd step—stop—2nd time 3rd step is topic—2nd discussion meeting in 14 years—I guess that you are trying to tell me something—finally I am just beginning little by little to turn my life and will (worries over to you and your care and I'm finding I don't have to be enslaved by sick, worried centered thinking) thanks Lord for healing, freeing up, and loving me so much, to the point of dying on the cross to save me and us all—may I become a message of your healing love—Thanks, I love you, Mike

Sep 13, 1997

Lord, I'm powerless over my brokenness and sinfulness, my life's a mess, I believe you love me and want and can save me—help me to turn myself—my life and will over to you and your loving care for me. Thanks, I love you, love, Mike

Sep 14, 1997 Sunday—Triumph of the Cross

"Lord, I do have faith—help the little faith I do have."

Lord accept me tonight—help me to turn my life and will and worries over to you and your care and love and rely on you—help me make a change in my diet without getting sick and bleeding—help me at work—help me to trust—thanks, I love you, love Mike

Oct 18, 1997

"Mike, the bread that I give you is Me, My flesh for the life of the world. I AM with you always, I AM your life, let Me love you, live in, with and thru you."

Lord, thanks for loving me so much that you died for me and give me yourself daily—help me to be more open to you and depend on you—can't make it on my own—I'm very sick physically, emotionally and spiritually—I'm a weak, selfish, sinful, and broken man—thanks for dying for me and reaching out to me in love daily—help me to be more open to you in the moment by moment in my life—forgive me for being so selfish, self-centered and worrisome—thanks for revealing you to me in silence and in others, especially the man that came up to me and asked for a smoke tonight—I didn't want to be bothered and was scared he might hurt me—all he wanted was to talk and be accepted—homeless living at VOA, "misfit" (like myself) looking for you—in him I saw your goodness—I saw him looking for you and for love and acceptance—help me to give myself as you did. Thanks, have mercy on me a sinner, I love you, love, Mike

Oct 26, 1997

"…Jesus have pity on me" "…your faith has saved you"

"Mike, its O.K. your faith in Me will save you—trust in Me"

Jesus,—help me to trust you and to work to take care of myself by facing my fears with your help—I can't do it on my own—I'm overwhelmed and stressed out—can't sleep, nervous, worried, obsessed with fear of change and guilt about how I have hurt my family, help me Lord—I'm sick—don't want to change but fear getting sick, losing job and going in hospital or dying—can't make it without you—help me—Thanks, I love you, love, Mike

Nov 5, 1997

Have pity on me Lord, "your faith in me is saving me"

I AM your God, and I AM with you, give thanks to Me for I AM good and my love for you is everlasting"

Lord, thanks and forgive me for being so selfish and weak and sinful and sick—thanks for loving me and being with me in my pain and emptiness—have mercy on me a sinner, thanks, I love you, love, Mike

Apr 17, 2000

Mike, its O.K. I AM with you" "you are My intimate friend"

"You shall love Me your whole being, love others and love yourself." Mark 12

"Take this, this is my Body"

"Father let it be as you would have it"

"Then they crucified Him"

"Know that I AM with you always"

Jesus, help—am scared—don't know what to do—fears—loss of job, security, vacation, schedule, Mass, sleep, digestion, health—am sad and scared, afraid—don't know what to do—help me to stop, pray, listen to you and love and let you guide me—help me to trust in you—thanks for 5 years of recovery and 6 years of sobriety and 16 years of human services—help me to love—Thanks, I love you, love, Mike

Lord Jesus Christ Son of God have mercy on me a sinner.

"I want you to be all mine"

Mar 18, 2000

"Know that I AM with you always" (End of Matthew)

Dear God, its 3:15 AM and I am up and can't sleep—very anxious, upset—got scary new Friday at 4:30 PM—may lose my current job as drug counselor at DAC—very upset, sad,—love job working with people, love counseling—Don't know what is going to happen or what my options really are—but glad I won't be jobless—just major change—that scares me—schedule change, having to dress up, trying to get to Mass—fear exhaustion, constipation, insomnia, missing Mass, being sick—not being able to counsel—it's really upsetting, scary, sad—I offer you me tonight—want to trust you and put this in your hands—you've never failed me—me to trust in your love, your will, your way for me. Thanks, I love you, love, Mike

Apr 19, 2000

Lord Jesus Christ, Son of God, Have mercy on me a sinner. Sad, worries, afraid, anxious—what is going to happen to my job, career, vocation? Use me as a missionary warrior in Binghamton, NY—Thanks for the options: CDSU/Case Manager, Jail Counselor, DSS Case Worker, DSS examiner, BC Office of Employment and Training. Help me to love like you. Thanks, Jesus, I love you, love, Mike

X.

MARRIED TO E.D. (EATING DISORDER)

MIKE'S JOURNAL GIVES GREAT INSIGHTS into the torment of his eating disorder and his deep relationship with God.

I wondered why God couldn't heal Mike.

Mike related his own life to Chapter 12 in the second book of Corinthians, where the Apostle Paul talks about the thorn in his flesh:

"…I was given a thorn in my flesh, a messenger of Satan, torment me. Three times I pleaded with the Lord to take it away from me. But God said to me, 'My grace is sufficient for you, for my power is made perfect in weakness'…for when I am weak, then I am strong."

Paul's passion for the Lord was incredibly intense, and we can only imagine how intense his suffering was as he pleaded with God for relief. People have wondered for nearly two millennia what the thorn in Paul's flesh actually was.

Mike pleaded with God to take his eating disorder away from him. He was made so weak—physically weighing around and eventually less than 100 pounds and suffering constant mental anguish.

Yet Mike's dependency on God made him so strong, and he allowed God to do tremendous things for others through the gift of his life in the midst of his own great struggle.

God's power was made perfect in Mike's weakness through Mike's incredible witness.

The same is true with each of us. The more we turn to God in our own weaknesses, the stronger we become.

Mike told me that if I wanted to understand his eating disorder, I should read the book *Married to* E.D., in which E.D. stands for Eating Disorder.

Mike explained that he was giving so much incredible time and energy to his eating disorder—like a marriage commitment to a bad spouse—that he was neglecting his loved ones and so many other things.

Although Mike indeed gave so much attention to his eating disorder, it is hard to imagine a person more focused on others and loving toward others than Mike was.

Like many with eating disorders, Mike's anorexia was rooted in guilt. But for years I didn't know the cause of this guilt.

Mike's eating disorder was manifested in four areas: not eating enough, exercising too much, abusing laxatives, and smoking.

For as long as I can remember, Mike had routines where he would eat the same exact thing every day. For years he ate oatmeal. Then I remember him switching to toast with cheese. He also ate a lot of eggs.

His one unhealthy habit was drinking caffeine-free Diet Coke, which he would mix with water.

Nutritionist Helen Battisti spent a great deal of time with Mike on his diet and worked with him for years. Helen gave Mike a strong protein diet and energy to carry out a vigorous daily routine.

Our family will always be deeply grateful to Helen for her incredible work with Mike. We believe she kept him alive for many more years than he otherwise would have lived.

For as much as eating consumed Mike and as little as he ate, he really enjoyed eating. While visiting my mom and dad's house on weekends, he would sit at the table and talk to my mom while eating toast—often semi-burnt toast—with cheese on it. He would enjoy every bite and every crumb and take his time doing so—taking fifteen minutes or more to eat a single slice of toast.

My favorite Mike eating story actually came one Thanksgiving when I was a teenager. Mom said Dad and I would be going to our Uncle John

DeVinney's house to prepare a Thanksgiving Dinner for him. John lived alone and was in a wheelchair.

With his stringent routine and weak health, Mike just couldn't handle overnight trips, and Chris stayed at home with him. Mom offered to prepare Thanksgiving food for Chris and Mike—even though she knew Mike wouldn't eat it—but they declined.

Mike and Chris celebrated their own Thanksgiving Dinner—peanut butter and jelly sandwiches—in what they joked was one of the best Thanksgivings they ever had.

It was sad that Mike couldn't enjoy the food at special meals like Thanksgiving with us, but our family accepted Mike fully and loved him unconditionally.

Although he didn't talk about it, Mike religiously monitored calories.

Through Helen Battisti's loving guidance and our ever-present family support, it meant Mike could eat a little more of the healthy food he was eating—one more piece of toast, one more egg, as he counted virtually every calorie.

We realized that change or improvement for Mike didn't mean he was going to wake up one day and start pounding down Wendy's Dave's Singles.

The second dimension of Mike's eating disorder was exercise. Mike walked and walked and walked—burning massive amounts of calories.

Mike loved walking, but it was also part of his obsessions and disorder. On a given day he might walk nearly two miles from his apartment to his office in downtown Binghamton, then a half mile to Catholic mass and back at noon. Then Mike would walk three miles across town to the Broome County Jail to see a client before walking two more miles home. This totaled nearly eight miles of walking in a single day. Some days he walked much more.

There was a time in his life that he actually walked seven miles from his apartment in Binghamton to my mom and dad's house. Mike and Dad liked to say that the distance from Jerusalem, where Jesus died, to

Emmaus, where his disciples saw him walking on the road, was also seven miles.

Mike walked in both extremely cold and extremely hot weather. He walked with Dad, our brothers, Flint, Julie when she was in town, and eventually me. When he was walking alone, he prayed and prayed and prayed.

For a time in the 1990s he also biked. He loved biking from his apartment in Binghamton to my parents' house, but he broke his elbow when a person in a parked car opened his door as Mike was riding by.

By the time I was old enough to play sports with Rob and Chris, Mike was too ill and frail to participate.

But there was one exception: Mike joined one of the thousands of back yard basketball games (my brothers and their friends and later my friends and I played so much) at our parents' house with me, Chris, Rob, and our nephews Robbie and Kevin.

I believe Mike was about forty years old then and barely weighed 100 pounds. We were all careful not to run into him for fear of severely injuring him. It was so fun, though, to enjoy that one basketball game with Mike. It is a memory I will always cherish. I was so little when he graduated from high school and don't remember his younger athletic days.

Even though Mike used excessive walking to lower his weight, it was also a positive activity in which he shared so much with family and friends and prayed so much.

Mike's abuse of laxatives—the third aspect of his eating disorder—was not so positive. He took them frequently for decades. His use of laxatives became a vicious cycle of dependency; he had trouble going to the bathroom without them. This abuse of laxatives wore away his digestive system.

Mike was always trying to save money to give to the overseas missions, so he always bought the cheapest laxatives—the CVS brand.

As we can see in his journals, Mike was dealing with constant abdominal pain, but he rarely mentioned this to family and friends. He was always so positive—a happy warrior.

One final way Mike kept weight down was smoking cigarettes, which suppressed his appetite. It was a terrible vice, and boy did Mike inhale those cigarettes.

Everything for Mike was routine, routine, routine.

He would wake up at the same time, walk to daily Mass at the same time via the same path, eat exactly the same things, and get to bed at exactly the same time.

He had obsessions and compulsions.

Our immediate family grew accustomed to Mike's strange eating habits and regimental routine. Mike would politely decline meals with Flint and his family. With Julie he was always coming up with excuses not to eat at their Pepper Mill lunches. She would let Mike have it for not eating—but couldn't break his habits.

Sleep was a great challenge due to his eating disorder. Being at such a low weight caused Mike to not sleep well. Mike talked frequently about and expressed great thanksgiving when he slept well.

Mike went to bed very early every night. In later years he would tell us not to call him after 7 p.m. Early evening was a time for prayer for him, and he would wake up very early the next day for more prayer. Rest was something his weakened body desperately needed.

Family and friends worried greatly about Mike, as he was so thin for so many years and we all struggled with how to help him.

A great memory I have was a story from Mary Jo Slavik, Julie Trasolini's sister, who after marriage bought a house on Norton Avenue only four houses away from our parents.

She told me that her son, Gabe Slavik Jr., would pray for Mike every night at the dinner table when he offered his prayers.

Like so many others, Gabe knew there was something very special about Mike, but also that he was suffering so much.

For someone who was such an outstanding counselor as Mike, you might ask why counseling wasn't successful in treating his eating disorder.

As mentioned, Mike tried counseling with a woman named Linda, whom he mentions in his journal. Years later Mike told me he did really try with Linda and she was a nice person, but he didn't make much progress and eventually stopped.

In addition to Helen Battisti, Mike had an extraordinary primary care physician named Dr. Richard Terry, who began offering a special program for eating disorder patients for those in our area.

Dr. Terry is a remarkable human being who has gone on to open a medical school in Elmira. Dr. Terry loved Mike so much and served him so faithfully for many years. Like Helen Battisti, our family will always be indebted to Dr. Terry for his instrumental work in keeping Mike alive.

Mike also had great priests as spiritual advisors—including Father Thomas Hobbes and Father Corey Van Kuren—who would help him battle this horrible disease.

XI.

THE SPIRITUAL LIFE OF A SPIRITUAL WARRIOR

THE CONVERSATIONS WITH JESUS AND beautiful prayers Mike wrote to God didn't just happen. They came about after years of dedicated prayer and continual steadfast efforts to grow closer to God.

Much of his spiritual life took place in his tiny apartment on 25 Cary Street, on Binghamton's North Side.

His second-floor apartment had a small bedroom, with room for a single bed and chair with a little space to walk. There were a tiny kitchen and small bathroom as well as a nice porch Mike enjoyed in the summer. Mike kept the furnishing sparse—the bare-bones minimum.

The rent for the apartment was only $175 per month, and the building was owned by an elderly man named Mr. Pierson, who lived a few blocks away. Mike loved Mr. Pierson—an old-fashioned man who grew up during the Great Depression—and felt he was getting a good deal on an apartment he loved and lived in for over twenty years.

Cary Street could be described as part of a rough neighborhood. Cary Street residents were frequently out in front of their houses or apartments. Many were on public assistance, and some were involved with drugs. Mike loved them all—whatever their life choices—and was friendly with everyone.

Mike would wake up at 5:00 a.m. or earlier to spend several hours in prayer—often on a prayer bench—before work.

The brown wooden bench was about two feet long and six inches wide. It had two short legs on it. The person praying—in this case Mike, for hours and hours—could actually kneel and sit back on this small bench.

Mike loved mantra prayers—repeating the same prayer again and again.

His favorite prayer was the Jesus Prayer, "Lord Jesus Christ, have mercy on me a sinner."

The prayer was from a book called *The Way of the Pilgrim*, in which the main character is struck by Paul's words to "pray without ceasing" (Thessalonians 5:17).

Mike would pray the Jesus Prayer for hours on end in his apartment or while walking. This prayer became a deep meditation for Mike and a way of becoming so close to Jesus.

If Mike walked alone from Binghamton to Endwell—seven miles or more—I believe he prayed this prayer the majority of the time.

There were many beautiful things about Mike's spiritual life, but I believe this one beautiful prayer that he prayed hundreds of thousands of times was instrumental in his transformation into a saintly man.

The Jesus Prayer calls on God's mercy for sinners. Mike would teach me that the great saints in the Church were the ones who were most aware of even the smallest of sins as they became closer to God.

Mike's dedication to the Eucharist and prayer led to the dramatic spiritual transformation I saw in him from my early childhood memories until his death in 2010.

Mike was always a very special, kind, amazing person. When he was younger, he might at times gossip or be judgmental, like most human beings.

As he got older, I saw a man who sanctified his life to the point where he was constantly praying or loving others and never made unkind comments or judgments.

Mike's love for the Eucharist was at the center of who he was.

Mike loved daily Mass, which he would usually attend at 12:10 at Saint Mary's of the Assumption in downtown Binghamton. He would carefully arrange all of his counseling meetings at work around this schedule.

If he could not attend the lunchtime Mass, he would attend St. Paul's closer to his house early in the morning.

Mike loved receiving Jesus in the Eucharist. Seeing him at Mass was seeing a man in a state of deep prayer and meditation uniting with the Lord and Savior he loved so much.

Mike would talk at great length how special it was for him to receive Jesus every day. He would be heartbroken if something came up in his schedule at work and he couldn't receive Jesus.

On a few occasions it appeared his work schedule might change, making him unable to get to Mass at all. This was a crisis for Mike. Things always seemed to work out, and he was always able to get to Mass.

One of my favorite quotes about the Eucharist comes from St. Augustine, who said, "See what you are and become what you see."

See the Body of Christ and become it. I believe this quote personifies Mike and the Eucharist. He threw his whole heart into this mission every day.

Mike also loved the Sacrament of Confession, which he would attend every Saturday afternoon with his spiritual advisor after a long walk from Mom and Dad's house.

Father Sixtus had had a profound impact on Mike during his time in the seminary, but he died sometime after Mike left New York City.

The first regular spiritual advisor after Sixtus I remember for Mike was Father Tierney of Saint Ambrose parish in Endicott. Mike loved Father Tierney, who came over to Mom and Dad's house for dinner several times. Father Tierney moved to Florida in 1998 and passed away a few years later.

Father Hobbes—longtime school counselor and former principal of Seton Catholic Central—became Mike's spiritual advisor from 1998 onward. Father Hobbes was also the Saints football team chaplain who had gotten knocked over by the coach in a story I told previously.

Father Hobbes loved Seton, loved being a priest, and was a tremendous spiritual advisor to my brother.

Father Hobbes was stationed at our home church—Christ the King—from 1998 until it closed in 2008 and was amazed by Mike's holiness and spirituality.

When speaking of Mike, he said to my father, who served as a deacon at Christ the King Church during this time, "It's hard and humbling to hear the confession of a Saint."

Mike was also close to and relied on Father Corey Van Kuren for spiritual advice. We were so honored to have Father Corey write the forward to this book. He said to me, "I want to write why people still need to hear from Mike."

Mike loved priests. He knew priests had the power no one else did: to take the simple bread and wine and turn it into the Body and Blood of Jesus Christ that he cherished so much.

Whenever he saw a priest, he would beam with a smile and say, "Thank you, Father, for being a priest."

Mike developed two other "Jesus Prayers" from the original "Lord Jesus Christ have mercy on me, a sinner."

The first was, "Jesus I love you: save souls."

Mike knew that the salvation of souls and getting to heaven was the most critical goal for every single human person.

The second was, "Jesus is my lover, and I am Jesus's lover."

This was an amazing prayer and showed how deeply Mike loved Jesus. Mike's relationship with Jesus was a deep, personal love that I believe few people have ever experienced on that level.

The evenings for Mike were reserved for spiritual readings and more prayer.

For at least six years he had no TV at all. Then he had an old black and white television with an antenna—so he could watch for free—that he used to watch the news each night.

He liked watching BBC News, because they had the most news about international humanitarian situations.

Mike read the entire Bible several times as well as every single book he could get his hands on about the Passion of Christ. He read intensely about Jesus's suffering and His last words from the Cross.

The only non-spiritual book I remember Mike mentioning were books by James Michener, who wrote incredible works of historical fiction.

Michener did a great job captivating the reader with the human experience, and I believe reading Michener helped Mike with his work with people.

Mike absolutely loved Lent. He constantly prayed, meditated upon, and talked about Jesus's great love for us as seen through his tremendous suffering during the Passion.

Mike suffered so much from his illness but was united so strongly to the suffering of Christ.

Mike prayed and prayed and prayed for others. I know he prayed so much for me, our family, and his friends, and I believe his prayers had a huge impact on me.

Mike prayed for the world's poor and for an end to abortion.

Mike prayed for his clients, co-workers, and bosses—even those who hurt him badly.

Mike prayed for the souls in purgatory and had a prayer list of old relatives from Hornell who had passed away whom he prayed for every night.

Mike had at least two mystical experiences that he seldom spoke about.

One time he was in deep prayer in his apartment and he saw a lighted globe floating in his room. He was not scared, but he wondered if it was from God or the devil. He asked his spiritual advisor, Father Hobbes. Hobbes thought it probably was from God.

On another occasion, upon leaving noon mass at Saint Mary's of the Assumption Church, he heard the voice of Mary, Jesus's mother. I can't remember what Mike said he had heard Mary say, but it was more just the fact that Mary said something to him.

For years at the end of his life he wore an old green Seton Catholic Central Saints football jacket, on which he drew a cross on the back. He had a heavy winter jacket on that he taped a gray cross on the back for colder weather, a gray flannel shirt with a cross he drew on it for warmer weather, and a T-Shirt for hot weather that said, "Love One Another—John 15:17."

Passersby wondered who this thin man was with the cross on his back. Many honked and give him a thumbs-up in support of his Christian mission. A number of people honked and gave him a thumbs-down.

Mike also loved taking retreats. When most people take retreats, they usually go to retreat houses and have a spiritual director for a weekend of prayer.

Mike's retreats were self-directed in his apartment. He would tell our family that he was doing a retreat and that he wouldn't be over on the weekend.

This meant Mike would be spending Friday night, Saturday, and Sunday in deep prayer and contemplation in his apartment—his spiritual fortress—leaving only for Mass and walks in which he prayed and prayed and gave glory to God.

My estimate is that Mike did retreats like this approximately every other month for fifteen to twenty years. This would be have been as many as 100 retreats in his lifetime where he was enjoying time with his lover—his Lord and Savior Jesus.

Mike's life of prayer brought him great happiness. Even though he suffered so much and had many moments of darkness due to his eating disorder, he also had much time of great, great joy.

He would frequently say, "I am the happiest person I know" and "I feel like million dollars."

Mike wasn't putting on an act. When he was around others, the happiness really radiated out of him. Everyone who knew him could attest to that.

I believe this rich spiritual life allowed Mike to live fifteen or twenty years more than he would have otherwise with such a severe eating disorder, and to work and function on an amazingly high level given his dangerously low weight.

Mike was truly a spiritual warrior. In addition to the clients he served as a social worker, Mike would be also be a champion for the poor in other profound ways.

Grandma Bernadine, Mike, and Aunt Gert. These two courageous women represent all of Mike's extended family from Hornell and beyond.

Dad, Mike (the tallest one standing), and Rob across the top; Mom sitting with me as a baby and Chris next to me

The Irregulars in my parent's basement—their frequent hang-out. From bottom left to right: Tom Gallagher, Wayne Tremark, and Vinnie Palmeri; the middle row, from left to right: Chip Koch, Rob, Mike, Jim Flint, and Chris; the back row: Bob Guyton and Steve Legge; The street sign Mike is holding, which is a little too shiny in the photo, says Norton Ave.

Julie Trasolini and Mike—the hopes and dreams of Saints Football

The Irregulars are ready to spring into action—Sean Keegan, Jim Flint, Mike and Andy Chambers (a.k.a. "Bear")

Mike's Birthday Party when he was home on break working for the Franciscans and Covenant House in New York City. He is wearing a Covenant House Under 21 shirt (the shelter took in kids under 21). I am looking at his gift—a religious portrait—and our dear Aunt Doris is next to us.

The four brothers—Mike, Rob, me, and Chris. Mike loved and guided each of us so much, and we had so many great times together.

Mike at the ceremony in which he won Broome County Counselor of the Year for his outstanding work as a drug abuse counselor in the Broome County Jail. Mike was not surprisingly looking shy and humble about this great honor.

Mike with my in-laws, the Quinteros. From left to right: Lucy, my mother-in-law, and one of the widows Mike ministered to; Mom, Dad, Chris in front of Diana's nephew Tomas, my wife Diana, me holding Diana's nephew Juan Miguel, and Mike; seated are my wife's brother-in-law Julio with my sister-in-law Edna, nephew baby Pablo, and nephew Luis David

Mike at baby George's baptism with Rob and his family. From left to right on the top row: me, Rob, Chris, and our dad in his deacon clothes; middle row: our nephew Kevin, our nephew Robbie, our niece Heather, my wife Diana with baby George, our sister-in-law Kathy, our niece Jessica; front row: our niece Rachel, Mike, and our mom

Mike with baby George in his apartment at 25 Cary Street in Binghamton, the place where he spent so many hours in prayer

This was a bittersweet moment. I was with two of Mike's best friends—from left to right: Wayne Tremark, Jim Flint holding baby Mike, and me—at Flint's daughter Amber's graduation party. After five miscarriages, Diana and I had baby Mike, but we had lost my brother Mike.

XII.

MIKE'S MISSION FOR THE WORLD'S POOR

WHAT COULD ONE SOCIAL WORKER in Upstate New York do to help the world's poor?

At the center of Mike's life and his mission to the poor was Matthew chapter 25, in which Jesus said, "Whatever you do for the least of these, you do for me."

Mike visited those in jail and served the poor and downcast for his entire adult life as a social worker.

But there was something else that bothered him tremendously, and he had to act: the fact that there are so many people who are hungry in the world—especially in Africa.

Mike was a young social worker in New York City when famous singers recorded "We Are the World" and international attention was placed on famines in Africa. Images of starving men, women, and children on TV shocked the nation and always stayed with Mike.

A hero for Mike was always Peter Daino, whose parents were leaders at Christ the King Church. Peter joined the Peace Corp in the 1970s and went on to serve for over forty years a Marianist Christian Brother in poor countries in Africa.

Mike desperately wanted to help in the fight against world poverty and found a great charity he would support to do so, Catholic Relief Services (CRS).

Mike loved CRS not so much because it was Catholic but because he believed it did the best job of any organization of keeping overhead low and making sure that the highest percentage of a donation goes directly to help poor people.

Mike said that 97% of your donation to CRS goes to those in need. CRS gives aid to 130 million people in 110 countries around the world.

I am not sure exactly when Mike started donating to CRS, but by the 1990s he was saving and giving literally every single dollar he could to the organization.

As mentioned, Mike's apartment only cost $175 per month. His electric and phone bills on top of this were minimal, and there was no cable TV bill or cell phone bill. He did not have a car. He never bought new clothes or new things and only gave a few gifts to family on birthdays and Christmas. He ate very little, and his food bill was small.

Dad estimates that in a given year when Mike made $35,000, he would give $17,000 to CRS, and that he did this for years and years.

Remember, out of $18,000 he had left, a portion of that would go to taxes. When Mike took the charitable deduction on his tax return and received a large refund from the IRS, he would immediately donate the money to CRS.

When leaders of CRS donor operations saw how much Mike was giving, they wrote him and offered to come meet with him in Binghamton.

Mike chuckled because he figured CRS thought he was a wealthy business leader they might meet with at a nice restaurant.

For Mike, his reason for giving was simple:

People were starving and needed food. He would give every dollar he could to save them.

If it was his niece or nephew or one of Flint or Julie's kids who was starving, he would do everything he could to save them.

Mike believed we should all do more for starving people in Africa.

Critics might argue that world poverty persists due to government corruption and instability in poor countries.

Mike didn't let arguments like corruption and the fact that the US government was already sending billions in aid to poor countries slow his work down. He knew people were in immediate need.

Millions of people in the world are malnourished and starving. What is so difficult about giving them food so they can survive?

When family members gave Mike new clothes for Christmas or his birthday, he would look at them and quickly check if the price tags were still on them, so he could quietly return the gifts. He would say, "Oh, thanks so much, where did you get this?"

Mike would take back the clothes, get the refund, and give the money to CRS.

Mom and Dad got the message and stopped giving him clothes.

Because of his eating disorder and a lack of nutrition, Mike's dental health deteriorated. He had a number of teeth that needed to be pulled or replaced.

He did not want to spend the money to replace them, and he declined Novocain when they were pulled because it cost too much money. It is amazing to think about the excruciating pain Mike went through to save a few hundred dollars to give to CRS and help a person he would never meet.

Mike's only major vice after he quit drinking was smoking cigarettes. Mike realized that cigarettes were expensive and cost him money that he could be sending to CRS. He cut down dramatically on smoking to save money, but could never kick the habit. He even cut cigarettes in half and tried to hand-roll cigarettes with tobacco to lessen the expense.

Mike didn't brag about his work for the world's poor. He just did it.

It was ironic that Mike knew hunger and the brutal impact of malnutrition through his own eating disorder and cared so much for hungry people in the world.

Mike knew the pain—at least partially, in some strange way—that an extremely impoverished person who was starving would know.

Flint recalls Mike saying one time, "How can I enjoy steak when people in the world are starving?"

Mike didn't frequently "preach" to others to make us feel bad that we weren't doing more, but he challenged us.

As he struggled with his own weight and ate very little each day, he was in solidarity with poor people in the world.

He loved the story about the priest who addressed his audience with a very short homily. I don't know if it is a true story, but the priest supposedly said, "I only have three points to make today: First, millions of people are going to bed starving every night. Second, you people don't give a damn. And third, most of you are more concerned that I said 'damn' on the altar than you are about the fact that millions of people are starving."

XIII.

THE WIDOWS AND OUR MOM

My Mom said to me, "Michael's friend Alice is coming over for dinner." I was about sixteen years old at the time.

I said, "Does Mike have a new girlfriend?"

Mom replied, "No, Alice is an eighty-year-old widow Mike met while walking in his neighborhood."

Alice was one of the widows Mike was so special to.

She was part of a tremendous ministry Mike had to widows, which I never fully realized until I was writing this book.

Think about the life of an elderly widow for a minute. A typical widow's husband may have been deceased for years, and their children and grandchildren may live out of town or be very busy.

A widow may sit around for an entire day or several days without actually seeing another person.

The first two widows Mike took a special interest in were our Grandma Bernadine and our Aunt Doris. Both would be predeceased by their spouses by twenty-five years or more.

Mike loved both of these wonderful women and enjoyed visits with them so much. They were a critical part of his life and our family.

Alice Maycock lived on Chenango Street in an old big brown house, where she often sat on her porch, where Mike began talking to her during his walks.

These conversations blossomed into a great friendship. Alice had white curly hair and a raspy voice. She was a witty spitfire. Mike had a great sense of humor and loved joking around with her.

Alice became a regular guest at Mom and Dad's house for several years. It was always a lively and fun dinner. Alice would tell you exactly what she thought.

Our brother Chris also became close to Alice and painted her house one summer.

Mike was a great friend to Alice for years. She eventually went into a nursing home and passed away.

Another widow Mike was extremely fond of was a deaf woman named Virginia, who attended daily Mass with him at Saint Mary's of the Assumption Church. Mike wrote very beautifully about her in a piece he wrote called "Three Saints I know," which I will print in the next chapter. Mike often walked Virginia to her house after daily Mass.

After Mass Mike would visit and eat lunch with Angelina Trasolini—Julie Trasolini's grandmother—who lived near St. Mary's Church and was in her nineties.

Two unique stories about Grandma Trasolini were that she ran a boarding house when she was younger and that she was so terrified during thunderstorms that she would hide in the closet.

Henry Trasolini—Angelina's son and Julie Trasolini's father—was so appreciative of Mike's daily visits to his mother. He said his mom was worried about Mike's weight and made sure he finished his lunch each day—usually just a toasted cheese sandwich.

It was special to think of Mike eating lunch with Julie's grandmother every day. But Grandma Trasolini came to love and talk about Mike so much that it actually made Julie a little jealous.

Another widow Mike ministered to was Charmaine Tremark, his great friend Wayne's mother.

Mrs. Tremark house was beyond Mike's normal walking route from downtown Binghamton to his apartment, but Mike still went out of his way to check on her. It was part of the inseparable bond of the Irregulars.

The final widows Mike took a most special interest in were our mom's best friend, who lived across the street from us, Florence Fertig, and another friend who lived three doors down, Ann Dunda.

Mrs. Fertig was a mild-mannered, kindhearted person who was an extremely devoted and hard-working wife, mother, and grandmother. She was about ten years older than my mother and a great mentor and friend to her.

When our mom moved to Norton Avenue, she did not have a driver's license. Mrs. Fertig insisted that she get her license and volunteered to watch my brothers so Mom could take driver's ed classes.

Her husband Frank, a World War II Veteran and IBMer, died in 2005. Because we were close to the Fertigs, this situation hit all of us hard.

Mike helped as much as he could.

Mrs. Fertig loved sitting in her garage in a chair to watch the cars go by on Norton Avenue. Mike would cross the street to sit and talk with her for long periods of time.

Mike also continually insisted that Mom invite Mrs. Fertig over for dinner. I had married and moved back to town at this point, and we enjoyed many, many family dinners with Mrs. Fertig due to Mike's thoughtfulness.

Mike wasn't as close with Mrs. Dunda, but he still had a soft spot for her and spoke with her when she was visiting Mrs. Fertig or walking by her house.

Mrs. Dunda was a remarkable woman whose husband died in a car accident when she was only forty-five years old.

I give a great deal of credit to Mike's care for widows to my mom and dad and how very caring they were of their elderly relatives in Hornell. Both had numerous relatives who were unmarried or widowed.

Mike cared for children—at times orphans—rescued from the streets of New York and Binghamton. He cared for those downtrodden in jail, and he cared for widows.

In this chapter, I also decided to talk about Mike's incredible relationship with, dedication to, and love for our mom.

As I mentioned, Mike was extremely close to each of his immediate family members—Mom, Dad, Rob, Chris, and me—but it has been a challenge to adequately describe them in this book.

With Mom, we have some incredible letters Mike wrote to her that she saved and that I will include in the coming pages.

Mom was not a widow, but I included her in this section because it fits into the example of Mike's special love for elderly women.

You might say that the men in our family were stars and got the attention. Dad was an IBM engineer, then a deacon and a teacher. Rob, Chris, and I were all standouts in sports and had careers that garnered a lot of attention.

Mike was our saintly brother and the incredible social worker.

It would be easy to say that Mom was just a housewife, but being a mom and a wife is the most important job, along with being a dad and a husband, and she did an outstanding job at it.

Mike was tremendous at loving, affirming, and appreciating Mom. He sat for hours around the kitchen table talking with and listening to Mom as she did her work.

Both Mike and Mom were witty, positive, and cheery during these conversations. Mike asked about all the things on Mom's heart—what was going on with her children and grandchildren, how her church friends and neighbors were, and how her health was.

I just remember Mom beaming with joy during these conversations with Mike. He cared about all the little things in her life, and he loved her so much.

Mike was incredibly defensive of our Mom and would get very upset at anything that would hurt her.

One time Mom and Dad attended a dance at a local dance club. The requirement was that the ladies in attendance must have floor-length dresses.

Mom had a dress she thought was close enough to floor-length to pass and didn't want to spend money on a new dress. Someone at the club told Mom her dress was unacceptable. She was embarrassed, as any woman would be, and word of this got back to Mike.

Mike was very angry. He couldn't believe someone did this to his Mom and wanted to confront the dance club.

Mike worried about how his eating disorder and health worried Mom and Dad. He worried that his appearance at public events would embarrass them, because he was so thin and looked ill.

I know Mom worried tremendously about Mike's health, but she wasn't one to share her emotions.

When Mike was first formally diagnosed with an eating disorder—which I believe would have been sometime in the early '80s—Mom said that she would prepare meals for him every day and bring them to his apartment so he would have enough to eat.

Both Mom and Dad's response to Mike's eating disorder was simply to love him unconditionally. And they were so proud of him. They knew he was an incredibly holy man who was a tremendous force for goodness in the world.

Mom never talked about her own childhood—her two alcoholic parents, a father who was physically abusive to her mother, and a mother who abandoned her.

If I ever got down and started feeling sorry for myself, she would say, "You don't know how lucky you are. You should think about people who really have problems."

She only said that to me a few times in my life, but it always stunned me and caused me to stop whining about my more trivial concerns.

Mike certainly developed Mom's mentality. He never felt sorry for himself and his tremendous health struggles. He adopted both Mom and Dad's optimistic approach to life.

But Mom never gave up on Mike. She never stopped loving him, never stopped immensely enjoying his company, and never stopped being so very, very proud of him.

Mike had the same sentiments toward Mom. She meant everything to him.

What follows are a few of the beautiful letters from Mike to Mom.

Jan 14, 2001

Dear Mom, just a quick thank you for all you do and are for me. God has truly blessed us all and especially with you for my "Mom."

You teach me much and your love and support bring me closer to Jesus, because the love you have for us all in your loving heart is from Jesus. Thanks too for great Christmas and Birthdays—you always make me feel like a million dollars. Hope your back gets better. Sorry I have been on your case about this.

Enclosed is a rosary ring and prayer card. I'd like to ask you a birthday favor: sit in your chair once a day, close your eyes, breath slowly in and out, realizing Jesus is in and with you. Don't think of any thoughts or images—just be aware of Him. Slowly pray as you breath in "Lord Jesus Christ, Son of God" and breath out "have mercy on me." Try doing 10—using the rosary ring to count. Simply be aware of Jesus who is with you now, call on His Name. Try it for a week.

He wants you to know Him more intimately. Thanks—you're in my prayers. May God bless you. Stay close to Jesus. He loves you very, very much. Love your son Mike

May 9, 2001

Dear Mom, Happy Mother's Day

Its 7:30—had a good night's rest and am happy to be alive this morning. Thanks for being my "mom." Thanks for teaching how to play baseball (Bet you never thought I would be saying that to you).

But seriously, I listened to Colleen and Kelly [his co-workers] talking about raising their children and how important it is to teach kids how to play the game of baseball—which is life. They are worried children today don't seem to know the rules of the game or how to play and it's not the kid's fault. They often have nobody to show them how to play.

Throughout my childhood and up to the present you have taught and showed me how to play and live the game of life and I want to thank you because today I'm happier than anyone I know. I like playing the game of "baseball" or life and learned how from you and Dad and my brothers. Mom you are a great and wise coach. Thanks for helping me learn the numerous rules of the game:

Respect:

I still call Mr. and Mrs. Fertig, Mr. and Mrs. Fertig. I still write and visit relatives. I still say please and thank you; hold doors open for women and men; respect old people; listen when someone talks; and am patient by taking turns with others

Teamwork and valuable social skills:

As kids you taught my brothers and me how to play together—to share what we have with others (maybe that is why I like Catholic Relief Services so much), to play fair and to not gossip or talk unkindly about anyone. If you could teach the rest of the world that, I think that maybe 1/2 the problems we have could be eliminated

Apologize, make-up and shake hands rather than hold a grudge if we have disagreements:

"Make up with your brothers" and "I'm sorry" are two essential words for our relationship with others and God.

Underneath these words is the most important love and which as my mom you have taught and showed me how important and essential love is. It determines whether we win or lose the game of life.

Jesus says, "Love one another" and "There is no grater love than to lay down your life for your friends"

Mom you have showed me God's love by your own love for me and my brothers. You have followed Jesus's example of laying down your life for "your friends"—your husband, sons, neighbors, sick people, relatives, lonely and forgotten by baking a cake, sending a card or visiting—the little rules of the game that lead to happiness—to share and care and give.

Also, when I was hurting and down you asked me, "Why did God make you?" and I knew the answer because of your love—God made us to know, love and serve him, be happy in life and be eternally in heaven with Him.

A few months ago, you told Christopher and me "We are all God's children." Too often I forget this. If all people tried to live out this game with that rule in mind, perhaps much of the other half of our world's problems could be solved such as hatred, violence, war, abortion, loneliness, addiction, greed, selfishness and starving people.

Thanks for teaching, showing me and coaching me. I don't have my own family, but I try daily to show and teach others, like my clients, what you taught, showed and gave me.

Big, tough guys coming out of prison seem to respond quite well to the #1 rule, "Love one another." Actually, everybody I know likes it when I play by the rules.

Mom, I am running out of time—there is much I've forgotten to thank you for—but thanks. You are still my coach and I am playing on God's team—can't worry about losing with Him as the owner of the team.

Thanks for being my Mom and loving me.

Time to go shower and pray so I'll be ready to go out in the world and play the game of life, happy to be alive.

May God bless you as you keep teaching, loving and being you and being my Mom. I love you a lot and Jesus loves you much, much more. Stay close to him. You are in my prayers and my heart.

Love, your son, Mike.

May 28, 2001

Dear Mom,

Happy Memorial Tuesday—Had a great night's rest—feel like a million bucks. I certainly have some problems, but I am happier than anyone I know. You know why?

Dad told me years ago when I was drinking, I can be as happy or unhappy as I want.

You told me that God made me to know, love and serve Him—that's my happiness.

Jesus is in love with us, you and me, and I'm in love with Jesus and His brothers and sisters. I am sad though that there is so much suffering in our world—people starving to death physically while others starve spiritually.

The only thing we can do is love. That's life's secret—Jesus taught love and you have lived it and the love you've given me. Thanks Mom I love you.

Memorial Day is time to remember victims of war and famine. Also—I am homesick for my family. We used to always get together at Grandma's—on this day [in Hornell]. It is sad but true we are spread out and too busy. But that's O.K.—what counts is that we love each other. That's what Grandma and Dad's family and Aunt Gert and your family taught me.

I'm happy to be part of our family and feel sad for people like Bob [my co-worker] who doesn't have one. My retreat was awesome—feel like crying because I want to share it with others—quiet time spent in love with Jesus and wanting to love others as He does.

Jesus said, "As the Father has sent me, so I send you." Then He breathed on them and said, "Receive the Holy Spirit."

"Come Holy God, come Holy Spirit, enkindle in our hearts the fire of your love. Glory to you Holy God, now and forever"

Guess that's all for now, am happy to be on my way to Mass to receive Jesus and then come home to you, Dad and Christopher.

How happy I am—even more that we got rain. People at work can't understand why I like rain so much. Rain is an important part of life and it makes me happy. It cleans things and helps things to grow. It kind of reminds me with my relationship with Jesus. I daily need Him to cleanse me of my sins and help me grow in His love.

Try and spend some quiet time with Jesus today. He's in love with you. You're in my prayers, thanks for giving me love and a home and family to come home to.

May God bless you,

Love your son, Mike

Nov 16, 2001

Dear Mom,

Happy 65th birthday! I hope this is a good year for you. Our family is all blessed by God to have you. You don't how much you mean to me.

Jesus only asks one thing of us. He says "love one another." I'm happier than anyone I know. People at work think that I am crazy because I am so happy and hopeful. I am always trying to see the good in others. I'm falling in love with Jesus and His brothers and sisters.

You have showed me His love and helped me to love him, others and myself. Thanks. You said we are all God's children. The more I see this, the more precious life is, because each one of us is a special and beautiful child of God, who Jesus loves so much.

He died for you also. You told me when I was hurting with my alcoholism that God made me to know, love and serve Him—that's the secret to life. I am sad when I see so many people suffer and want to do all I can to help them know Jesus and His love for them. I fall very short, but He forgives me and helps me keep loving more and more like Him.

I apologize for all I put you thru and want you to know how much it means to have you and Dad and Rob, Kathy, Christopher and George. You are my family and always make me feel like a king returning home from a long trip.

I had a great visit with Helen today. She sees me making a lot of progress. Eating regular bread instead of the light bread is a major accomplishment for someone like me, and I even had an extra slice of bread today. I've never done that before.

Your love, support and prayers are paying off for me. Thanks a million Mom!

God's healing me a lot and I'm happy to be me today—as Popeye the sailor used to say, "I am what I am and that's all that I am." Today I can say that like Popeye I am happy to be me despite my sinfulness and shortcomings, because God is helping me love Him, others, and myself more and more.

Thanks again, Happy early "Turkey Day" from a real live turkey. "Gobble, gobble."

Happy Birthday Mom. I love you!

You're in my prayers.

Stay close to Jesus and Mary His Mother—Jesus and His Mother love you very, very much.

Love, your son,

Mike

May 9, 2003

Dear Mom,

Happy Mother's Day!

Thanks for being my Mom and loving me. God has blessed me by giving me you for my Mom.

You are always there for me and make me feel like a king when I am at the house. I wish weekends did not go by so fast.

The greatest thing a person can do in life is love. You have shown me this. Love is the secret to life. Without it we are miserable. I'm happier than anyone I know because I'm falling in love with Jesus and my brothers and sisters.

I am blessed to be at the jail and feel God's calling me to a deeper love. That's the reason I'm doing retreats. He is my lover and is letting me get to know Him more personally.

He is in love with us and longs for us to let Him love us and know Him more intimately.

Mom—thanks for loving me on sunny and cloudy days, ups and downs and in betweens. Your love has helped me give up drinking and be able to live with my eating problem.

I'm sorry for you because I imagine it's not easy being my Mom because of all my problems—but that is what love is all about—loving unconditionally. You never stop loving and I hope I can do the same with my life.

Thanks, Mom. "I love you" Happy Mother's Day!

You're in my prayers—

May God bless you and reveal Himself to you more intimately.

Love your son,

Mike

***

There is one last widow Mike ministered to.

In 2005 I married Diana Quintero—whom I will tell you more about in the coming pages. Diana's dad had died when she was fifteen years old, leaving her mom—my future mother-in-law, Lucy—a widow at a young age.

Lucy stayed with us during long periods of time and could not speak English. Family gatherings were tough for her. Mike always took time to try to speak with her through Diana's or my translation.

Mike bought a Spanish-English dictionary and tried to teach himself Spanish so he could communicate with Lucy. He was always so incredibly kind to her.

Mike's incredible outreach to the widows and my Mom were all part of his heroic virtue.

XIV.

EVANGELIZING AS A WRITER—FOR JESUS AND THE POOR

I CAN PICTURE MIKE SITTING AT Mom and Dad's kitchen table with his electric typewriter, writing *The Passionate Love of Jesus: Reflections on the Gospel of Mark as Experienced by a Sinner.*

This powerful piece represents Mike's experience of Jesus's radical love for us and a call for us all to a radical love.

Mike printed his *Passionate Love of Jesus*, made copies, and shared them with everyone he knew.

As mentioned, in 2018 we published them and Mike's other writings into a book called *The Passionate Love of Jesus as Experienced by a Sinner.*

Below are excerpts of these powerful writings.

> Chapter 1:1 Here begins 'the Gospel of Jesus Christ, Son of God.'
>
> Open our hearts, Jesus Lord, and reveal Yourself to us in Your Holy Word, help us listen to You. Your Holy Gospel is good news for us sinners because through it You reveal the passionate love You have for each one of us. Jesus, Your name literally means "Yahweh save." O Holy God, save us and reveal Yourself both to us and through us. Thanks—we love you.
>
> Chapter 1:7 The call of the first disciples

"Come after me and I will make you fishers of men," You said to Simon and Andrew, and "immediately" they "abandoned" their work to follow You. Help me to act like them—it is urgent to abandon what stops me from following You and being in Your "company" as they were.

Chapter 2:17—"The healthy do not need a doctor, sick people do. I've come to call sinner, not the self-righteous."

Lord, help me admit my sins to You and through sorrow find Your healing. Only as a humble sinner can I know You; it is only in my "need."

Dear Reader: Please Note: Evil exists, and you and I are in a holy war against Satan, the father of lies, who wants to steal our hearts and souls from Jesus. How? The Devil convinces many of us that he does not exist! Perhaps you don't believe this? He lies to you and me saying: racism, abortion, world hunger, materialism, greed, hating, resenting the poor or the rich, holding a grudge, gossiping, indifference, murdering others (physically, socially, emotionally, financially or spiritually) is ok or that that it is okay to hate pro-abortionist, pro-lifers or persons who think abortion is okay. Hatred kills us and others—he pumps up our heads with so many lies, hoping we become discouraged or apathetic or stop trusting Jesus to save us. He tells me it is okay for me to keep smoking even though I am murdering myself. Bet you he told the paralyzed man's four friends that Jesus could not heal their companion. That it was pointless to bring him to Jesus because the house was too crowded to get into. They fought a holy war and won by lifting up their friend, tearing open the roof and lowering him down to Jesus who did heal their pal, and gave us an example to fight Satan and win by going to and relying on Jesus. We must not do nothing, which is all the Devil asks at times. We must act, or risk following him to hell. It is up to each of us to begin making our homes, communities and world places where Jesus's compassion, care, love, healing and action happen through us. Alone we may feel helpless, but together with Jesus we can "do something beautiful for God" as Mother Theresa said years ago. Lord, forgive me for being a coward and not acting against evil for fear of being called a "religious nut." (Dear Reader: Thank you for taking this journey through Mark's Gospel with me—it is good not to travel alone, because too often we are very lonely people. Jesus is always with us. He is with you now as you are reading this…)

Lord, too often, I am paralyzed by my sins and by deep secret, painfully ugly things I would rather not think about. Selfishness, pride, jealousy, murderous resentments stop me from feeling or caring. Jesus, help me to see that no matter how bad and ugly this garbage in my soul is, no sins of mine are too big for you to tackle, forgive, heal and purify. Daily I must tell you and my sisters and brothers I am sorry, forgive me for what I did, said, thought or did not do. Save me from the ugly stuff in me that wants to murder me—I cannot save myself; I am suffocating under all my garbage. Only You can heal my soul. Forgive me, Jesus. Forgive me for doubting your forgiveness. You saved me when I was drowning in alcohol and will save me if I ask. Thanks!

(Dear Reader: This is embarrassing, but I need to hear Jesus and you say, "I forgive you." Daily He prompts me by His grace to confess my sinful selfishness. And when I tell Him I am sorry, I am blessed, forgiven and healed to hear Him say to me, another paralyzed man, "My son, your sins are forgiven." Oh, what healing love you have for such a broken sinner. Thanks. "O my God, I am heartily sorry for having offended you and my brothers and sisters…Lord, Jesus Christ, Son of God, have mercy on me a sinner." Jesus, thanks, I love you!)

It is Saturday; looking forward to going into the confessional booth at church where God welcomes me home—it's a safe, dark, quiet place where, with head bowed on my knees, I'll meet you, Jesus, not as a judge, but as friend, companion, comforter, protector, savior, lover and God. Oh, how glorious to be touched and healed by You, Jesus. Thanks for being so kind to me. Special thanks to the special Priests who have welcomed me home to you, like Msgr. B and Fr. C at St. Mary's; Fr. H at Christ the King; Fr. Sixtus, a Franciscan Missionary who died years ago; and Fr. T, who now ministers in Florida. May we have their enthusiasm and fire as we bring Jesus to each other. Confession helps me get rid of the garbage in my soul to make more room for you, Jesus. Confession may be embarrassing, even scary, but it is well worth the hurt and healing. If you have never gone, give it a try, even if you are not Catholic. God will understand and offer you a powerfully cleansing encounter with His Son.

Chapter 8:31 The First Prediction of the Passion

Lord, You taught Your follower You "must suffer much, be rejected, be put to death and rise three days later." Why must You do this? Because Your burning desire to save us. You corrected Peter, who tried to talk You out of sacrificing Yourself for us, saying, "Out of my sight, You are not judging by God's standards but by man's." Perhaps Your language is so strong to wake Peter and me up. You loved Peter greatly (with his failings) and want us to know not to listen to Satan, the father of evil and lies, who lies to us telling us sacrificial love is worthless. Help me to not listen to the tempter when he tries to tell us You cannot save us or that our efforts to give ourselves to our hurtful, unborn and starving brothers and sisters are worthless. No sacrifice saves—help me to give until it hurts, like You.

Chapter 8:34 The Conditions of Discipleship

Lord, You call me to deny my very self, take up my cross and follow in Your steps, pointing out that if we lose our lives for Your gospel and will be saved. O Lord forgive me for rejecting my cross—help me to accept and bear my suffering like You—help me to kill the parts of me that stop me from following and loving—I am so selfish and proud and need to change. Help me to die from being cruel, to abstain from gossiping and taking out my hurts on others. Help me to be patient with those who appear "ugly" to me, like family, friends, neighbors, and coworkers whose ugliness is only a reflection of the sin in my own heart. Help me to listen, to care to be there in order to give glory to Our Father for His goodness.

Yes, you ask us to love to the point of suffering and dying for the "sinful me." You are our hope, for when You were transfigured before Your friends, You revealed to them the glory that follows our dying to ourselves. You tell us You love us so much that You will, and do, die for us. From Heaven Your Father cries out to us that You are His "Beloved Son," and for us to "listen" to You. Help to listen and reveal You to others, O Holy God.

Chapter 10:17 The Rich Man

Jesus, the rich young man asked what he had to do to get eternal life—You "looked at him with love" and said he must not only keep the Ten Commandments, but "must go and sell what you have and give to the poor…after that, come and follow me…" The man went away sad for he had many possessions. Help me to be like him, to listen to You and feel sad that I too resist giving up my possessions, which are unhealthy for others and me.

Lord, I offer You my pride, vanity, self-centeredness, jealousy, envy, indifference and judgmental-ness that stop me from loving—free me from these sinful possessions. Help me to feel sad that one in four unborn American babies are murdered due to legal abortion. They are my children too, and You ask me to do something for them and for all who suffer. Yes, help me to be sad and cry for my greed of earthly pleasures like smoking, buying expensive clothes, spending money on things I want—while millions of brothers and sisters literally starve to death! Yes, daily individual people starve to death due to my greed and indifference—help me to express my sadness by giving—money, sacrificing luxuries and giving more until it hurts—until I feel. Last year a horrible famine plagued the Sudan in Africa. 2.5 million children of God facing starvation—millions of innocent people die. Help me to cry and abandon my riches. Lord, how many die daily? How many are starving right now as I read? Oh, forgive me for not wanting to get in touch with this "holocaust" of unborn and starving people—help me to not continue to partake in the American holocaust of indifference and greed. Help us to give until we hurt for them. Help me to know that You look upon me with love and sadness, hoping I will give of me to others—it is the only way I can be Yours. Dorothy Day notes, "True love is a harsh and dreadful thing." May I come to know the mystery of this kind of love by giving, like You, until it hurts? In 1928, a famine killed 25 million people in the Soviet Union and in 1958, 20 million people in China—did we know or care? Do I know now or really give a damn? (It is a scary question.) It would be easy to get discouraged—because You made it clear how us rich people cannot enter eternal life on our own, but it is possible with Your help, for "with God all things are possible." With You, I can make a difference—shake me from my apathy. Thanks for calling us to You for others.

Chapter 10:46—The Blind Bartimaeus

Blind Bartimaeus called out to You, "Lord Jesus, Son of David, have pity on me." Bystanders, like me, told him to shut up and turned him out. But he cried out more passionately and You healed him. Oh, heal me of my blindness when family, friends, neighbors, co-worker or stranger appear ugly to me. Too often I am okay with the crowd—help me to see others as You do and answer their cries for pity. If I don't, who will? Only by calling on Your holy name can I be saved (Acts 2:21)

Chapter 14:22 The Supper

Jesus, You took bread, blessed it, broke it and gave it to us saying, "Take this, this is my Body." You also gave wine to us as saying, "This is my Blood, the Blood of the covenant, to be poured out for you." Holy God, You give us Your Body and Blood to nourish us, feeding our starving souls with You. You want us to experience Your passionate love and call us to do as You do—give You to me and to others—to feed others as You feed me. You call us in Holy Communion to receive You, Jesus, and enter into the Holy Mystery of Love—life in You, O Holy Trinity Glorious God—Father, Jesus and Holy Ghost—Glory to You, Glory to You…! It is too much—may I approach You in humble, loving fear knowing how You have stooped so low to be with me, feeding me with Your sacred flesh and blood—and what love! Daily at Mass, the Holy Sacrifice, the sacred wedding banquet, You call us to know You more intensely, saying, "Take this…this is my body." I want to cry because I am so unworthy, and Your love is so great! You give man and woman Your true entire self, Holy God-heart, body, mind, soul, divinity, longing to reveal You to others and me so You can live with, I and through us. O, Lord, I am definitely not worthy…help me to humbly open my broken self to You, Jesus. Again, at this sacred meeting, You call us a passionate loving union with You, saying daily, "This is my Blood"…to be shed for me and all. You shed Your scared Blood while hanging in torment on the cross, paying for my sins, for which I deserve the death You endured. How holy, merciful and loving You are, Jesus, for You took on our sins, shedding Your very Blood to pay for sin and cleanse us of the dirtiness and disfigurement it causes our souls. Continue to heal, forgive, save, cleanse and love us as You offer Your Body and Blood, Your entire person, dying to be ours. What can I say? Maybe it is better for me to shut up and just be silent—and enjoy You—Wow!

At the Holy Sacrifice of the Mass, Jesus, You take bread, bless it, break it and give it to us, saying, "Take this, this is my Body." You give us the chalice of wine to drink, saying, "This is my Blood, the Blood of the covenant to be poured out on behalf of many, do this in remembrance of Me." Please…Holy Jesus, You give us Your very self, Your flesh and blood to nourish our starving souls with Your loving presence—You want us to experience the union of You in me and communion in You with others—Your passionate, personal love for us, Your mystical body on earth. You call us to do as You—giving, loving, and seeking union, in a communion of love with our sisters and brothers. You call me to enjoy and experience and share in the divine love of community which Your Father, Self and Holy Ghost dwell in as One Holy God—it is too much—May we worship, thank, adore and give glory to You in humble, fearful love. Come and live in me, Jesus, and make us one with You.

At the Last Supper, He washed our feet. God blessed me much by giving me a chance to know him more as a drug abuse counselor. It is an awesome privilege to get to know another person. My clients often wash my feet. Years ago, a woman who had an abortion (over 20 years ago) and who had never talked about her pain, shared herself with me—her grief, sense of loss and love were intense. As her heart was opening up, I saw God's love; she shared Him with me, and I was blessed by her. The two best things in my life are to be there with another person and to sit in silence with Jesus—true chances to taste Heaven. Abortion and world hunger have many victims. We need to work to make them non-options and show our love, care, support (give some $) by washing feet as Jesus did and still does through his followers. Perhaps the saddest people in life are those of us who refuse to have their feet washed, or to wash the feet of another, because that is where Jesus is at. How do we wash feet? By listening, smiling, holding a door, laughing or crying with a friend or refusing to laugh at another, letting someone go ahead of us in line, not giving the "bird" to someone who cuts us off in traffic, asking for help or giving it. By doing so we all share in God's goodness. We can pray, feed hungry people, offer comfort to those who, in hopelessness, consider abortion, like a person considers suicide—no needing my judgment, but my compassion and physical, financial and spiritual support. We can comfort those who mourn the loss of a loved one by simply asking, "How are you doing?" vs. ignoring their pain. We can simply be there with others. We all can do something. (St. Francis washed feet by hugging persons with leprosy and caring for them. When dying, he told his friends, "While we have time, let us do good.") Lord, help me to wash the feet of the next person you put in my life, and thank them for giving me a boost towards Heaven because I cannot get there alone. What joy! Many spend their lives washing feet. Both my parents in their 60's and still do so. Years ago, as a broken alcoholic having once again fallen off the wagon, I was submerged in guilt, shame, hopelessness. While visiting my mom she sensed my hurting and, in compassion, touched me, asking, "Do you know why God made you?" (I had no response.) She shared the answer to life with me, saying, "God made you to know, love, and serve Him, be reasonably happy with Him in this life, and eternally happy in Heaven with Him." Thanks for washing my feet, Mom. It is good to enjoy life and be a bit happy, but never really happy because ten thousand people die daily from starvation, malnutrition and my indifference. Life has happy moments, but I can't be really happy as long as so much of humanity suffers and waits for us. One of us can make a difference. One man did. He was just out of prison, recovering from alcoholism and addiction, and working a low-paying job. He took great joy in being able to buy things for his kids, and greater joy in donating $15 a month to sponsor a child in a third world country. He made a difference. So did Jesus and so must you and me.

Jesus, daily you call us to "do this in remembrance of You"—yes, at Mass we get to receive You, but that is not the end. No, to do what You did is only possible with You—for You ask me to give my life, my blood, myself in love for and to others. How awesome—we are called to receive You and bring You to others to truly be "Christ-bearers"—help me to be a "Christopher." In this we enter Your Holy Heart, O Loving God!!! Jesus, continue to feed us with Your Body and Blood. Thanks!

Chapter 15:21 the Way of the Cross

Jesus, they "pressed" Simon into helping You carry Your cross because they feared that You would die attempting to carry the beam by Yourself. Forgive me for not wanting to help those who still carry the cross. Thanks for the many "Simons" You give me to help when I am overwhelmed. And help me to push on, like You, carrying our cross, falling, bleeding and dying on the way to Calvary. You fell but did not give up—the weight of the crossbeam crushed You to the ground, ripping open Your shoulder and arm, tearing open Your knees and elbows—and how You kept getting up, and embracing this heavy wooden burden even though it only opened the wounds in Your shoulders and arms more deeply, killing You. O Holy Love. Thanks for not quitting on us, Jesus—I want to cry, recalling how You struggle up a steep, rocky hill, dying from loss of blood each step of the way. What a holy privilege to be able to follow You!

Lord, at this point I need to look back for a few minutes. A month ago, walking to Mass on Sunday, I walked past a man sitting on a curb. He tried to speak to me—he was revolting—skinny, old, filthy, spit and vomit dripping from his beard, dripping down his coat. Out of force of habit, I told him I had no money or cigarettes (I lied twice, denying You just like Peter did). He called to me, saying, "No, that's not what I need. I can't get up. I have emphysema. Can You help me get up off this curb? Suddenly, I was ashamed of myself, not wanting to touch this beautiful child of God who was obviously sick and hurting—couldn't make it on his own—much like You when Simon was forced to help You carry the cross. I wish I could say I reached out to him out of love, but no, I helped him because of my own guilt issues. I took his hand and helped him up and he healed me—by touching him and letting him hang on, something powerful happened. I think he broke my heart, and I was able to love and asked if he wanted me to get an ambulance to go to the hospital. He said, "No, I'll be okay." He was okay, but I was not—I still think of him and wish I could thank him for breaking my heart. How dare I rush past someone suffering on my way to church? How dare I not want to see victims of famine and starvation on TV? Sad, but true, I am more upset when my toast gets burned than when I think about the fact that one fourth of this planet's 6 billion individuals are hungry, starving, dying—like You, Lord. Every 37 or 52 seconds a person dies somewhere due to starvation (I read this someplace). But does a person die due to starving or due to my indifference? It is upsetting but I still keep spending money on cigarettes, candy, chocolate…somehow enjoying these is spoiled by knowing that a child, a brother or sister starves—but what can we do? We cannot give to everything. Or everyone. Or can we? What would Jesus do? He would visit my friend in a nursing home instead of going to the mall. He would listen when someone needs to talk and be heard and helped. But what about the issues of racism, children dying by gunfire? They bleed and die daily, just like You did, Lord. It is sad. A few months ago, a Youth was shot dead in McDonald's parking lot of State Street. (Our kids and families need us and You, Jesus.) I could be politically active—oh, but that would mean giving my time. But Lord, You would do something—You want us to be "Simons" to each other, offering help, whatever that means. Three thousand seven hundred abortions happen daily in our nation—1.4 million pre-born babies are being murdered yearly. What about the millions who starve to death while I enjoy myself? We spend billions of dollars on bombs and McDonald's, thousands on redecorating our churches, homes and faces. We even spend thousands to help a beached whale get back to sea, so it does not die. Now I am part of this mess and am responsible to act. What will it cost me to care? What did it cost You, Lord? What does it cost me not to care or not to act? A woman once told St. Vincent DePaul how seeing the poor frightened her. The Saint responded by letting us know that we should be frightened when we look at the poor (or refuse to see them) for they remind us of God's justice. (Maybe I should stop and think about this?)

Problems are overwhelming, but that is why You came for us and ask us to do what You would do. Maybe pray, or listen, or visit, or vote, or speak, or give money. But You would not walk away and do nothing. Lord at the last judgment You might ask if I fed You in Your hunger—what will I say? (Matthew 25:3-46) Perhaps I can send some money to Catholic Relief Services (CRS, P.O. Box 17090, Baltimore, Maryland 21298-9664). Maybe I could tithe, which is what the Bible asks—if I gave one tenth, I would not really need it, so You want more from me. There will be hell to pay for my indifference. Lord, You are my only hope—only You can save me from myself and give me the grace to be a modern Simon—it is actually a blessing to be able to reach out to others—their needs and my action will help me to develop a stronger heart. Help me, Lord, I am weak and selfish and sinful. Prayer does work. A close friend's newborn has taught me much about suffering. This child has had ongoing medical problems and she is bringing many of us closer to You, Jesus, because in praying for her, You once again have broken my heart and the hearts of many calling us to a more passionate love of each other, her and You. Yes, in our weakness we can experience Your power. Thanks for this beautiful little girl.

Each of us is looking for You, Jesus (whether we know it or not—it's that empty feeling, deep in our hearts). If you don't think so, next time you walk through the Oakdale Mall spend time looking into the eyes of your fellow pilgrims. We seem to have it "all," but we don't. Smile, share some joy, become a blessing for others, (as Fr. C. at St. Mary's says) be a missionary of charity, like Mother Theresa—all she did was love—and attracted many to Christ—can't we do the same? Lord, help us see You in the faces of each person who is looking for You today, and may they see You in us as we become "community." Christian fellowship—true church—Your mystical body in Binghamton, New York. We can do it with You, Jesus! By living out the "Thy will be done" of the Our Father. Do I really mean it and want not my, but Your will, O Holy God? To seek Your will over mine causes tension, similar to a person lifting weights. Am I willing to begin seeking Your plan for me, even when it really costs? Maybe I can start seeing my neighbor as You do. What do You see or feel when You look at me? Too often You see me sitting in judgment of another, looking down the end of my nose at her or him—it must break Your heart. How dare I, who has been forgiven so much and been given so much, demand others to be perfectly what I want, while it is okay for me to have my own "little" imperfections? Your will is to love the person who seems unlovable to me. Who do I look down at; perhaps persons on Welfare, or who are HIV infected, single mothers with beautiful children, the religious right, the liberal left, President Clinton, the gay and lesbian community? In John 13:35 You tell me to "love one another just as I have loved You." Who is this other person You want me to love by "washing his or her feet? I have given You an example…" (John 13:15) Recall Matthew 25:45, "…in so far as you neglected…one of the least of these, you neglected…me." Guess I better get down on my knees and wash the feet of the next person You introduce me to, and the next one, too! Service not talk. Maybe I should thank the person I look down at because he or she is the person who can teach me to love. I need to look up into that person's eyes while washing his feet and care, especially if I want to get to Heaven, for there is no hatred allowed in that Holy Place. Sad, often I show more care to my friend's dog than my brothers and sisters. Shake me up, wake me up, knock me off my pedestal—make me uncomfortable with me so I can begin to amend my life while I have it. Handshaking scares me—fear of catching a disease. A person at work is HIV positive, and each time I shake his hand his love heals me, touches me (healing me of my disease which is sin). He blesses me and I love him for that. Help me to shake more hands, Jesus, so I can touch and be touched by You and others—you both still carry the cross—forgive me for refusing to help for slapping, hitting, spitting on You when You fell. Forgive me, Jesus, help me start loving and not stand by and watch You die again as an outcast, a troubled soul, a starving child or unborn baby. Sad Planned Parenthood argues that killing an unborn baby is "cost-effective" for every $1 spent by our country to pay for abortions, $4 is saved in public medical and Welfare expenses. Jesus, You also were reduced to a dollar sign, being sold for 30 pieces of silver, the price paid for a person who was to become a savior, and You died for this. Our greed and my indifference are killing You and other innocent persons. My two nephews, ages 5 and 8, live out of state—two of the neatest little guys You ever want to meet. If they were hungry, unborn or starving. I would do all I could—sending food, money, praying, asking others to help. How are they any more deserving than my nieces and nephews who are hungry and starving to death (as I write) in India, Bangladesh, Iraq, Sudan, or Ethiopia? Lord, I know I should do something but…(CRS gives about 94-97 percent of donations to those who suffer.) If I am lucky someday, I hope to meet these little nieces and nephews of mine. Jesus, exhausted, You work to get up after falling under the crossbeam on Your shoulders which crushed Your bloody body into the dirt, yet we have hoped to share, for it was our weakness, sufferings and sorrows You carried. (Isaiah 53:4)

Chapter 15:22 The Crucifixion

Jesus, when You reached the end, "they tried to give You wine drugged with myrrh," but You "would not take it." Help us to feel and experience suffering and pain with love and dedication rather than trying to escape them and number them out through destructive ways of escape. Jesus, today through Your amazing grace I am grateful to be an alcoholic who is getting better—still I find other unhealthy ways to medicate and numb my nerves when I am hurting or those who I care about are suffering. Help me to see in Your choice to suffer and feel mine fully, because of Your great love, that pain and suffering can be sacred if united to You in love. Thanks too for the many alcoholics and addicted persons You have let me get to know—Each of them reflects Your goodness, glory and love in a unique and beautiful way—Help me to love them like You—It is Your love in suffering that heals us.

Chapter 15:24 "Then they crucified Him…"

Jesus, how horrible it must have been—for me it is comfortable to read this verse of the Gospel and move on—help us to stop, ponder, be quiet, reflect and be silent before You as You are being crucified. Please reveal Your passionate love as we remember…crucifixions were common at Your time, but we are far removed and unaware of how terrible such an execution is.

Jesus, You were stripped—how humbling and painful, for as You were stripped, Your clothing caked with blood and dirt, tore open the wounds on Your back, legs, arms, sides and chest—skin, scabs, and flesh ripped off to You—pain intense enough to cause one to pass out, but You didn't. Rather, You laid Yourself down on the crossbeam and offered your hand to Your executioners—what love—no resistance, loving, painful, terrifying submission, like a lamb—offering Yourself, body, blood, heart and soul—to be sacrificed for our sins. What does it fell like to be bleeding to death? Your right hand was held tightly against the wood and a hammer blow drives a spike through Your wrist—the metal spike pressed on a raw nerve in Your wrist and You were engulfed in horrendous agony and pain…Then, You offered Your left hand, knowing what would follow—how much pain, how much love. Then, Your feet were pressed on top of each other, held to the wood and hammered flat—as a man. You can no longer walk away or escape or defend Yourself—You gave up freedom to gain us ours.

Jesus, Your being raised up on the cross is too much to fathom. Lord, the full weight of Your body falls and hangs against the nails in Your wrists and feet, rubbing against raw nerves. How horrible it must have sounded and felt to fall and hang in an ocean of pain. Hanging by the nerves in Your wrists. You began drowning in agony, drowning in my sins, our sins… Then begin Your slow dying. Jesus, to breathe You must press on nerves in Your hands and feet, and each breath costs You horrendous agony—it is easier to not breathe, but then suffocation slowly begins, and slowly over three hours, every muscle in Your body cramps up due to diminished oxygen and blood. You push and pull on the cramped muscles and live nerves to stop from suffocating—Jesus, what did it sound and feel like to gasp for air? How could You endure three hours of cramped muscles, slow, slow suffocation prompted only by willingly pushing on raw nerves? (Lord, a little cramp in my leg or stomach causes me intense pain—what could Your cramps have felt like?) But raising Your head, neck and back to breathe renews these wounded parts of Your body as they rub against and press upon the wood—the thorns in Your crown stabbing deeper into Your head and skull—how was it You did not pass out? (I'm nauseous just trying to think about it).

Jesus, for three hours You took on hell, death, evil, suffering and hatred—choosing to continue to writhe, breathe and love in immense agony. (Three minutes or 30 seconds of pain are too much for me to endure—three hours is unfathomable to me). Your love is conquering brutality, for You are loving those who are killing, mocking and rejecting You, not only them, but me too—I want to cry, for so many times I have been brutally cruel to You and my brother and sisters. While dying, Jesus. You are forgiving us—returning love for hate—Oh help me to learn from Your Holy Heart how much You love us and how to forgive and love others (including myself). Lord, struggling to breathe, crowned, scourged, pierced, bleeding and hanging from an altar of wood, You did not ask "Why me?" or lash out in anger at such injustice. Dying, You experienced the consequences of the sins of humanity—You are experiencing our brokenness and desolation to the depths of Your soul, and thus You cried. "My God, My God, why have you abandoned me?" No Lord, You did not ask, "Why me?" Instead, You were looking for Your Father, who for the first time in Your life, is not there—You experience desolation and are totally alone. You experience and pay for my sins second by second, minute by minute, for what feels like eternity.

It feels like an eternity. You took our place—what can we say or do? Is each of us worth this much to You and Your Father? Yes. Lord, You not only prayed these words to Your loving Father, but lived eventually died them, hanging on between Heaven and earth for us all to see. Your holy suffering makes us sacred, healing and cleansing us if we allow it to in obedient love. How can I respond? What stops me from giving a "yes" to loving as You do? Yes, You want me to love. How awesome—You are with us in our suffering, broken hearts—we need not suffer along like You dying on the cross. How glorious is Your call to follow and be more like You who are dying, giving Yourself totally in love to Your father as us? O Most Holy God, Abba Father, Loving Jesus, pour into our hearts and souls Your most Holy Spirit. Only then with You can we enter into the divine mystery of Your love.

Jesus, Your muscles twist and writhe in agony as You struggle to breathe. But now, Jesus, You are slowly suffocating, each attempt to breathe is not strong enough, engulfed in pain, covered in blood, agony and suffocation, pressing on Your hands and feet becomes too much. It has become too much for You to stay alive. But how can this be, for You are God?

Chapter 15:37 "Then Jesus, uttering a low cry, breathed His last."

Silence. Death. Your sacrifice is finished, Jesus. Your lifeless body now falls and You hang, Your sacred face is caked with blood, spit and dirt, as is Your back, hands and limbs—You do not look human, insects of the desert start to prey on You while the silence causes holy fear and terror in Heaven, earth and hell. Jesus, forgive my impatience and wanting to move on. Help me to spend a minute, at least a few of my precious minutes or seconds, in silence before You—so that You can touch my soul. Lord Jesus Christ, Son of God, have mercy on us all. Lord Jesus Christ, Son of God, have mercy on me a sinner.

How is it You saved others, yet did not save Yourself? Through the gift of faith and love the centurion, on seeing You die, declares, "Clearly this man was the Son of God."

(Please read Psalm 22 and Isaiah 52:13—52:12 in order to enter more deeply into Jesus's passionate love for You.)

Thanks, Jesus, and keep giving me Your body and blood daily. Lord, You ask us to go back to Galilee to meet You—You want us to go to You, to meet You in the Gospel so You can speak to us and reveal You to us and through us. Hey, He wants You and me to know Him more deeply—Wow! Sad, but true, I make excuses—I "don't have time" to read the Bible—maybe I fear getting to know You more, maybe that is because that might mean I have to change. Perhaps it is because my heart is too full of "my selfishness" to have room for You. You call each of us to be "another You," "another Chris," a "Christ bearer." Oh, how holy, glorious and frightening—called to think, love and act like You, not letting pain stop us but make us into stronger lovers. How can I be a "little You"? By listening, caring, not lashing out at a person who knows how to "push my buttons" but seeing every person as my brother or sister who You chose to die for. But that is easier said than done—help—I'm weak. Help me to give me to others—maybe cut back my luxuries (like spending $3.75 for cigarettes, $1.07 for two candy bars) and give to You, to individuals who are starving... These thoughts make me uncomfortable, but that's okay—maybe there is hope for me yet. Thanks for making me uncomfortable with me—that is Your way of calling us to more intimacy with You, O Holy Jesus.

Show us the open wounds in Your hands, feet and side as You did Your other friends 2,000 years ago on our first Easter. Why were Your wounds still open and not healed? Perhaps these open wounds of Your undying love invite us to know You more personally. Jesus, this very moment in the "sacrament of now." Your side is still opened up. You invite us to enter Your undying love, invite us to enter Your wounded side where Your pierced, beating, throbbing, glorified and loving heart beats and longs for us to come home to You. Wow—it's too awesome—Listen...You can hear the heartbeat of God's only Son who is dying on the cross for us. Jesus, Sacred Heart of the living God, consumed and burning with love for us, waiting and wanting… Years ago a girl I wanted to be with broke my heart, and for years I drowned my sorrows in alcoholism, which almost killed me. Jesus, my heart and soul were so sinful and sick and only broken by selfish self-pity because I wanted her to make me feel good about me. Now I know only You can do this—only You can save me. I ask You to continue to bless, heal and break my heart in saving ways. For it is by being opened up like You that I can be touched, pierced and suffer with my sisters and brothers who suffer now that You live and love in and thru us and me. This is what Your heart asks me to do—enter into the mystery of Your self-sacrificing love. Jesus, You who are crucified and whose heart is pierced for love of each human soul, help me to choose to love and, yes, suffer with You and my hurting sisters and brothers, starving for You. Forgive me, Jesus. Too often I am a selfish coward—scared of Your sacred wounds calling me to glorious love. Help, I am weak and want to love more.

Oh, thank You Most Holy God, Abba, Our Father, for Jesus Your only Son.

Lord, Jesus Christ, Son of God, have mercy on us all.

Lord, Jesus Christ, Son of God, have mercy on me, a sinner.

Come, Holy God, O most glorious Holy Spirit, and enflame our broken hearts with the glorious fire and passion of Your intense love for us.

Glory to You, Holy Father. Glory to You Jesus, Glory to You, Holy Ghost. Glory to You, Most Holy God, now and forever. Amen!

In the name of the Father, and of the Son and of the Holy Spirit. Amen…

May God bless You.

I would like to thank God for his help. Thanks, too, for family, friends, priests, and several Catholic writers who contributed to these reflections, especially the author of *A Doctor at Calvary*, Pierre Barbet, MD, whose research was essential to the reflection on the crucifixion concerning the physical and medical suffering of Jesus, our Crucified God.

Dear Reader, I would like to ask you for a favor this next week. Take a moment once per day to say:

"Jesus, You love me."

"Jesus, I love You."

(He will change your life.)

Thanks,

Michael Phillips

2/18/00

Source: *The New American Bible for Catholics*, Revised 1991

***

Saturday March 25, 2000

Dear Friend,

I just got home from Mass and am enjoying a cigarette and getting ready for lunch. Before eating I want to share a little more with you. Its's the season of Lent, a time to get in touch with the crucified Jesus and his passionate love for all persons. Today, we rejoice because it's the feast the Annunciation. Thank Jesus for becoming an unborn baby through the power of the Holy Ghost in the womb of Mary, yours and our Mother. Jesus came down from heaven to take away my sins and save me from the fires of hell (my selfishness) and lead me home with you to live in heaven with your loving Father. Thanks, Mary, for saying "yes" to God and please pray for me that He'll give me the grace to start saying "yes" to Him as you do in order to bring your Holy Son Jesus to others.

Have you ever met a saint? I think I may have met a few right here in Binghamton, NY—inspirations of how much Jesus loves us and can do in our lives. I thank him for revealing Himself to me through them.

Virginia G, a good friend, died several years ago. She was 97, lived alone, was deaf, and on fire with God's love. She was a daily Mass goer. Daily she walked across Court Street which hummed with lunch time traffic—to go and receive Jesus. She used to talk with me after Mass (she was a good lip reader). She used to kiss me after we crossed Court Street hand and hand. And as I left to go back to work she would always joke and say—"be true to me." She is one of those special souls who always smiles, is happy to see you and make you happy to be alive. She really cared. Never once did she complain about her hardships—having been deaf due to a childhood injury. Looking back, maybe it was Jesus holding my hand and asking him to be true to him too. She was weak, feeble, lived alone and was not well-off, yet she warmed everyone she touched. She inspired much of these reflections. Our church, like Virginia, was very old and was seeking pledges to renew the church—thousands of dollars are needed. After mass, she said to me as we walked up Court Street—"I think raising a thousand dollars to fix up our church is a waste, because our money could be better used by feeding the hungry people in our world. Although she was deaf, she seemed to be able to listen to Jesus better than me. Thanks Virginia.

Another inspiration was Pasquale. He literally went to as many Masses a day as he could, using his disability checks to pay for cab rides from church to church several times a day so he could receive Jesus's Body and Blood. He was what some of us call a "simple person" not gifted in worldly information. He taught me much (and I'm a SUNY graduate—big deal). In his simplicity, he was open to Jesus. He told me one day after having received Communion, "Jesus is in my heart, and I'm on fire with love for Him." Thanks for teaching us and me about what really counts. He died recently on Court Street, no doubt coming from and going to Jesus.

Brother Peter [Daino], a missionary, spends himself in loving service. He currently works with a nun in Africa caring for children whose parents have died from AIDS. I've been blessed to hear him preach when he comes to visit. He's on fire with Jesus's love for us. When he talks about his kids, he makes me realize they are my kids too! Thanks Brother Peter and keep setting our hearts on fire! (Jesus wants you to be a saint too!)

Dear Friend, can't wait for you to get this, and have just one last reflection for you. It's so important we share this glimpse of Jesus together, and just how much He can do with and through you and me. Recall Mark 6:30-44—it's about Jesus feeding 5,000 men with only 5 loaves of bread and 2 fish! Jesus you love each of us so much, and seeing vast crowds you "pitied them" and taught them and then told your disciples and us: "You get them something to eat." (How can we feed so many people?) Jesus you are asking us "how many loaves to do we have?" (or how much can you give?) Jesus is taking what we give… "Then Jesus, taking the 5 loaves and 2 fishes, raised His eyes to heaven, pronounced a blessing, broke the loaves and gave them to His disciples to distribute. He divided the 2 fishes among all of them and they ate until they had their full… Those that had eaten numbered 5,000 men." (This didn't include the women and children! Wow—what power you have Jesus and are waiting to show through us!) Jesus wants each of us to give what we can no matter how large or small, and with our gift He will feed our hungering sisters and brothers. It's essential for us to know this because another person's eating and being able to stay alive depends on me, you and us. Thank for listening. May God bless us all and our gifts.

Its 12:45—I'm finishing writing and looking forward to having grilled cheese with jelly for lunch. Can't help but thinking—got paid Friday, my checkbook is across the table and my father has shared with me that 40 million persons will continue to die yearly due to starvation unless they are helped. I'm financially very comfortable but am beginning to feel "spiritually uncomfortable." My checkbook seems to be waiting and so are my hungry sisters and brothers. What do you think I should do?

Please share these reflections with others.

Thanks!

May Jesus bless you and me and us all as we come to know Him more deeply.

Peace,

Mike P.

***

REFLECTIONS AFTER SEPTEMBER 11, 2001

10/30/01

God enjoys seeing us happy. He also is unhappy when we are unhappy and when we love even when God enjoys seeing us love and be loved; giving = loving = God living in with and thru us. 1 unborn baby dies due to abortion every 20 seconds …a human being dies every 40 seconds due to starvation… 16 million of our sisters and brothers die every 40 seconds due to hunger… "WWJD?" Terrorists killed 3,000 innocent people in NYC, DC and PA on Tuesday, September 11, 2001… 1 in 5 children in Afghanistan dies before his or her 5th birthday due to hunger and disease… over 2 million innocent people in Afghanistan are fleeing upcoming violence but have been stopped at the border of Pakistan—trapped… what would JESUS want our government to do? What would He want us, you and me to do? He says "love one another"…but I am afraid to get involved…I'm too selfish (John 15:17) A priest shared how his nephew is a reporter in NYC covering the Trade Center tragedy, and told him reporters break down and cry when they look at the rubble. Seeing numerous body parts of victims of the terrorist attack September 11, 2001—the media will not let us see these things because it is too horrible. How can we as followers of Christ respond to terrorism?

A woman in a central American country plagued by civil war lost her husband and 3 sons due to the fighting. A reporter interviews her and asks, "how come you are not bitter?" She responds, "there is no life in hatred." (My brother told me this).

Jesus help me join You now…feed me with Your Body and Blood. You are all I need…Jesus crucified, dying on the how very much You love us and want us to be Your witness to our suffering brothers and sisters who You died for…He longs to love and heal others thru you and me…help me love like You do…May I embrace You, my brothers and sisters and Your cross daily…Jesus You wait with Your suffering little sisters and little brothers for Me. "And I, once I am lifted up will draw all people to Myself." (John 12:32)

10/30/01—"He must increase, while I must decrease." (John 3:30) in El Salvador 3/4 of kids under age of 5 suffer malnutrition. 1/2 do not have safe water and sanitation. Only 1/2 of all babies born make it to age 1…most persons only get 2/3 of calories they need. Malnourishment is a leading cause of death…the use of violence by our government to protect U.S. interests while neglecting hungry children is so sad…13 million people face dying by starvation in East Africa due to those who are ignoring them…1/2 of children in Afghanistan die before the age of 5. War, draught, famine and winter

7.5 million little sisters and brothers of Jesus in risk of starving to death…our government is spending billions on war and millions on helping feed strong people. What would happen if we spent billions on feeding, teaching, loving? "Love one another" (Jn 15:17)

"When did we see you hungry and not feed you…" As long as you neglected to do so for the least of my brothers and sisters you failed to do so for Me. (Mt 25:31-46) "…her many sins are forgiven her, hence she has great love. (LK 7:41-50) "Lord, Jesus Christ, Son of God, have mercy on me a sinner." The answers to hatred, hunger, abortion and evil can be found in John. "He had loved His own in the world and would show His love to them in the end." (Jn 13:1) (Jn 13:14) "Then you must wash each other's feet." "I am indeed going to prepare a place for you and then I shall come back to take you with Me." (Jn 14:3) "…if you really know Me, you would know my Father also. (Jn 14:7) "As the Father has loved Me, so have I loved you. Live on in My love." (Jn 15:9) "The Bread that I will give you is My Flesh for the life of the world. (Jn 6). "thank You, Holy Father…Lord Jesus, Son of God have mercy on us all…come Holy Spirit…glory to you Holy God!" Recall St. Paul's words: "God made Him who knew not sin, to be sin, so that in Him we might become the very holiness of God (II Cor).

The answer to evil

Hatred is always self-destructive, and unfortunately, it harmed thousands of innocent people. May God have mercy on them, their survivors and on us all. Love is the only answer to such evil.—Michael Phillips, Binghamton

(published in the Binghamton Press & Sun Bulletin sometime after 9/11/01)

Bread, not bombs

What would our world be like if our country spent billions of dollars on humanitarian aid and developing self-sufficiency projects for the suffering of our world, instead of on bombs? One person starves to death every 40 seconds in our human family.—Michael Phillips, Binghamton

(published 12/13/01 in the Binghamton Press & Sun Bulletin)

Feed them instead

It is estimated that a war against Iraq would cost the United States $100 billion to $200 billion. Would it not be a truly Christian act to use this money to promote life, by helping developing nations to feed millions of individuals who wait for a Christian response?

(published in the Binghamton Press & Sun Bulletin sometime after 9/11/01)

XV.

CONVERSATIONS WITH MIKE—MY GREATEST TEACHER

MY LAST DESCRIPTION OF MYSELF was as a little kid playing with my Star Wars toys all the time who looked up to Mike, Flint, and Julie as heroes.

At this point, I would like to give a fuller biography of myself and talk about the incredible life lessons Mike shared with me from my teenage years into young adulthood.

After my parents, Mike was the most profound influence on my life. My values and decision to go to Catholic colleges, serve in our nation's political system, and become an educator were all influenced by Mike.

As a teacher I can say that writing and sharing this book is the ultimate education experience.

Learning about Mike's life means learning about God's love.

And as someone who has been in politics, this is my ultimate campaign—promoting a book on the life of my amazing brother Mike to touch as many souls as possible.

I attended St. Anthony's Grammar School and Seton Catholic Central Middle School.

As mentioned, like Mike, Rob, and Chris, I attended Seton Catholic Central High School, where I am a teacher today. I did extremely well in school and sports, serving as both Key Club and Senior Class president and graduating in the top of my class in 1994.

I loved sports and played football and basketball all four years in high school. I played baseball for the school for two years and then ran track—the sport I excelled at most— my last two years, while still playing American Legion Baseball during the summer.

When I was in high school, Mike's health was already greatly weakened due to his eating disorder. He was on a strict routine and needed to go to bed early for the sake of his health.

It meant so much to me when Mike came to my games, because I knew he was struggling.

He came to a few of my football and basketball games, but they were later on at night and tough for Mike to attend.

Mike also went to some of my track meets. The meets took hours and were different from other sports in that you could go talk to family and friends in the crowd during breaks between events. I remember talking to Mike at the fences just off the tracks I was competing in. I knew he had been a great runner and understood the pain, drive, and thrill of running.

Interestingly, the sport he may have enjoyed watching me play the most that he attended frequently was baseball.

Our American Legion baseball games for our Post 80 team—founded by Coach Dave Ligeikis—were usually held in the afternoons in June and July at Veterans River Park in Kirkwood.

Mike found the games to be peaceful and relaxing, and I have great memories of him there on those lazy summer afternoons.

We began walking regularly together near the end of my time in high school, when we could talk about mature topics. We would walk from my parents' house on his usual route down Watson Boulevard, down McKinley Avenue, through the IBM plant, and before stopping for a bathroom break at Wendy's on Washington Avenue, where Mike bought a cup of coffee.

We talked about the classes I took in high school and college, my work in Congress as an aide, my work as a teacher, politics, and most importantly faith and family during many long walks.

We talked a lot about my teachers and classes. Mike loved hearing about what I was learning.

I obtained my undergraduate degree from Villanova University, where I majored in history and minored in political science and theology. A scholarship from IBM landed me a summer job working in manufacturing for three summers at the plant where Dad had worked for three decades. IBM was my first job, besides being a paper boy for years in a route on Norton Avenue I shared with friend Steve Krol.

After doing so much and so well in high school and being raised like an only child, freshman year in college was rough. It took me a while to develop the confidence I had in high school. One of the most special things Mike did for me was to travel to Villanova and visit me with our brother Chris in my freshmen year.

Travel was hard for Mike because of his health. He never stayed overnight away from his apartment, and he didn't care for long car rides. The fact that he made a three-hour trip to and from Villanova near Philadelphia on the same day and was there to support me during a difficult time will always mean so much to me. I'll never forget Mike and Chris in my small dorm room in St. Monica's Hall.

When I was away at college, Mike said he always thought about me when he was walking and looked at the hills to the south—going toward Pennsylvania and Villanova. He was pulling for me—and praying for me at college.

I ended up having an incredible time at Villanova. I made friends to last a lifetime and got really into my faith and politics after an internship with Congressman Chris Smith of New Jersey after my junior year.

After Villanova, I obtained a master's degree at the University of Notre Dame through their Alliance for Catholic Education (ACE) teacher training program.

ACE sent young Catholic teachers into Catholic high schools in the southern United States, where the Catholic population was a small minority and Catholic teachers were needed. For two years I taught at Loyola College Prep in Shreveport, Louisiana, where I had an incredible experience as a young teacher in an amazingly friendly, hospitable Southern town. I made more friends to last a lifetime in Shreveport and at Notre Dame.

Mike was a great support during my Shreveport years. Teaching high school at age twenty-two was a real challenge. Mike loved to hear about what I was trying to teach and gave me many great suggestions.

I landed in Washington, DC, in 2000, teaching in inner-city public schools before returning to work for Congressman Smith, whom I had the honor to serve for four years.

Since leaving Washington in 2005, I have taught at Seton Catholic Central High School and Broome Community College, been a summer schoolteacher at the MacCormick Secure Center—a maximum security youth detention facility—and even taught grammar school part-time at All Saints Catholic School.

Since Mike's passing I have done work for the Jack Kemp Foundation—and was actually mentored by Jack Kemp, the former Buffalo Bills football star and New York congressman—a good government group called Reclaim New York, both the New York State Republican and Conservative parties, the Joint Landowners Coalition of New York, the Broome County Legislature, the Binghamton Mets and many other political campaigns and projects including fighting for the right to life, term limits and election integrity.

Mike taught me so much. First and foremost, he taught me the importance of family.

He continually told me how special Mom and Dad were and honored them every day of his life.

He loved his brothers and was always there to support each of us.

He loved his extended family and relished chances to visit them in Hornell.

He always focused on the needs of Mom and Dad and his brothers—not his own needs.

As mentioned, Mike's love for his immediate family members was also extraordinary, but many of the stories that exhibit this love are too personal and don't fit as well into this narrative.

In addition to our talks during those great walks I learned much from Mike while he was sitting at my parents' kitchen table.

Mike taught me about honesty and integrity.

I vividly remember him saying, "Don't get in trouble. But if you do, be honest and take responsibility for your actions."

Mike's advice would serve me well on a few occasions.

In junior high school our track coach and social studies teacher, Mr. Rush, heard us whipping a ball around in the locker room before practice—a really bad decision because of all the mirrors there.

When he assembled the team and asked those involved to step forward, I was scared to death. But I followed Mike's advice to be honest and stepped forward. Others followed my brave lead.

Mr. Rush gave me and the others a stern talking to, but he applauded us for being honest and let us off the hook without punishment.

In the locker room in high school I accidentally shattered the overhead lights throwing my comb into my locker.

Rather than running from the scene of the crime, I turned myself in to the janitor, Mr. John Terry, who I thought would then turn me in to the vice principal, Mr. Deus—who I was scared to death to see.

Mr. Terry applauded me for turning myself in and said if I helped him clean up the debris, there was no need to talk to Mr. Deus. Again, thanks to Mike's advice, I was off the hook.

Mike taught me about friendship.

I've written so much about Mike and his friends, the Irregulars, already.

Flint and Julie remained great friends, and Mike would do anything he possibly could for them.

Our walks would often take us to Flint's house in southern Endwell, a few blocks from Christ the King Church.

After his service in the Army, Flint settled down to life as a family man with a woman named Tam, whom he had four children with: Amber, Julia, Justin, and Jared—also known as "Moose."

Seeing Jim and his family gave great joy to Mike. Flint's kids really looked forward to Mike stopping by every Saturday afternoon. Justin would go stir crazy waiting for Mike—"When is Mike coming? When is he coming?"—as he bounced off the walls.

When I was with Mike, Flint told a lot of stories about Saints football. Mike didn't say much but just listened to Flint and his passion.

When Moose was a baby he loved to fall asleep on Flint's chest while Flint was sitting in a La-Z-Boy. Moose was so big and warm that Flint said it was like having a heated electric blanket on him. His chest often became covered with sweat.

Mike loved this story about Moose. I can picture Mike laughing and laughing when he talked about Flint and his "electric blanket."

Flint was a truck driver with limited income. Every year before Christmas Mike would give him an envelope with $400 inside for Christmas presents for his kids. If Flint didn't take it, Mike said he wouldn't come back around.

Flint said his kids looked so forward to Mike coming over that Mike hated to let them down. But at times Mike would have other family commitments or be slowed down by his health problems.

If he wasn't going to stop on a Saturday afternoon, Mike would call Flint on a Thursday and say, "Flint, I am taking a retreat," or "Flint, I have something with my family and I can't make it over this weekend."

A lesson I learned from Mike was to always get back to people.

Unfortunately, great tragedy struck Flint when Tam left him for another man.

Flint was devastated and angry beyond belief. It is hard to imagine how terrible this would be for any person to experience. With Flint and his tough football player, fighter mentality, it made matters even worse. In his youth, Flint was prone to fights, and a violent response was certainly something everyone worried about in this most difficult situation.

At one point Flint—full of rage—was following Tam's new boyfriend in his car and thought about ramming into him. Seconds before he hit the accelerator he heard Mike's voice say, "Don't do it!" and he stopped.

Miraculously, Mike convinced Flint he had to make peace with the situation for the sake of his kids.

Not only did Flint make it through this most trying time, but he also eventually extended forgiveness to become friends with Tam and her new husband, whom he jokingly referred to as his "replacement"—as if Flint had been substituted out of a football game.

And most importantly, Flint continued to be a great father for his children—having a special role in raising his boys.

Mike's great friendship with Julie also persevered through the years.

Mike and Julie cherished the times they spent together when she was back in town visiting from her nursing jobs in Philadelphia.

Mike continued to be very protective of Julie when she had boyfriends, but in a positive way, as opposed to in high school when the Irregulars were beating the snot out of Julie's boyfriend in football practice.

Julie finally found the right man to marry in Mark McWright, who was also from the Binghamton area. Mike was extremely happy for Julie and Mark.

I will always remember the enormous smile Mike had on his face after the wedding when talking about it. He kept telling me afterward that the best part was that he got to dance with the bride. Mike loved Julie so much and their great friendship continued to endure.

After marriage Julie and Mark settled in Baltimore and had four children—Elena, Olivia, Luke and Mary Christa. Mike wouldn't have the chance to see Julie's children as frequently as he did Flint's, but he loved them so much. He talked to me about Julie's family frequently.

Flint's children and Julie's children would be like beloved nieces and nephews to Mike whom he held in his heart most dear.

I give Mark McWright tremendous credit for how well he treated Mike, and I really appreciate how Mark allowed Julie's friendship with Mike to continue to flourish in a positive way.

One special memory Julie has is from when she brought her son Luke home to visit for the first time. They met at Julie's sister's house. Mary Jo live just a few houses down the street from my parents. Mike burst with joy holding Luke.

The story reminds me of how excited Julie was to hold me as a baby for the first time in my parents' house.

Mike was so happy that Julie had found happiness and done well in life.

He had prayed for Julie and Mark so much during their first years of marriage when they struggled to have children.

His mission became to pray for Julie's mom, Mary, who developed a rare, excruciating lung condition called Idiopathic Pulmonary Fibrosis, which would cause her lungs to slowly wear away.

It was an extremely painful condition with no cure, and it was agonizing for the entire Trasolini family.

Mary Trasolini was an amazing woman, full of the same vigor and warmth that make Julie so special. She also was my mom's hairdresser and closest friend on Norton Avenue after Mrs. Fertig.

For years, every single time I saw Mike, he would say to me, "Please pray for Julie's Mom."

He said that each time you see her will be the best you see her. The next time she would be a little worse.

Julie had a miraculous experience in Baltimore one Sunday after Mass. There was a deacon at the Mass whom she had never met before and had great spiritual gifts.

After Mass, as people gathered to talk, friends said to Julie, "The deacon is looking at you."

The deacon said, "I know your mother is very ill. Please take this Miraculous Medal (a Catholic icon with an image of Mary the Mother of Jesus on it) and give to your mother."

Then the deacon said, "I know you have a friend who is a man who is very holy and very close to Jesus, but is very sick as well. Please give him this Miraculous Medal."

When I was in the middle of a difficult decision as to whether to keep working in Congress or return to teaching, Mike gave me the Miraculous Medal.

After putting the medal on, I felt a great sense of peace.

Mike loved his other friends so much as well. As mentioned, he like to call Vinnie "Skirny" and saw him frequently at my parents' house.

Vinnie is so close to our family, he often stops at my parents house on Christmas Day. When he comes to my parents' house, he doesn't have to ring the door bell. He is welcome to just walk in.

Mike and Vinnie laughed and laughed when they were together and they were always there for each other.

Vinnie's and his wife Karen had two children, Vincent and Valerie. Vinnie's family was very important to Mike.

When Wayne came to town it was so special. Mike didn't get a chance to see him that much, but when he did, the joy of their great friendship abounded.

I learned laughter, joy, and humor from Mike through his friendships.

Mike could joke about himself and others in a positive, gentle way.

Mike taught me the incredible dignity of every single human person and their soul.

He believed the three most urgent issues of grave importance facing our world, in order of importance, were the salvation of souls, abortion, and world poverty.

Mike realized that nothing was more important than the salvation of one's soul.

As I stated previously, one of his most beautiful prayers was simply, "Jesus, Save Souls."

He wanted everyone to know Jesus as he did and make it to heaven. He was very humble about the state of his own soul. If I were to say, "You are so holy. You are going to heaven," Mike would scoff at it.

Mike never made judgements about the future of the souls of others.

He taught me that the Catholic Church has never said for certain who is in hell. They have never said that Judas Iscariot, who betrayed Jesus, or a murderer, or any other person who committed horrible acts was in hell.

We don't know what state of mind a person is in and we don't know what the mercy of God would have in store for a person who has committed evil.

If someone Mike knew had fallen away from their faith or was living a life of sin, he would pray for them. He had made his own mistakes in life and sympathized greatly with struggling sinners.

Mike also taught me that the Catholic Church teaches that the only people we know are in heaven for sure are the canonized saints.

Everyone who is in heaven is also a saint though, and part of the Communion of Saints. Hopefully this includes many people.

As mentioned, Mike prayed for the souls in purgatory—especially our relatives from Hornell.

Catholics believe that purgatory is a place for souls to be purified before getting to heaven.

Abortion was the second most serious issue facing society in Mike's mind. He could not believe and repeatedly focused on a statistic that held 3,600 children die from abortion every day in the United States of American alone.

It just broke Mike's heart.

Mike felt that this loss of innocent human life was so tragic and needed to be stopped through prayer from individuals and action by political leaders to make laws to protect human life.

Mike did not take a judgmental stand toward women who had abortions or men who participated in them. He prayed and felt sympathy for those involved with what he considered a most tragic decision.

Mike taught me a great spiritual lesson with regard to abortion that applies to so many other areas of life: the Devil cannot create, he can only distort that which God has created.

What is more beautiful than a couple on their wedding day joined by God in marriage?

What is more beautiful than a newborn baby?

Only God can call new human beings into existence and allows men and women to participate in this sacred gift.

The Devil distorts the good God has created in human sexuality with pornography, prostitution, sex outside of marriage, adultery, divorce, and the taking of precious innocent human lives through abortion.

The third area Mike believed needed to be addressed most urgently was world poverty. I have already dedicated an entire chapter to this topic and why he literally gave every single dollar he had to helping poor people in the world.

Mike would spend much time talking about these three critical issues—the salvation of souls, abortion, and the world poverty—with family and friends, and much more time praying about them.

Mike taught me the importance of being passionate about your work. He absolutely loved his job as a counselor but told me that many of his colleagues got burned out.

It is hard listening to people's problems all day. For the population Mike was working with at the Broome County Jail, success rates were poor.

Mike told me that as many at 90% of people in detention facilities are there due to drugs and alcohol—selling drugs illegally, buying drugs illegally, or doing something illegal while under the influence of drugs and alcohol.

Mike always pointed out to me that statistics show those who have the best rates of recovery from drug and alcohol addiction are those who have had religious experiences.

As a government employee, Mike could talk about his faith only if his clients first brought up their own faith. I know he cherished those opportunities when he could talk about faith.

Mike loved his co-workers. I already mentioned Bob and Colleen Sullivan. There was a great bond between the three of them for many years.

Mike loved trainings, which he had to attend to maintain his certification as a drug abuse counselor. He was always looking to learn more about his trade and improve his efforts to better serve his clients.

He loved his clients and, as mentioned, would always say, "People are special."

Mike just loved his work and was really good at what he did.

I remember walking the streets of Binghamton with Mike near his house and running into his clients. He didn't want to engage them with me present because it would breach their confidentiality, so he would wave and keep going.

I will never forget one guy with shaggy long hair and a scruffy beard who was missing teeth.

He was so happy to see Mike and yelled out with a big smile, "Mike, I have been clean for six months now!"

Flint said when he was walking with Mike in Binghamton, Mike told him he would put his hood up just so clients wouldn't see him. He loved them but didn't want to break confidentiality.

There were several occasions when it appeared that funding for Mike's program would be cut and that he would lose his job. This caused him great consternation. An instrumental figure in saving funding for his programs was State Senator Tom Libous.

Another lesson I learned from Mike about his work was loving those who hurt you.

Mike had many difficult times with bosses he struggled with. I will not mention their names.

Dad had said that Mike's bosses and even some co-workers may have been envious of Mike, because he was so happy and he loved his clients and his job so much.

Mike continually made requests about his schedule so that he could get to daily Mass and meet Grandma Trasolini each day, which may have rubbed supervisors the wrong way.

My recollection is that one boss in particular was constantly nitpicking and complaining about Mike making his life as difficult as possible, when he just wanted to meet with clients and do his job. It sounded like bullying to me.

Many people allow a difficult work situation to eat away at them. Mike said, “Don’t let other people rent space in your mind.”

Mike talked to family members and friends about how difficult his bosses made his life and work, but he prayed for and forgave his bosses time and time again. This was part of Mike’s sanctification and his great example for all of us.

Mike was forced into a major sexual harassment lawsuit in which he had to testify as a witness about a comment a supervisor made about a colleague of his. Mike absolutely hated being dragged into the middle of this conflict and testifying in legal proceedings, but he had no choice. He knew he had to testify and tell the truth. He continued to love and pray for his co-workers during this difficult time.

Mike taught me the importance of defending the dignity of life in the political system.

He wanted politicians to defend unborn children from abortion and always voted as a single-issue voter for pro-life candidates.

He thought that our government was spending too much money on defense and should be feeding poor people instead. He hated war.

Mike was extremely conservative on social issues—a steadfast prolifer—but a liberal social justice advocate for the world’s poor and a pacifist.

Flint, a proud Army veteran, realized that Mike hated war and was critical of how much our nation spent on our military, but he said every year Mike would be the first person to call and wish him a happy Veterans Day. He was also proud of Wayne’s sacrifices in the military.

Mike realized were tremendous problems with the American welfare system, but he was very careful not to judge poor people.

Mike and I had some fierce debates about politics that we both enjoyed during our walks.

Besides Mayor Ed Koch, the only national politician I remember him really liking was President Ronald Reagan.

He liked both of these men not because he focused on their policies, but because of their personalities.

Mike loved hearing stories about the congressman I served, Chris Smith, a truly remarkable man and the greatest defender of human rights, the unborn, and the dignity of all life in the history of Congress. Smith is still serving in Congress today.

A great inspiration for Smith's human rights work was *Tortured for Christ,* by Richard Wurmbrand, a Romanian minister who was tortured in the Soviet gulags during the Cold War.

As mentioned, I interned for Congressman Smith in 1997, and after several years of teaching, I was fortunate to return to his staff in 2001. Top aides Mary Noonan and Andy Napoli allowed me to help with part of Smith's incredible human rights work, which included oversight on Smith's landmark law, the "Trafficking Victims Protection Act of 2000," and fighting for human rights around the globe, including in China, Vietnam, and Cuba.

Smith's personal mission—like Mike's—has been Matthew 25: "Whatever you do for the least of these." He and his wife Marie have been such an incredible personal inspiration to me and so many others.

My first day working for Congressman Smith was April 23, 2001—the feast of Saint George and the anniversary of the death of my Grandma Bernadine. Her husband, son, and grandson were all named George, and she died on the day of this feast.

I went to daily Mass that day and the priest said, "We don't know a lot about St. George, but we know he was a fighter. Sometimes we have to get in there and fight against evil."

Wow. That was and is Chris Smith—fighting against evil.

Mike fought hard against evil in his own way.

Mike was a great support during my time with Congressman Smith, which also brought me into a great group of friends in Washington who helped nurture my faith.

During one of our walks, when I was visiting home during my time working for Congressman Smith, Mike said, "I am reading a book about St. Francis, and you remind me of St. Francis."

Mike said that whenever Francis saw a problem, he threw himself into it. Mike thought the same could be said for Smith—and my work on projects for him.

I responded by telling Mike, "You're the one like St. Francis."

And he was. Mike was a spiritual giant who threw himself into helping others.

Mike helped me in my work in politics when I would get too worked up by telling me, "Christ died for all of our sins."

Christ died for our closest friends and worst adversaries.

Mike taught me healthy living.

Yes, he walked too much, and yes, he did not eat enough and he exercised too much. However, I still learned so much about the importance of exercise and healthy eating from him.

Whenever I saw Mike he was in a great mood. I attribute this to his deep relationship with God, but also exercise.

Mike taught me that when you walk briskly or exercise, it is a great way to relieve stress and feel great.

Mike also taught me about the "Holiday Blues" on Thanksgiving and Christmas. Families gather together for joyous celebrations, but eating too many sweets and too much food and being cramped up inside can make people anxious and moody.

Walking and exercise are great ways to counter the "Holiday Blues." Even if it's very cold, Mike taught me that you just have to dress for the conditions and go out there or find ways to exercise indoors.

Mike about told me to avoid sweets and caffeine. They give you a "sugar high" and a "caffeine high" that are then followed by lows and irritability.

Mike also taught me how to read food labels to avoid sugars and fats that you don't need.

Following Mike's advice and focusing on a protein diet (Mike ate a ton of eggs) has helped me lose 50 pounds since Mike passed away.

Sleep is critical. Mike struggled with sleep because of his illness and was always talking about the need to get enough sleep. He told me if you don't, your brain won't function correctly.

Exercise, eating healthy, getting enough sleep, and, of course, prayer were keys to Mike's success amid his health struggles. They are great recipes for success for any person.

I learned and experienced firsthand what made Mike such an incredible counselor.

He was so good at listening to and affirming me. Despite his struggles he was so positive about his own life and always saw the good in others.

Utilizing Carl Rogers's counseling style, Mike often repeated what you said to him to affirm you.

He would say, "Yep. I know" in a special way that connected with you where you were at.

If you were struggling, he was there for you, but he always tried to help you see the light at the end of the tunnel.

If you were angry with someone, he reminded you that person was hurt or broken in some way.

As I mentioned in the section on my parents, Mike avoided gossip. He had a way of presenting negative stories in a gentle, charitable way.

I learned overcoming disappointments from Mike.

Things did not go well for Mike in his goal to be a great football player or in other areas of his life. He made it through the tough times and kept his eyes on the prize in Christ Jesus.

I learned simple living and humility.

At first it was shocking to think how simply Mike lived and how little money he used, but he was able to do it.

One time when my wife Diana went to Colombia with our kids and I was unable to join them, I spent as little money as I possibly could, ate simple meals, thought about Mike's simple living, and felt purified by the experience.

I learned contrition and redemption from Mike.

Mike talked to me about the many mistakes he made in his younger days with the Irregulars. He was embarrassed. He had let my parents down and caused them a lot of pain. However, he also did so much for so many years to be a great son and become a holy man.

Thanks in part to Mike's witness and testimony, I avoided alcohol and many of the bad decisions he had made.

The story of Mike is a story of redemption. He knew in different ways this was the story of all of us—his family, friends, and clients, and people everywhere.

Mike's tremendous awareness of sin—and serious transgressions—made him all the more compassionate toward others and all the more appreciative of God's great mercy for him.

Much of what I learned from Mike's spiritual life and mission for the poor he served as a social worker and his donations to CRS I have shared already.

Whenever there is a mission appeal at church or an opportunity to give to the world's poorest, I always dig a little deeper for a bigger donation because of Mike.

I learned the most from Mike about faith and his love for Jesus. Everything else in Mike's life stemmed from this.

Although Mike was a devout Catholic, I've always felt his witness was for all Christians and all people.

Catholics talk about Mary and the saints a great deal. We don't worship them. We honor them, reflect on how devoted they were to Christ, and ask for their prayers. Their mission is to lead us to Jesus.

In my conversations with Mike, I never remember him talking about the saints too much.

For Mike it was Jesus, Jesus, and Jesus. He was totally focused on Jesus's love for him and his love for Jesus.

It is interesting to note that deacons in the Catholic Church need to have a spiritual advisor. In virtually all cases this would be a Catholic priest. Mike was actually my dad's spiritual advisor.

Dad would have Mike read his homilies in advance and ask for comments. Dad still laughs about how thoughtful and gentle Mike was in his critiques.

Mike would say to Dad, "You may want to say it this way instead."

Even though my brother Rob, Chris, and I weren't living a religious vocation with a required spiritual advisor, Mike was our spiritual advisor too.

I learned so much from a man who studied in Franciscan seminary, read a steady stream of rich spiritual readings, prayed without ceasing, and dedicated his life to Christ.

Mike taught me so much about the Passion of Jesus, which he read about and reflected upon for hours and hours.

He believed that Jesus sweated blood during the agony in the garden.

He would meditate for hours on each wound of Jesus—the scourging from which Jesus probably would have died in a few days had he not be crucified, due to a massive number of wounds and probably infection; the crown of thorns; the wounds on each of his hands and each of his feet; and the spear in his side.

He loved reflecting on the "Seven Last Words" of Jesus.

They are:

"Father, forgive them, for they know not what they do." (Luke 23:34)

These were Jesus's words to the Pharisees—the Jewish religious leaders and soldiers who put him to death.

"Before this day is out you shall be with me in paradise." (Luke 23:43)

These were Jesus's words to the repentant thief. Mike told me his name was Dismus, and things were looking dismal for Dismus before he turned his life to Christ.

"Woman, behold your son. Son, behold your mother."

These were the words of Jesus to John, the beloved disciple and only Apostle who stayed with Jesus during his crucifixion.

"My God; My God, why have you forsaken me." (Matthew 27:46 and Mark 15:34)

Jesus was quoting the beginning of Psalm 22—a famous Jewish prayer that starts in doubt but ends in hope and trust.

"I thirst." (John 19:28)

Mike believed that Jesus was thirsting for souls.

"It is finished." (John 19:30)

This was the prayer the Jewish high priests said after sacrificing the Paschal Lamb.

"Father, into your hands I commit my spirit." (Luke 23:46)

This prayer is also from the Psalms—Psalm 31 was a bedtime prayer that Jewish mothers taught their children.

Mike believed that Mary smiled when Jesus died because she was relieved that his intense suffering was finally over.

Mike wrote a song about Mary being with Jesus at the crucifixion to the tune of the "Little Drummer Boy," which I wish I had a written version of.

Hearing the song, the "Little Drummer Boy," during Christmas time always brings tears to my eyes because it reminds me of Mike. Mike's version of the song seemed to have the following lyric, "Mary saw her son bah rum pa pa…"

Mike said that it was all of our sins that put Jesus on the cross and all of our sins that Jesus died for. His sins, my sins, and your sins—Jesus died for all of us.

An incredibly special experience was watching the movie *The Passion of the Christ* by Mel Gibson with Mike when it was in theatres in 2004. The movie was based on scripture but also *The Dolorous Passion of Christ*—visions from an eighteenth century mystic named Anna Catherine Emmerich that Mike had read and recommended to me.

The Dolorous Passion of Christ showed what Jesus was thinking throughout the Passion and scenes not in the Gospels. They include Jesus telling his mother that he would die and seeing inside his mind as he continually prayed for those who were mocking and torturing him.

I hadn't been to the movies with Mike since he took me to *Star Wars: The Empire Strikes Back* when I was a kid, and I was excited to see his reaction.

Mike sat silently in deep reflection throughout the movie and thought it did an incredible job portraying the Passion of Jesus he had spent so much time meditating upon.

In addition to the Lord's Passion, Mike loved the Eucharist. I loved going to Mass with Mike and just being in his presence as he was so focused on God and the miracle of receiving Jesus during Communion.

At St. Mary's Church he loved sitting in the cry room—which was also a confessional in the back—or in one of the pews in the back left side of the Church.

I can still picture Mike in both of those places in deep, deep prayer as he prepared to receive Jesus.

Mike knew scripture well and shared with me his favorite scripture passages.

Mike loved Isaiah 53—the passage in which this great prophet predicted the suffering of Jesus—and could recite it by memory:

> "Who has believed our message
>
> and to whom has the arm of the Lord been revealed?
>
> He grew up before him like a tender shoot,
>
> and like a root out of dry ground.
>
> He had no beauty or majesty to attract us to him,

nothing in his appearance that we should desire him.
He was despised and rejected by mankind,
a man of suffering, and familiar with pain.
Like one from whom people hide their faces
he was despised, and we held him in low esteem.
Surely, he took up our pain
and bore our suffering,
yet we considered him punished by God,
stricken by him, and afflicted.
But he was pierced for our transgressions,
he was crushed for our iniquities;
the punishment that brought us peace was on him,
and by his wounds we are healed.

Mike told me that he prayed Matthew 11:28-30 every single day. The passage reads, "Come to me, all you who are weary and burdened, and I will give you rest. Take my yoke upon you and learn from me, for I am gentle and humble in heart, and you will find rest for your souls. For my yoke is easy and my burden is light."

This was a profound prayer for a man who suffered so much for an eating disorder.

Mike loved the story about Peter sinking in the water before Jesus when he called out, "Lord Save Me" (Matthew 14:30). He told me this is the shortest and most important prayer in the whole Bible.

As mentioned, Mike told me the story about Saint Paul and the thorn in his side, and how begged God for relief. God would not remove the thorn but instead told Paul that His power is made perfect in weakness.

I can picture walking with Mike near the railroad track crossing between Watson Boulevard and Main Street, saying, "When I am weak, I am strong. We need to depend on God more when we are weak," and that God tells us, "My Grace is Enough."

Don't we each have some thorn or burden we suffer from that won't go away? How can we become more dependent on God through these thorns? How can we be made more perfect in weakness?

Mike never complained about his own suffering, but he often told me, "The Church is full of suffering people."

I have thought about that phrase frequently with regard to Mike's life, but also so many others. When I go to church, I sometimes glance around at the congregation and look at their faces. I think about what suffering inside of each person might have brought them to church to look to Jesus as Mike did.

Mike frequently told me the closer you became to Jesus, the more spiritual attacks you would receive from the Devil. I know that this is true in the lives of many of the great saints and recently listened to a book on a tape entitled *Saints who Battled Satan*, by Paul Thigpen.

Mike kept becoming closer and closer to God but kept getting attacked more and more by Satan through his eating disorder, which continued to become more and more severe.

Mike had an incredible awareness of sin and taught me the importance of confession—an incredible sacrament he received once a week—usually with Father Hobbes or Father Corey.

He said theologians theorized that God allowed sin to give humans humility and that the great saints had an incredible awareness of the even the smallest sins. He also said the saints were the sinners who just kept trying.

Mike repeated to me many times the advice he received from our mom that shaped his purpose of life and that she learned in Catholic grade school, "The purpose of life is to know, love and serve God; to find some happiness in this life and eternal happiness in the next."

Mike loved a wise saying from Fred Picciano, a great and humble man who was a religious education teacher and leader at the Christ the King Church. Mr. Picciano taught students, "Each day you either move closer or further away from God. You are never the same by the end of the day."

Mike loved the theological concept of the "Sacrament of the Now." Catholic sacraments are signs of God's love and profound ways of connecting with Him.

The "Sacrament of the Now" means that embracing the present moment—in prayer or by being fully present to the person you are with—is a profound way of experiencing and sharing God's love. The "Sacrament of the Now" personified Mike's approach to counseling and how he treated all people.

Mike told me that the saints were those sinners who just kept trying, and the only requirement to be a Christian was to be a sinner in need of God's mercy.

This was a profound statement from someone who was so conscious of sin and was doing everything he could to battle and avoid even the smallest sins in his life.

Mike also told me that God called some to lead the others.

Mike directed this lesson to me specifically and always reminded me that God was calling me to lead in a special way. This has meant a great deal to me in my life as an educator and in politics.

With the cross he put on the back of his jackets, Mike taught us all not to be afraid to witness to the faith.

He witnessed to the faith in so many ways and loved the saying of St. Francis, "Preach the Gospel at all times, and if necessary use words."

Mike told me a lesson our mom had shared with him. He said Mom said to him, "Michael, you can choose to be as happy or as unhappy as you want in life."

Mike said he chose to be happy every day, and we all should too. His great happiness stemmed from his Christian faith and his love of God.

There is a famous song with the chorus, "They will know we are Christians by our love."

Mike paraphrased it and said, "If you are really a Christian and put your whole heart into it, you will shine brightly—it will radiate out of you. People will know you are a Christian. You will be better than the best."

This is how I remember Mike—as an incredible Christian man and witness to Christ who was so humble and holy, yet shined so brightly.

XVI.

THE CRISIS

IN 2002, AT A LUNCH ceremony in downtown Binghamton, Mike was honored as the Broome County Counselor of the Year for his incredible work.

His fellow counselors submitted the reasons for his nomination for this award. Their testimony is as follows:

> "In a field that is relatively new and continually changing, as new theories and treatment modalities are explored, we would like to acknowledge this individual's consistencies.
>
> "Michael subscribes to the highest ethical standards. He thoroughly and thoughtfully considers all aspects of situations to be dealt with. His regard for the total well-being of his clients is evident. Michael is non-judgmental, seeking the best in people, and meets his clientele where they are at. One may say that he epitomizes Rogerian philosophy.
>
> "Michael has an enviable knack for engaging his clients. He excels at establishing rapport. He has long been known at this agency for the units of service he produces. His clients seldom miss appointments and will return to treatment specifically to work with him, as he instills a sense of trust. Michael has been willing to make personal sacrifices to continue in direct counseling with a clientele that he feels committed to.
>
> "As a co-worker and employee, he is simply 'the best.' He is professional, loyal and a team player. He has been and continues

> to be flexible and adapts to the changes within the agency. He has wonderful interpersonal skills and always maintained a positive working relationship with all referral sources.
>
> "We feel fortunate in having had an opportunity to work with him. The treatment community can always count on Michael to give his all and serve as a wonderful representative of this field; the bottom line is that Michael Phillips is a 'good egg.'"

Local political leaders—including my future political opponent, Congressman Maurice Hinchey, County Executive Barbara Fiala, State Senator Tom Libous, and Binghamton Mayor Rich Bucci—wrote proclamations for Mike. The then deputy mayor and future mayor Rich David spoke and presented a proclamation to Mike.

A short time after the award ceremony, we almost lost Mike.

People with severe eating disorders are always susceptible to having a fatal imbalance in their electrolytes. Dehydration from a flu or upset stomach or even drinking too much water can cause this imbalance.

Mike's electrolytes were off on a late spring day from drinking too much water, and he collapsed at work. Our parents and Chris met him at the emergency room. He was very near death, but luckily the doctors brought him back.

When I got the news, I was at the Memphis airport flying from Washington on my way to Shreveport, Louisiana, for my good friend Trey May's wedding. Dad called me and told me the news, but he said Mike had been stabilized and was probably going to be alright.

Mike was fighting to survive in the emergency room, but he felt his life slipping away as he was losing consciousness. He heard our mom's voice say, 'Michael, your feet are cold,' as she rubbed his feet.

At that moment, Mike said, he made the decision he could not die in front of Mom. He fought his way back to life.

On a trip home after Mike's run-in with death, Mom showed me the video of the ceremony for Mike's Counselor of the Year award. Mike had been too embarrassed to have Mom and Dad at the ceremony, but we all loved the video.

At the end of the ceremony Mike gave a brief but beautiful acceptance speech. He said, "I can only accept this award on behalf of my fellow workers, who with their help made this possible. It has been an awesome privilege to get to know my clients."

His co-workers could be seen and heard cheering wildly in the background for Mike. They just loved him.

Mom broke into tears after showing me the video. She said, "Michael never won an award before."

I never saw Mom cry before. The survivor of a brutal divorce, domestic violence at the hands of her father, abandonment by her mother, and severe alcoholism was always so unshakable.

The fact that Mike had never won an award also brought tears to my eyes. I went to the basement to work on my laundry and started to cry myself.

The tears from both Mom and me were partly from the award ceremony but more from the fact that Mike had almost died.

Back in Washington, I loved my work with Congressman Smith, my friends, and going to daily Mass, but I couldn't seem to meet the right girl.

St. Patrick's Church near Ford's Theatre had a night once a month for young adults called "Christ in the City." In was an hour of prayer, Eucharistic adoration, music, a sermon by a priest, and Confession.

I was really tired at work one day and debated going to "Christ in the City" that night. In the end, I decided to go.

After an hour of prayer, when I was leaving, I saw that beautiful woman for the first time on the steps of St. Patrick's Church. Her name was Diana Quintero, and she was there with a friend, Oscar Dussan, who was studying to be a Catholic priest.

I introduced myself to her but she could not speak English, so I used the Spanish I knew, and we got a lot of help from Oscar translating.

Oscar had been pestering Diana to go to "Christ in the City" to meet up with one of his friends who would be there, whom he hoped she would date. Diana didn't like Oscar's friend romantically and finally said, "I'm not going for your friend, but I will go for Jesus."

The three of us walked to the restaurant together and talked and talked. I bought her a drink and invited her to the big annual St. Patrick's Day party the next week at my friend Timmy Carney's house.

Diana came to Timmy's party, and I asked her out on our first official date. We went on several dates before I had to leave town to work on President George W. Bush's re-election campaign in Pennsylvania on a Catholic Outreach project.

Diana was and is such a beautiful woman. Her middle name, Milena, means "to shine"—perfect for her. Beauty, faith, and goodness radiate out from her.

During my absence from Washington, Diana was praying a novena to Saint Teresa the Little Flower—a cloistered nun who died at the age of twenty-four around the year 1900 but has had an incredible impact on the world through her writings and many miracles associated with her intercessory prayers.

Diana was praying the novena to St. Teresa that our relationship would work out. During this time she visited a nursery school staffed by religious sisters that her nephews were attending.

A sister said to her, "You are praying to St. Teresa? Here is a statue of St. Teresa."

Then, from a vase of roses at the foot of the statue, she gave Diana a rose.

"This rose is from St. Teresa for you," the sister said.

Diana learned that if you receive a rose while asking St. Teresa for intercessory prayers, it is a sign that your prayer request will be answered.

When I returned to town from the campaign, I picked Diana up at her sister's house for another date. I will never forget that moment when I saw her for the first time in months. It was like the light of God hit me and I was given a revelation. I knew we were going to get married.

During this time I had lunch with Brian O'Brien, a friend of mine from Notre Dame and a seminarian who is now a Catholic priest. He was in Washington for a visit.

He said, "You're in love with a girl who prays the rosary and goes to daily Mass? I hope you can marry her soon."

When Mike met Diana, he would have the same advice. Our whirlwind romance was in fact rapidly moving toward marriage.

I saved for the engagement ring and planned to propose that summer. Dad contacted me and said there was an opening at Seton Catholic Central to teach American History—one of my greatest passions. Dad was teaching physics there as a retired IBM Engineer.

Diana and I got engaged on July 23—my brother Rob's birthday. On the same day, I accepted the teaching position at Seton—which has turned into years of great joy serving so many incredible students and their families.

Our wedding was in Bogota, Colombia, on December 30—the Feast of the Holy Family.

Amazingly, Diana's old friend Oscar, our translator who was no longer a seminarian, met my college friend Katie Bronson at the wedding, and Diana's cousin Juanita met another of my friends from college, Gary Chon Hong. Both couples eventually got married.

Given Mike's severe health issues, he couldn't make the wedding in Colombia, but he was with us in spirit. Mike loved Diana like a sister the first time he met her.

Ultimately what brought Diana and me together was the deep Catholic faith we shared. After her father died when she was only sixteen years old, Diana got very involved in a missionary program called Central de Joventudes based in the small town of La Capilla near her house.

Diana took a year off from college and traveled around Colombia as a missionary after extensive training. She gave talks and did spiritual formation for teenage girls.

She also became very involved in an incredible rosary group for young people led by a Catholic musician named Felipe, who had visions of Mary that have been investigated by the Vatican.

Diana's faith has and continues to radiate out from her and is at the center of our lives together. When I told her about Mike, she said, "This guy sounds so special, I can't wait to meet him."

Mike was so excited for me and so happy to meet and bring Diana into the family. They were like a match made in heaven as far as sisters- and brothers-in-law go. Mike would call Diana "Hermanita," which means "little sister." Diana lit up every time she saw Mike. They loved talking about their faith and life in general.

After we had our actual wedding in Colombia, my parents planned a Mass to renew our vows and celebrate our marriage in the Binghamton area.

Mike was designated our driver for the day. It was such an honor to have him with us.

My nieces, Heather and Jessica, were doing Diana's hair at my parents' house in Endwell. Mike had to drive Diana back to our apartment in Johnson City, and he actually took a wrong turn—making Diana a bit late for the celebration.

As mentioned, Mike was so kind to my mother in-law Lucy. He was also so kind to and loved by Diana's sister, Edna, her brother-in-law, Julio, and their four children, Tomas, Luis David, Juan Michael, and Pablo.

Edna and Julio's kids loved Mike. He shaved his head in those days. They were little and they asked him if they could touch his head. They laughed and called him "Chicken Head."

At the end of our first year of marriage, Diana and I were blessed with our first son, George Joseph. We enjoyed so many joyful moments with Mike and our new baby. Not surprisingly, he would walk more than an hour from his apartment in Binghamton to our apartment in Johnson City to spend time with us.

After a year and a half, we moved to a house in Endwell—five houses down from the Church of the Holy Family, where our Dad was a deacon.

We wanted to be close to Mom and Dad, but also the 24 Hour Adoration Chapel at the Church. We have spent so many great hours at the chapel through the years.

Diana and I had a regular 3 p.m. hour at the chapel on Sundays. We often needed a substitute when we were traveling or had other activities. Mike gladly subbed for us many times.

I can still picture him walking from the Adoration Chapel one day in the rain with his green Saints football jacket with the homemade cross on the back and a smile on his face.

But by the spring of 2007, I was troubled. Mike was not looking good. He was getting thinner and thinner and looking bonier and bonier. He looked like a cancer patient getting crushed by chemotherapy.

Mike's bones were getting so brittle that he was cracking his ribs just by coughing. And his cracked ribs were tremendously painful.

There were a few times in my life when I was with people I knew were going to die. The first was with our Grandma Bernadine in a nursing home when I was in high school.

We were told she had only a short time left. When I looked at her during our final visit, I just knew this was it, and I said my goodbyes to her.

Aunt Doris, who had been so special to our family for so many years, was battling cancer in the early 2000s. I visited her several times in New Jersey in the apartment she lived in with her cousin Gladys.

The last time I visited Doris she was upbeat about her prognosis, but as I walked out the door, I looked at her and knew it was the last time I would see her. She passed away a short time later.

I was having similar feelings about Mike. He had also been dangerously thin and nearly died five years prior. He just seemed to be losing so much weight, and I didn't think he was going to make it.

I thought about my life thus far. I had put tremendous energy into sports, academics, my work in politics, and my relationship with my wife.

As a congressional aide before I met my wife I remember working until 11, 12, 1, or even 2 o'clock in the morning. Couldn't I bring the same energy and drive to saving Mike's life?

I couldn't bear the thought of losing someone who meant so much to me, and I couldn't bear the thought of having my parents lose their beloved son.

I talked to my close friend Brian Coveleskie, who worked in the insurance industry on mental health coverage. He had seen many eating disorder cases through the years.

When I told Brian that my brother's weight was under ninety pounds, he became greatly alarmed. He told me Mike's Body Mass Index (BMI) was 14 or lower. He had never seen a number this low and agreed that the situation was dire.

My goal was to do everything possible to keep Mike alive—so he could at least outlive Mom and Dad.

The person I put my hopes in to achieve this goal is a truly remarkable man—Mike's doctor, Richard Terry.

Dr. Terry agreed with my concerns about Mike's grave condition. Mike had hovered around 100 pounds for years—a dangerous weight that he was still able to survive at. Unfortunately, plummeting to ninety pounds or less was not sustainable.

I talked with my wife, Mom, Dad, Rob, and Chris, and we decided we needed to have an intervention in which we would force Mike into treatment.

The idea of treatment was just impossible for Mike. He needed his routine. Being in a hospital or rehab center with forced weight gain, when his mind had fought for so long to either lose or not gain weight, was just devastating.

Mike had to be admitted to Wilson Hospital in Johnson City to stabilize him until a spot opened in a rehab facility for an eating disorder patient.

In addition to Dr. Terry, Helen Battisti, and hospital staff, our family will always be grateful to Matt Salanger, the CEO of United Health Services and Wilson Hospital, for their care for Mike.

It was unusual for Wilson Hospital to house eating disorder patients for the long-term, and Matt was very generous in getting the hospital to lend its help. I had the honor of teaching Matt and his wife Mary Ellen's four children.

I felt like Dr. Terry and I had developed a great plan to save Mike's life, but I simply could not comprehend what was going on in Mike's mind.

Mike's severe eating disorder had become a personality disorder that was an inseparable part of who he was. Asking Mike to subject himself to forced feeding and weight gain was so extreme for him and ran counter to how he had lived his lived for twenty-five years. I didn't realize how difficult it would be.

Mike had been receiving forced feeding in Wilson Hospital for a day or two when he just snapped. He couldn't take it anymore and left the hospital.

Worried terribly about him, I finally found out where he was from my brother, Chris. Mike was at the Endwell Motel—where the Irregulars had hung out and played so many late-night card games—running from the torturous treatment trying to separate him from a disease that had become so much a part of who he was.

When I found Mike in his room at the Endwell Motel, it was a surreal moment. He was extremely weak from his dangerously low weight.

I still had no idea what caused the eating disorder. Anorexia in males is so rare. What caused my brother to have such a serious illness?

In this moment of anguish, I said to my brother, "Mike, what's causing all of this?"

Shaking with trepidation and shame, he could barely look at me. He uttered the name: Ben Hendrickson.

XVII.

THE ABUSE

His name was actually not Ben Hendrickson. I have used this fictitious name in the spirit of this book—not mentioning his name or the names of others who may have hurt Mike. I am also not using his actual name out of respect for his family and friends who might hear about this story.

I will continue to refer to the person Mike referred to under the pseudonym Ben Hendrickson.

When Mike said the name Ben Hendrickson, I knew exactly what happened. I had never met Ben personally, but I had heard stories about him.

Mike couldn't even bring himself to say what Ben did to him, but I knew.

Ben had sexually abused Mike when he was a young boy.

This is what had been torturing Mike so much for so long.

This was the deep secret Mike was trying to hide with his drinking.

The false sense of guilt that so many sex abuse victims tragically experience manifested itself as a severe eating disorder for Mike.

To be abused as Mike was at such a young age—the age of sexual innocence and purity—would profoundly impact on any person.

When Mike said Ben's name to me, it was such an awful and surreal moment. I felt as if Mike pulled back a curtain, and behind that curtain I could see a horrible, terrible open wound filled with disgusting and poisonous puss and scabs that he had been covering for so long.

We were both overwhelmed. Neither of us could say more. The pain of all those years for Mike came rushing over me—like a huge wave, yet small in comparison to what he had personally faced for so long.

Without releasing his true identity, I can assure readers that he is no longer in a place where he can harm children. This would mean he is either deceased, incarcerated, or in a nursing home.

After that night at the Endwell Motel, I spoke to Rob and Chris, and they confirmed what Ben Hendrickson had done to Mike so many years ago.

When writing this book, I asked Mike's two best friends if he had ever spoken to them about the abuse by Ben Hendrickson.

Flint said one time when they were younger and drinking, he said, "Mike, why are you always carrying a flask of 57 proof gin with you?"

Mike told him it was to cover the pain of what Ben did to him.

As you might imagine, Flint offered to find Ben and beat him up. Mike declined. He said he just wanted to put the incident behind him.

Julie said he never talked about it, but she discovered it after her son Luke was born. Mike took her on a long walk, and he was adamant with her, pleading, "Julie, please don't ever let Luke sleep over at another family's house. Anything can happen."

Julie said it hit her at that moment that something had happened to Mike.

There were three experiences in Mike's life involving sexual abuse or unwanted sexual advances.

The childhood abuse by Ben, which I know very few details about, was by far the worst and most damaging.

The second experience was during a trip with Flint to St. Mary's of the Plains in Kansas, a semester after Flint left the school. Flint and Mike drove out to get a TV and some other of Flint's possessions from Flint's ex-girlfriend. In the long drive back in the middle of a snowstorm, they stopped at a restroom. Mike was in there alone, and a man made advances at him. Nothing happened, but because of Mike's abuse at the hands of Ben, the Kansas experience shook him more than it would the average person.

The third experience was the sexual assault in the seminary from an older seminarian that I referenced earlier. In light of the Catholic Church facing a sex abuse scandal for years, I want to address this incident in greater detail.

Like so many other family members of victims of sex abuse that occurred within a Catholic Church setting, my initial feelings were of anger.

How could this happen in Catholic seminary when Mike was trying to consecrate himself to God in the religious life?

Why did Dad tell me that a report was filed, but he never followed up on it?

Why did the Catholic Church do such a terrible job handling so many sexual abuse cases in the past?

Father Sixtus—Mike's beloved spiritual advisor in seminary—must have known about this. Why didn't he do anything?

Even though Mike never spoke to me about the sexual assault—he had only told me that he faced unwanted advances by men in the seminary—he did talk to me about the sexual abuse scandal in the Catholic Church.

As I mentioned previously, Mike told me that the Devil doesn't create. He only distorts what God has created. The building blocks of the Catholic Church are the family and the priesthood. The Devil has attacked the family with the temptation of so many sexual sins and other sins that have broken families apart. The Devil has attacked the priesthood through this horrible scandal. What is more horrifying than a priest betraying his call to holiness by sexually abusing a child?

Mike also said the Catholic Church had dealt with sexual abuse in ways that families have dealt with them.

Let's consider a fictitious story of a man name Lou. If Lou sexually abused his nephew Johnny in the 1980s, and Johnny's parents found out, in most instances they would not turn Uncle Lou over to the police.

They might say, "This is horrible," and keep Lou from their children. They might add, "Lou always seemed different," and "Let's make sure this doesn't happen again," but they would not properly confront this devastating crime.

Mike said the Catholic Church did the same thing with so many priests. They tragically failed to respond—often enabling sexual predators to abuse more innocent victims.

Mike did not justify the actions of the Catholic Church when explaining this to me. He simply said this is what happened.

I don't know what Father Sixtus could have done to help address this case, but again he was working with Mike in a period of tragic inaction by all.

Unfortunately, Father Bruce Ritter, the founder of Covenant House, whose talk at Seton inspired Mike's vocation in social work, was accused of sexual misconduct and had to leave the organization in 1990.

Ritter denied all allegations against him. An argument in his defense was that organized crime wanted to see his downfall, because he was taking kids off the street, away from their businesses in the prostitution industry.

Mike said that in reading Ritter's writings, he was concerned by the great detail Ritter gave in his physical description of young men. Mike's intuition told him that Ritter probably had been involved with misconduct. Ritter died of cancer in 1999 at the age of seventy-two.

As horrible as the sexual abuse scandal has been, I am impressed by how the Catholic Church is dealing with it today through admitting past sins, removing priests who have committed crimes against children, cooperating with prosecutors, compensating victims, and working to prevent future abuse.

Mike remained a devout Catholic despite the scandal for the same reasons I have. He knew the overwhelming majority of priests are good people who have not been involved in these horrible crimes. A love of the Eucharist kept him a devout Catholic.

In addition to alcoholism and anorexia, the abuse caused Mike to struggle with his own sexuality and live a life of celibacy.

In high school, Mike had fallen in love with Julie. Shortly thereafter he entered seminary, where he would be committed to a life of chastity and celibacy.

Even though he left seminary, Mike never left his commitment to chastity and celibacy.

As with those in the religious life, celibacy was a way for Mike to sanctify his life and turn his full attention toward God.

Out of his experiences with sexual misconduct, the one Mike actually talked about the most was the bathroom incident during the Kansas trip with Flint. I remember him mentioning it numerous times to me.

I believe it was his way of warning me and saying the world is a dangerous place.

Even after reflecting for years on Mike's life, I can see no easy solutions for his pain and trauma, and I know the same is true of many victims of sexual abuse.

As story after story of sexual abuse has come forth in recent years, my heart has been broken for the victims.

Mike's abuse was linked to the drinking problem he overcame.

With his eating disorder, Mike turned the guilt and shame of the abuse inward—punishing himself and his body.

It would have been great for Mike to get counseling for his eating disorder when it first manifested in the late 1970s and early 1980s, but this would have been extremely odd. A young man going to counseling in general, much less for an eating disorder, was just not common.

My advice for anyone struggling with abuse or an eating disorder is to seek counseling as soon as possible.

God's gift of sexuality is so dear. I am thankful that I met and have been married to such a devout Christian woman.

But I've seen the Devil distort God's gift of sexuality many times. In high school, so many of my classmates were making poor decisions with sexuality. I saw hearts broken and heard stories of sexually transmitted diseases and abortions.

I highly recommend the website www.chastity.com, run by dynamic speakers Jason and Chrystalina Evert, to everyone. They address remaining chaste, starting over and healing from past mistakes, addiction to pornography and other sexual addictions, and same-sex attraction.

No matter what mistakes we have made with regard to God's gift of sexuality or in other areas of our lives, God's love is there for us, and we can experience redemption.

Consciously, Mike knew this. But, as mentioned earlier, Mike's eating disorder was a personality disorder that became who he was.

Sexual abuse, alcoholism, and anorexia could have been the only story lines of Mike's life, but they were not.

Romans 8:28 states, "We know that in all things God works for the good of those who love him."

God worked through the pains and sorrows of Mike's life—and the evil acts others had committed against him—to make him an amazing soldier for Christ.

Back at the Endwell Motel, this soldier was in the midst of a courageous struggle for his life.

XVIII.

HEROIC WARRIORS

Mike agreed to go back to the hospital, face his demons, and fight for his life.

Battling an eating disorder for many years made Mike a heroic warrior. Our family and Mike's friends who shared in this struggle were heroic warriors with him.

The plan Dr. Terry, our family and I had in my mind when I brought together the intervention for Mike was simple: physically stabilizing Mike through weight gain, then helping him get the psychological treatment he needed for recovery.

The point I am so deeply sorry about was failing to comprehend how deeply seeded the personality disorder was for Mike.

All the efforts I engaged in ran counter to who Mike was as a person at that point, and they would be torturous.

Mike was subjected to forced feeding tubes through his nose to gain weight. He couldn't walk—which he loved to do—because it would burn calories and prevent weight gain. He could have Communion brought to him, but he could not go to Mass. He couldn't smoke. These were all excruciating sacrifices.

And his digestive system was so scarred from years of abusing laxatives, he needed to rely on medicines prescribed by doctors in the hospital to have bowel movements.

Mike's mind constantly centered around burning calories, and under tremendous constraints in the hospital, he still looked for ways to do this. Little things—like chewing gum and doing crossword puzzles—would be ways for him to burn calories and fight weight gain.

Amid his pain, Mike remained a shining light as a Christian. He was angry about his situation, but he respected what I was trying to do. He knew his life was at stake.

Mike was so special to all the nurses who served him during each of his hospitalizations, and they quickly came to love him. Most nurses would light up with a big smile when they came into his room and saw him.

When Mike introduced us to one of his nurses, he would say, "She's the best."

Mike was so positive with family. I still remember his saying to my wife during his different hospitalizations, "Diana, I am taking a retreat." This meant that Mike would be praying all day—the Jesus prayer and so many others—for the salvation of souls.

I vividly remember the visits Flint and Julie made during this time.

Flint sat very close to Mike, speaking very seriously to his dear friend, whispering sincere and earnest words of thanksgiving for Mike's friendship and support.

This may sound strange, but their closeness and seriousness of manner in a profound moment reminded me of the famous scene where Pope John Paul II was huddled with Mehmet Ali Ağca, the man who tried to kill him.

Obviously, Flint was not needing to give Mike forgiveness, but encouragement—telling Mike, his best friend in the world with whom he had shared so much, how he could pull through this.

When Julie visited, she was in tears. She held Mike and was without words for her great friend.

Chris, Rob, Mom, and Dad were all so supportive of Mike during this most trying time.

I tried everything I could to help. I went to the Healing Mass at St. Mary's—Mike's home Church—and asked those there to pray over me for Mike.

I brought a visiting priest from Africa who was gifted in the healing ministry to the hospital to pray with Mike.

Mike was moved to a rehab facility near Albany for eating disorder patients after a few days, but he was quickly returned to Wilson Hospital because he was deemed too medically unstable.

After a few more days at Wilson, Mike was moved to a rehab facility at New York Presbyterian Hospital in Westchester County. Chris drove him for this next excruciating part of his journey and forced weight gain.

Below are Mike's journal entries from June of 2007, when he was in Wilson Hospital. The letter from July of 2007 was when he was in New York Presbyterian.

June 9, 2007 Friday

> When I woke up this AM I did not know where I was. I was happy to be alive and well rested. I thanked God. I became anxious thinking about wanting to smoke and go home and back to work.
>
> I'm upset because I have to comply with therapy, or I cannot get a doctor's statement to go back to work. I have to comply in order to get my medicines—it sucks being dependent. Wish I could find a way to have a bowel movement without taking a laxative. Wish I could sleep without medication.
>
> Don't want to gain weight but know I have to stay alive. I can gain some weight and not be fat and if I feel I gained too much, I can get rid of it when I am free.
>
> I'm hopeful. I'm sad for my family. I'm embarrassed because I am such a mess-up. I'm happy because God is good. And thankful for the people here who are so kind. I'm blessed.
>
> Want to love and be loved. Want to make family happy. Enjoy drinking energy or apple juice. Tube feeding (thru nose) is bittersweet, wheelchair is too. Embarrassed to take up so much time of workers if others resent me. It's weird to write about me…seems so selfish. Getting in touch with a lot of things.

The opposite of anorexia is eating healthy and happy and socially not caring about calories, weighing—being free to eat and live-, work- and sleep-in peace—being able to live without sadness, accepting my illness, need for God and others.

Do you want to die?

Do you want to change?

Will you change?

What do you want?

Will you let go of anorexia, or at least try?

Why do you hang on to it—it hurts your family?

You cheat on yourself.

Why do you still want to lose weight?

Or stay at an unhealthy weight?

Isn't anorexia a sick way of getting down, using others and feeling my sinful self?

What does God want?

Gain a little weight, stay alive, and don't die

Realize I don't have to gain a lot

That I can take it off if I want, but do not have to

Pray to Lord to have strength

Best way to be today—in hospital

Try talking to others

I am hopeful I can stomach tube feeding—is very good

June 10, 2007 Saturday

Don't want to die and don't like this. I want to be able to have a BM. I might need to use laxatives safely—I'm O.K. with that. It's scary and upsetting but somehow if I try to honestly change, I will be O.K.

I don't want to gain weight and know as soon as I am free, I can play the game and gain some. It's insane but it's O.K. because I am starting to accept the idea of gaining a few pounds—wish I could go away where no one knows me and start again.

Embarrassment, guilt, shame and sin suffocate me. I live to eat enough just to not gain weight and help me stay alive. It seems like I am in a dangerous place—I'm being tube fed.

Maybe they think I am going to die—I want help but I can't smoke and want to get the hell out of here.

I need to comply with MD to go back to work—so I am forced—without MD I got no job, no meds, and will end up dead.

I cling so tightly to thinness. I have got to gain 5-10 lbs. which would still leave me thin. Need to be healthier for family. They desire me and it is selfish to cut them out of my life because I am choosing to be sick. I'll try—its O.K. to make a little progress.

June 11, 2007 Sunday

Forgive me for cruelly hurting my family

Help me to change

Help me to love

Help me to let go, even if it is a little

I'm scared about BMs, cigs, sleep, weight, work, and playing the game—being a liar.

Help is on the way in this place. Its O.K. to be sick and imperfect. Tonight, I'm happy. I did not leave. No medicine is hell. If I leave I will lose my job so I have to stay and get Dr T to write letter to state I'm O.K. to work.

I'm in a fight for my family, job, clients and life—scared but O.K. right now

June 14, 2007

I'm scared—Dr. said he wants me to go to a rehab and said is not willing to do paperwork for me to return to work. I'm scared, tired, constipated, and nervous. I'm angry that I have so little control. It's not fair that after all my difficult work this past week that he can deny me my livelihood. I'm embarrassed, humiliated, but guilt ridden for what I put my family through. I'm messed up and a loser. I'm angry that I got put in the hospital against my will even though it may save my life.

Help me love, help me live, help me listen, help me to go home and back to work.

From New York Presbyterian in Westchester County

July 9, 2007

Dear Mom and Dad,

Hope all is good. I miss you both a lot and look forward to your phone calls. Reminds me of Staten Island. I miss Sat and Sun with you both. Thanks for all your support, kindness, love and acceptance. You two mean the world to me.

I am sorry I have put you guys thru some really rough times in life. I hope I can make some of those times up by getting closer to you both. Slowly I'm getting better. God is good. He is helping me change. The people here are very special, both clients and staff. Sad but true, too much suffering and not enough Jesus. He is our only hope. I am blessed very much because you have given me life's greatest gift—faith in Jesus and His love. So sad so many don't know Him.

I am happier than anyone I know because of Jesus, His love, your love and being able to love others. Thanks for giving me and teaching me to care, love, serve and listen. I'm working on eating more on a daily basis. God is helping me, and I have hope.

Two new girls just came in, one bulimic and one anorexic. The one seems very scared. I said hi and helped her take her dishes to the window to be washed after dinner. The other girls are really reaching out to her. She does not seem as scared. She is even smiling. I keep all the girls name in my notebook and try to pray for them during the meals.

Guess that's about all for now. I miss you guys and look forward to coming home. You're in my prayers.

May God bless you both. Love, your son, Mike

I called Mike as much as I could to encourage him while he was in rehab, but he did not want any visitors and felt ashamed.

Most of the other patients struggling from eating disorders were teenage girls. Mike ministered to the teenage girls and they loved him.

They would write him letters and he would write them in the years that followed. Mike didn't talk about them much—abiding by the same standards of confidentiality he held with his clients.

What happened to Mike in the Westchester rehab seemed to be a miracle. He returned home after a few weeks of forced feeding weighing almost 130 lbs.

When Diana and I returned from a trip to Colombia and saw him for the first time, we couldn't believe how incredible he looked. Mike had always shaved his head for years, but he was unable to in Westchester.

His hair grew back very thick and looked like the hair of a teenage boy. He had not one gray hair.

I had hoped that the intervention had worked.

Unfortunately, Mike faced bad news with work when he returned. The labor union and laws protecting sick workers guaranteed that Mike would still have a job in the Department of Social Services. However, he was moved from the job he loved, working with clients at the jail, to a position at the main headquarters of Social Services, screening clients receiving government assistance for drug use.

Mike said his new clients were special people made in God's image and likeness like everyone else, but he did not get to see and work with them on a regular basis as he did with his clients at the jail. This broke his heart and mine, but I tried to remind myself that we were trying to save Mike's life.

Mike also said the workload at his new job was extremely slow and there would be hours at a time when he would have almost nothing to do. He said he used that time to pray.

Mike just couldn't stand being 130 pounds. Through walking and his old eating habits (and I imagine severely abusing laxatives), he was dropping weight rapidly.

In conversations with me when we were walking, he said he just felt so uncomfortable with all that weight and couldn't stand it. He felt bloated. He felt huge. He was just so uncomfortable.

Mike continued to take bold steps to make a difference in the world. At this point he had not had a single drink in fifteen years and had no desire to drink, but he started going to AA meetings as much as he possibly could to support others.

For years he had wanted to get back in touch with his eighth grade teacher, Sister Michelle, and thank her for helping him develop a personal relationship with Jesus, but he couldn't find her.

Finally, they connected. She was living in Utica—two hours from Binghamton—and was no longer with her religious order.

They met at a restaurant in Norwich, halfway between Utica and Binghamton. Mike enjoyed seeing Michelle so much.

At one point during the meeting he got up to use the restroom and left her a note. In it he explained to her that he had an eating disorder.

He hadn't wanted to let his parents and family down with the eating disorder. He also didn't want to let down his beloved grammar schoolteacher.

When Mike returned to the table, Michelle had read the note. She said she still accepted him.

In the Spring of 2008, Mom's cousin, John DeVinney—who had been like a brother to her because they lived in the same house after her parents' divorce—passed away.

Mike rode with Diana and me and baby George to the funeral in Hornell. I reflected a great deal about Mike's life during this trip. He had been born in Hornell and spent so many great times there. He loved our relatives so much and prayed for our deceased relatives every day.

Something kept telling me that this would be Mike's last trip to Hornell. We had a great time, and I will cherish that trip forever.

By the summer of 2008—a year after Mike was in rehab—his weight was returning to dangerously low levels.

I was running for Congress, and we were doing a lot of door-to-door campaigning, dropping off campaign literature.

Mike wanted to help and he joined us in door-to-door. Because he looked so frail, he wouldn't actually knock on doors and talk to people. Instead, he just dropped off the literature.

I will always be deeply grateful to have had Mike's help when he was so sick. But by September, I was really worried about Mike. It appeared that he dropped down to under ninety pounds again—a dangerous level.

We had become close family friends with Pat and Mary Ann Dorner. Mary Ann is the older sister of Mike's close friend, Vinnie Palmeri.

Pat invited me to his Christian men's prayer group at Union Center Christian Church. I told the guys about my brother and my concerns about him.

They said, "Look, your brother's illness is making him incapable of making good decisions on his own. You have to intervene again to save his life."

I talked to Dr. Terry and my family and said that we needed to intervene again to save Mike's life. I forced Mike into the hospital again.

I will always remember that night with Mike in the emergency room in the fall of 2008. I watched Congress vote against the bank bailout in the midst of the financial collapse on the TV screen in the lobby.

Mike hated being in the hospital. He was angry at me for forcing him in again, but he forgave me and was still, as always, extremely kind to me.

He continued to be wonderful to the nurses who served him, brightening up their days. And he continued to joke with my wife, saying, "Diana, I am taking a retreat."

Mike gained some weight, got out of the hospital, and got back to work.

I lost the election in 2008 badly—by over 30 points—but I was determined to come back in 2010.

By the spring of 2009, Mike was doing extremely poorly. He looked worse than ever, and I sensed he was around 80 pounds.

I vowed I wasn't going to force him into the hospital again, but I was really worried. I remember going to Mass with him, and he was so weak he could barely open a door.

I was at Mom and Dad's house, and Dad said to me, "Mike is not doing well. You should go check on him."

When I arrived at Mike's house, he was standing out front. He looked horrible.

He said he was having trouble breathing and needed to get to a hospital as soon as possible. At his request, we went to Lourdes hospital.

As we sat together in the emergency room, Mike was so weak and seemed just awful.

He started talking about Julie and their great friendship. He remembered in high school they would spend hours sitting together at the mall, talking and just watching people walk by.

After a decent amount of time waiting, the ER staff began to treat Mike. His situation was dire, and his lungs were actually shutting down. Had I not picked him up sooner, we might have lost him.

I often thought about what a special testimony this was to his friendship with Julie. In what might be the final moments of his life, he was thinking about her.

As doctors evaluated Mike, there was concern that his kidneys were failing, and that it might be irreversible. Mike weighed less than eighty pounds.

In the hallway, while waiting for an elevator, I asked a nurse what was the down the hall in the next wing. She said, "That's where the cancer patients are. There is a lot of courage in that wing."

I can't imagine what it was like for so many of those brave patients battling cancer. But I know Mike was so brave and courageous in his struggle as well.

Thankfully, his kidneys were not failing. But Mike was still in terrible shape.

I believe Mike's greatest physical problem at the end of his life was that he had abused laxatives so badly for so many years that his digestive system was not properly functioning. No matter what he did, he couldn't seem to gain and maintain weight.

After a few days, Mike was slightly more stable and left Lourdes hospital—still at a dangerously low weight.

Our family came to an agreement with Mike and Dr. Terry. Mike would stay at Mom and Dad's house and do a weight check-in at Dr. Terry's office once a week, which I would attend with him. If Mike's weight was too low, he would have to return to the hospital.

Mike stayed in a tiny room in my parents' downstairs. As mentioned, the previous owners had used it as a beauty parlor, like in Aunt Gert's house in Hornell.

Mike was too sick to work—which was just heartbreaking. He could no longer give money to CRS, which was also so heartbreaking.

The weekly weight checks were very hard for Mike. As difficult as they were, it was still a tremendous honor to accompany him to those appointments with Dr. Terry. Those weekly meetings with Mike and Dr. Terry were moments I will cherish for the rest of my life.

Dr. Terry loved Mike so much. He continually went above and beyond the call of medical service to help Mike and did everything he could to save his life. He remains a true tribute to his profession.

The weekly check-ins were very intense. Mike would drink large amounts of water before the check-ins to inflate his weight. He always seemed to make weight and avoid hospitalization—barely.

I can't tell you how much our family enjoyed being with Mike at Mom and Dad's house for the next sixteen months. Even though he was suffering so much, Mike was just so pleasant to be around, and we cherished every moment with such an amazing person.

Diana, little George, and I were over visiting on most days. Diana had taken a job at Broome Community College, and I was teaching at Seton.

Mom, Dad, who was teaching just part-time at Seton, and Mike had babysitting duties with little George.

I am so grateful for the amount of time George got to spend with Mike. Mike worked with him on learning his numbers, the alphabet, and so many other things.

They loved watching cartoons together. There was a cartoon character nicknamed "Sneaky Pete," who was always causing trouble. George and Mike laughed so hard when "Sneaky Pete" got a cigarette caught in his pants. George knew that Mike smoked and started calling him "Sneaky Pete."

I'd call my parents in between the classes I was teaching at Seton, and I'd ask George—then three years old—how Mike was doing. He'd usually say, "Mike is sleeping," or "Mike is praying."

Mike's body was worn out. He was too sick to go on the long walks he loved, but he would still walk four or five houses down the street with George. George would say, "Mike are we going to King's house? Are we going to Dunda's house?"

Mike's ministry to widows continued with Mrs. Fertig, and he would go across the street to accompany her for long talks.

I remember Mike going to AA meetings all the time. He took the bus. He didn't want to be dependent on others for transportation—as sick as he was.

It hurt so much not being able to work his old job, but the AA meetings gave Mike some solace, and I'm sure he touched many lives there.

I remember him carrying around an AA book along with a beautiful old Bible he had from seminary, which I believe Sixtus gave him. He had read it several times and written beautiful notes in it.

Mike's health struggles continued. One night in bed he couldn't feel his feet, and my parents had to call 911. He was stabilized at the emergency room.

In May of 2010, I met with former New York City Mayor Ed Koch about my congressional race.

My opponent, Congressman Maurice Hinchey, had come under fire for lack of support for Israel, and I was seeking an endorsement from this big-name Democrat who was known for crossing party lines to support Republicans like me who supported Israel.

It was surreal meeting with this legendary mayor, and it was a lot of fun talking to Mike about the meeting when I returned, because I had long connected Mike with Mayor Koch from Mike's New York City days.

In late August of 2010 I vividly remember sitting in our parents' garage talking with Mike. He said, "I think I could write a book about almost kicking the bucket."

Flustered, I quickly responded, "You don't think you're going to die, do you?"

Mike assured me he wasn't in danger of dying, despite his weak condition. He said on those several instances when he almost died, he did feel peace and that he wouldn't have to fight anymore.

Mike was always good at spinning the situation on his health. He said he was actually planning on moving back to his apartment in Binghamton after nearly a year and half at Mom and Dad's house.

He said he wanted to live and get better, and I believed him.

I had a lot going on with my campaign for Congress. For months, with a stalwart group of volunteers, we had knocked on doors and made phone calls throughout our massive eight-county congressional district, which included Ithaca, where Cornell University is, my own area in Binghamton, and large parts of the Hudson Valley that were over three hours from our home.

Our internal polls showed we were only down seven points—an amazing surge from the more than thirty points we had lost by in the previous race.

In September Diana and I had big news: She was pregnant again. Since George's birth almost four years earlier, we had suffered five miscarriages, and Diana had two tubal pregnancies. We told Mike and our family the great news and entrusted our baby to his prayers.

Each of the previous miscarriages had occurred early—around our first ultrasound. I will never forget the call I got from Diana when I was driving in Sullivan County in the Hudson Valley.

She was in tears. She had just finished the first ultrasound, and the baby looked alright.

She joked, "Would you rather win the election or have a healthy baby?"

I quickly responded, "Have a healthy baby. of course."

I remember Mike coming to our house in Endwell and looking very weak. He was very sick, but he got on his hands and knees to play with George on our deck.

In early October I saw Mike at my parents' house. George was jumping around yelling, "Michael! Michael! Michael."

A few days later, after a long campaign trip, I just missed Mike at Mom and Dad's house. It was Diana's birthday—October 8. She was so happy and said, "I can't believe it. Michael ate a small piece of cake for me!"

It was a wonderful gesture by Mike, but he really shouldn't have been eating cake. His digestive system was simply too weak. The sugar and chocolate were not good for him in his condition.

With my race for Congress in its final weeks, I kept calling major figures, frantically asking for help for our campaign. Key supporters would come through, including Matt Schlapp—currently the chairman of the American Conservative Union; Ed Cox—the New York State Republican Party chairman and President Nixon's son-in-law, and his executive director, Tom Basile; and Allen Roth and David Goder—advisors to Ronald Lauder, a major political donor, of the Estée Lauder cosmetic company.

News came from the national level that both campaigns now considered our race a dead heat. Amazingly, former president Bill Clinton came to Binghamton to campaign against me at the Holiday Inn on the evening of Columbus Day.

Two days later in Kingston, I campaigned with Mayor Koch and Ronald Lauder at an incredible campaign event. Lauder had arranged my long-sought-after endorsement from Koch.

The next day American Crossroads, a premier Republican super PAC founded by Bush advisor Karl Rove, announced it was pouring $500,000 into our race.

I didn't know Karl at the time, but I met him the next year at an event at Cornell University sponsored by businessman Roy Park and the Young

Americans Foundation. I have been most impressed by his work as an author and historian.

Politico, a top national political journal, listed us as the No. 2 race in the country to watch.

I called Mike at the end of this amazing week and said, "Things are crazy. Are you going to be alright until after the election?"

He assured me he would and said that he wanted me to get a yard sign to Dr. Terry. He said, "Dr. Terry is really well respected in town and has done a lot for us. Please get him a yard sign."

I told him I would, and I made sure we got Dr. Terry a sign.

At this point in my life, besides taking care of my wife and son, the two central goals of my life that I had relentlessly pursued for several years were to win election to the United States Congress and keep Mike alive.

I trusted that Mike would make it the few days until the election. I needed to do everything I could to win this incredible congressional race.

The evening of Monday, October 18—one week after Bill Clinton campaigned against me and the fortunes of our entire campaign changed—I was in New York City speaking at "The Monday Meeting," a major event that attracted national conservative figures.

I thought about Mike so much that night, my visits with my parents to see him in New York City when I was little, and the amazing time he had spent in this incredible city.

I was speaking in a lineup that included Peggy Noonan, the famous speechwriter for President Reagan. Reading her book, *What I Saw at the Revolution*, in college had a major impact on my love for history and politics.

I had a really fiery campaign speech and got to talk to Noonan afterward. She said she liked my speech. I told her about President Reagan's trip to my town and the "Which Way EJ Speech." She remembered the speech and that her colleague from my area, Peter Robinson, had written it.

The next morning, we had a candidate forum at Traditions at the Glenn—the old IBM country club—hosted by the Greater Binghamton Chamber of Commerce.

In the audience I was surprised to see Julie Trasolini's niece, Julie Ann. She was there with her Maine-Endwell High School government class.

That evening I was on my way back to the Hudson Valley for two events in Ellenville. Diana almost never traveled with me, because she was usually taking care of little George, but I had an event with the Hispanic community and wanted her to attend with me.

We drove with Joe Malek, the younger brother of Matt Malek, a good friend of mine from Villanova. Joe had come in to help in the final days of the campaign.

Just before 5:30 p.m., as Diana and I were walking into the event, my cell phone rang with a call from Mike's number. I didn't take the call as the event was beginning, but I planned to call him after.

After the event we began the ride home, and Diana and I were flying high. We had all the momentum, and I felt certain we were going to win the race.

I decided to check my voice messages before returning Mike's call. He often left messages saying he was going to bed early and to call him back tomorrow.

As I checked my voice mails, there was no message from Mike. Instead, it was my brother Chris calling from Mike's phone, telling me the terrible news:

Mike had died.

XIX.

HIS LIFE IS A LESSON

DIANA AND I STARTED CRYING. I told Joe Malek to pull over the car. He found a field on the side of the road. I grabbed a rock and threw it as far as I possibly could.

I was just devastated to lose Mike and so angry to have failed in my mission to keep him alive.

I called my family as well as my good friend and mentor Jeff Coghlan to tell him the news.

Chris explained to me what had happened. Mike called him at about 5:00 p.m., saying he wasn't feeling well and had spilled some juice. He asked Chris if he could come over.

Chris got to Mike's apartment about fifteen minutes later and found him. He'd been kneeling in prayer on his chair when he passed away.

I originally thought that Mike had called me at 5:30 p.m., but it was actually Chris calling from Mike's phone to tell me our brother had died.

It was fitting that Chris found Mike. Even though I have written extensively about Mike's incredible relationships with Julie and Flint, it was Chris whom Mike was closest to and spoke with every day.

Mom and Dad were watching George when they received the news. Dad went over to accompany Chris. He was so moved to find Mike kneeling that he called Mom and said she had to come over as well to see Mike.

They had raised him, taught him the faith, supported him in all his struggles, and seen him develop into the most remarkable of human beings and Christian men.

To see him finish the journey praying on his knees was amazing in the midst of their great sadness.

The night Mike died, Rob drove in from Connecticut. Mom, Dad, Chris, Rob, and I wept and told stories about Mike at Mom and Dad's house, where we had enjoyed so many great times.

It is sad that Mike never recovered from his eating disorder but as Rob frequently said about Mike and others, 'sometimes healing doesn't come on this side of heaven.'

Dad told me that shortly before Mike died, he had taken little George to visit Mike in his apartment. It meant so much to me that George was one of the last people to see Mike alive.

My last memories of Mike were of him playing with George at our house, then at Mom and Dad's house, and eating birthday cake for Diana. In my last phone conversation with Mike, he praised Dr. Terry and insisted that I get him a yard sign.

When I talked to Mom in the days after Mike's death, she said Mike called her the night before he died and said, "I love you."

As she reflected on his life, she told me she took great joy in the fact that Mike was such a happy person. It is hard to describe in the midst of great suffering just how happy and joyful Mike was.

Julie heard the news and left me a voice mail before I was able to call her. In a sad but gentle voice she said, "Our beloved Michael has passed from this world."

When I spoke to Julie, she said that Mike had attended a wake for her aunt only a few days before. She said Mike looked so sick and it meant so much to her that he came. They just held each other and cried.

Rob and Chris were able to contact Vinnie before Flint. Vinnie was devastated for the loss of his beloved friend whom he had grown up with and was like a brother.

Vinnie called Flint, who was driving from work at the time. Flint was totally distraught and pulled over to the side of the road. His mentor and best friend, whom he had shared so much with and who had done so much for him, was gone. He just couldn't believe it.

We learned after his death that Sister Michelle had driven all the way from Utica to visit Mike in his apartment shortly before he died. She had made a huge difference in his life from introducing him to Jesus in a new way so many years before.

Amazingly, October 19, the day Mike died, is on the Catholic calendar as the feast of St. Paul of the Cross, an Italian mystic whose great devotion to the Passion of our Lord inspired him to found a religious order called the Passionists.

St. Paul of the Cross's devotion to the cross was so intense, it was seen as eccentric. Mike had witnessed to so many thousands of passersby while walking for so many miles over the course of many years with the cross on his back. The Passionist priests actually wear a cross over a heart on their clerical clothes.

October 19 is also the feast of the North American Martyrs. Jesuits St. Isaac Jogues and several companions were martyred by Mohawk Indians in Upstate New York. I visited a beautiful shrine where they died and learned that Jogues told the others that if they were being executed, it was most important to utter the name of Jesus at the moment of their death, which they did.

It's hard for me to imagine a scenario where Mike was not calling upon the name of Jesus when he died praying on his knees, after he called upon the name of Jesus hundreds of thousands of times during his life.

Mike's death was also one day after the feast of Saint Luke. The theme of Luke's Gospel—an outreach to the poor and sinners—was the theme of Mike's life as well.

My emotions in the immediate aftermath of Mike's death included regret. How could I take my eye off the ball on Mike's health in the middle of a political campaign?

But I also knew that Mike was in such bad health for so long, and his body was so permanently damaged, that barring a miracle, he would not recover.

In some ways I feel as if my intense focus on the campaign finally allowed Mike to die. I wasn't there to push him back into the hospital, which might have prolonged his life but also his suffering.

Memories came rushing back from my life with Mike immediately after he died.

Mike died during the peak of the beautiful colors for fall trees in a time of year that was so special to him. The day he died was an absolutely beautiful fall day bursting with colors.

Fall marked Mike's hopes and failures in football, the beginning of his friendship with Flint, the coming together of the Irregulars, and so many events that followed.

I kept thinking about that picture I loved so much of Mike, Julie, and me in front of that beautiful fall tree bursting with color—with Mike in his football jersey and Julie in her cheerleading outfit.

I thought about that ride to visit Mike at seminary in Holyoke. All I could remember was all those beautiful fall colors I had seen during the ride as a small child.

I thought about Mike in New York City. I can't believe that I was in New York City—a place so special to Mike, where his incredible career as a social worker began—the night before he died.

And amazingly, Ed Koch, the mayor Mike liked so much and was in office when Mike lived in New York, endorsed me right before Mike's death.

I was still teaching at Seton in the middle of the campaign and went to school the day after Mike died. I parked in the side parking lot of the school and came in a back door, near the janitor's office.

Emotions flooded through my body once again as I thought about hanging out with Mike in that room in the years after high school, when he was a summer janitor and I was a small child.

Amazingly, Mr. Wheeler's Stage Band down the hall was playing "Don't Stop Believin'"—the great song that reminded me so much of Mike and his work in New York City with young men and women at Covenant House.

It seemed like Mr. Wheeler and Stage Band were playing "Don't Stop Believin'" all the time for the next few weeks, and it gave me great comfort.

A day or so later I stopped by the school library and grabbed a copy of the local newspaper. When I opened it to find Mike's obituary, I broke into tears. Mr. John Colonna, an incredible guidance counselor who was close to our family, was there to comfort me.

Going by our Phillips for Congress campaign office at the bottom of the Hooper Road ramp the day after Mike died was surreal.

Volunteers making phone calls were literally out the door. A trailer had been pulled up into the parking lot, and more volunteers were calling out of the trailer. Helping to spearhead the effort was Vinnie's sister, Mary Ann Dorner. She brought together so many great friends to help us, including our top caller, Kathy Koffs, who seemed to make calls for days straight.

The next afternoon another big name entered our race with an endorsement for me—former New York Governor George Pataki.

What was even more special for me than having a governor campaign for us was seeing State Senator Tom Libous. On a number of occasions Mike had told me that Senator Libous saved funding for his drug counseling program at the jail and the job he loved.

I was able to thank Senator Libous for what he had done for my brother and the community by saving the drug treatment program.

Tributes poured in for Mike immediately after his death.

The first tribute came from the people on Cary Street hours after his death.

Mike had walked down that street thousands of times and was always so friendly to the neighbors in what most would refer to as a rough neighborhood that Mike loved so much.

Neighbors from up and down the street came out in large numbers to see the ambulance take Mike's body out of his apartment for the final time. It was moving for Dad and Chris to see the love and respect the neighbors showed at this moment.

Next were the online tributes—many from coworkers that our family did not know—posted on Mike's obituary.

Here are what some of the mourners wrote as they paid tribute to a great man:

October 22, 2010

> Dear Mr. and Mrs. Phillips,
>
> I enjoyed the privilege of working with Mike as the Program Director of the Salvation Army shelter for homeless boys. Rarely have I met a more Christ-like servant and human being. His personal example of understanding, goodness, and humility inspired the entire staff and endeared him to clients and co-workers alike. I'm deeply saddened at his loss and extend my most sincere and deepest sympathies to you at losing a son at such a young age.
>
> Joseph Hein

October 21, 2010

> "Lord, as we mourn the sudden death of Mike Phillips, show us the immense power of Your goodness and strengthen our belief that he has entered into Your Presence. Amen."
>
> I loved my cousin Mike and will miss him. He was truly a good man and the closest to a living saint that I'll ever know. I will always be thankful for all the special moments that we had. I know that he has touched many lives.
>
> In 30 years, I never heard him utter a single word against anyone and I never heard another person say a single negative thing about him.
>
> Mike spent much of his time in prayer. He enjoyed writing his Gospel reflections, often times mailing his thoughts and reflections to loved ones, they were beautiful. I never had a

conversation with him, where he did not mention his love for God. He was on fire for Christ and madly in love with Him and his fondness for His mother, Saint Mary, was very apparent.

Mike loved God with all of his heart, soul, mind and strength and he was like this his entire life. When he was found this morning, he was in a position of prayer. I've never known a person like Mike. He was the closest I have ever been to a real saint. He will truly be missed. I'm certain he is with Jesus now, the one he loved with all of his heart.

Please pray for his soul and pray that God will comfort all those who loved him so very much.

I love you Mike and will miss you very much!

Jimmy Brousseau

October 21, 2010

I have been blessed to have Michael as a friend and co-worker. His sense of humor, his positivity and his genuine regard for everyone touched all who met him. He gave 100% of himself to everyone—always sharing a kind word, a smile, and a prayer. Michael saw the good in everyone. I have many, many memories of Michael that I will treasure forever. I am so saddened by his loss, but am comforted knowing he will never leave us—His love for his family, and his devotion to his work and his beliefs was always an inspiration. I know he is watching over you all now saying that it is alright. Michael will be truly missed.

Kelly Nojaim

October 21, 2010

Mike was ALWAYS willing and able to do what the good lord asked of him. Mike helped me out at my internship and answered every and all questions. Mike also gave me a rosary when I was going through a difficult time. I still have the rosary and will never forget the kindness that Mike had for me, and everyone who he came in contact with. There is no doubt in my mind that he is in heaven!

Jason Kratochvil

October 21, 2010

Anyone who met Mike Phillips met a true gentleman; a person who exemplified kindness, compassion and generosity. His intentions and actions were obviously based in his strong faith. He was conscious of not hurting others and gave hope to those who felt hopeless. He is an excellent role model of a human being. I am most fortunate to have known and worked with him. He will be missed by all who met him. My prayers and sympathies to his family.

Valerie Ann Jones-Giles

October 21, 2010

It was my privilege to have worked with Michael for a brief time. He always made people feel good about themselves. Always a kind word and a smile. He made a lasting impression on me, and I will remember him fondly. I felt that I was in the presence of a very special person when I was around Michael. My prayers are with him and his family and the many friends who will miss him so very much.

Kathleen Kimble

October 21, 2010

To Michael's Family,

I worked with Mike at the Salvation Army Youth Shelter. He was such a special soul. He will never be gone from my thoughts and prayers. He helped so many young boys in the time I worked with him. I am so saddened to hear of his departure from this life. I am positive he is at peace and with the angels for he was one of them here on earth.

Beth Putrino

October 21, 2010

I don't think I've ever met another person on this earth that was more caring, giving, self-sacrificing, kind, and the epitome of Carl Rogers, i.e., of giving "positive regard" to his clients…most people were "good eggs" in Michael's eyes and his clients… according to Michael they all did "phenomenal work"…he would always find the good in a person…and his wonderful sense of humor…I'll never forget…Michael will always hold a very special space in my heart…we all loved Michael…I am very sad he has left us but know in my heart he is watching over us…telling us "it's okay"…My sincere condolences to Mr. and Mrs. Phillips, Chris, and the rest of the family…Michael was a true gem…

Colleen Sullivan O'Neil

***

Friday evening was time for Mike's wake at Allen Memorial Funeral Home. I had not seen his body since he died.

As I looked at him in the coffin for the first time I was overwhelmed with a tremendous sense of peace and grace. Mike looked so peaceful, and his long struggle was over.

Two additional thoughts came to my mind. For some reason I thought, "Will his body be incorruptible?" and "Is Mike a saint?"

The answer I had in my mind to both of these questions was a resounding yes.

Only our immediate family and Aunt Ellen were there at this point. Rob, Chris, and I stood over Mike's coffin together. To cheer Chris up, Rob quoted my campaign theme, "Had Enough?"

He joked that Mike had "Had Enough" of this world. We all laughed.

Aunt Ellen—who was Mike's godmother—said, "Michael, you were the best person I have ever met."

A prayer group from our church came to the funeral home to lead the rosary.

Then it was time for mourners to come in and pay their respects.

I was deeply honored by the hundreds of people who waited in a very long line to pay their respects to our family.

The Irregulars were there. Of course, Flint, Julie, and Vinnie were there, but Wayne joined along with Cucci—who was battling health issues of his own and was in a wheelchair. Legge—whom we hadn't seen in years—was there as well.

The Koch sisters, who lived in town, were there with so many friends from Norton Avenue.

We were deeply thankful for how many friends of Mom and Dad came from Christ the King Church—which had closed two years previously—and the newly formed Church of the Holy Family.

Our aunts, uncles and cousins from Hornell and elsewhere journeyed to town to pay their respects for the first cousin from both sides of the family to pass away.

Chris said a few of Mike's clients were there. This meant so much.

Mom, Dad, Rob, Chris, and I truly appreciated this tremendous outpouring of support. I have thought about this in every wake I have been to since Mike passed and have tried to attend as many wakes as I can.

The next day was time for the funeral at Church of the Holy Family.

Flint, Vinnie, and Wayne were pallbearers, along with our nephews Robbie and Kevin and our very loyal and special cousin Sean Ragiel.

The two highlights of the Mass that we were all waiting for—besides the Eucharist, which is always the most important part of every Mass—were Dad's homily in the middle of Mass and Chris's eulogy at the end.

Dad had a copy of his homily typed up and saved. Here are Dad's words about Mike's life:

"On behalf of Michael's family, I would like to thank each and every one of you for the kindness you have extended to us in this time of pain and sorrow. The day Michael was born was one of the happiest days of my life. When the nurse came out and showed that little 5-pound 10 ounce bundle of joy, I was ecstatic. This past Tuesday was one of the saddest days of my life when I received that phone call from his brother Chris that Mike was dead. I rushed over to see Michael kneeling motionless in a prayerful position.

"In the natural order of life, the parents usually predecease their children. When the child dies first, we often ask why and struggle to understand God's rationale. There is a story that might help us understand more, it is about a shepherd that was tending a flock of sheep in a pasture. The sheep had grazed a long time in that particular pasture. There was a pasture on the other side of the river that was much greener. The shepherd tried many times to lead his sheep over the bridge to the new pasture. But they wouldn't follow him. So, he finally picked up one of baby sheep and carried it over the bridge and set it in the new pasture. When the mother sheep saw her offspring on the other side, she immediate led the other sheep over the bridge. Sometimes God uses our young to lead us to his heavenly kingdom.

"The gospel we selected for Michael's funeral Mass was a scene from the last judgment. Jesus said when I was hungry you fed me, when I was thirsty you gave me to drink, when I was naked you clothed me, when I was ill you cared for me, when I was a stranger you welcomed me, when I was in prison you visited me. Whenever you did this to the least of my brothers, you did it for me. Come, you are blessed by my Father.

"I couldn't imagine using any other Gospel. This was Michael, it summed up his approach to life. Michael worked as a substance abuse counselor for the last twenty years. After paying his living expenses, which were very meager, he donated the rest of his income to Catholic Relief Services to feed the poor. When he was forced to retire with poor health, he wrote Catholic Relief Services that he could no longer contribute to their cause. They wrote back and thanked him for his previous support and inform him that he was their longest large-gift contributor.

"When Michael graduated from high school, he spent two years in the Franciscan seminary in Holyoke, Mass. After spending a year at home, he returned to the Franciscan community at Covenant House in New York City, working with homeless kids. On his first visit home from Covenant House, he told me he had found his niche in life working with these young people in need. He said he didn't have the training and skills he needs to care for them, but what he could do is love them, and that is what he did.

"Michael eventually learned those skills when he returned home and continued his education at Binghamton University, while working as a case worker at the Salvation Army. For the past twenty years Michael was a drug and alcohol counselor for Broome County. When he was honored as the Counselor of the Year in 2002, he said at the ceremony that he could only accept the award on behalf of his fellow workers, who he felt made it possible.

"Michael was easy to recognize when he was walking, with the black cross on the back of his clothing. The guards at the prison he worked used to call him 'Big Mike.' Michael wore his faith on his back as his frail body shared in the suffering of Jesus. Michael prayed constantly, and he prayed daily for all his friends and relatives.

"Michael was my spiritual director; he was my mentor. We walked a lot together and shared a lot. In fact, when I retired from IBM in the early nineties, we use to walk every Sunday from downtown Binghamton to Endwell, which is about seven miles. The same distant that Jesus traveled on the road to Emmaus as he shared with the two disciples the meaning of his ministry. It was at a time when I was discerning my call to the diaconate ministry. Michael encouraged me to be open to God's will in my life. I look back at the joy I have experienced in serving God's people these past fifteen years.

"Michael had a very deep spirituality. He suffered almost constantly from his eating disorder. On one of his many visits to the doctor, his doctor shared with him that he treated many patients that had eating disorders and that they were usually quite unhappy and wondered why Michael always seemed to be so much at peace. Michael told him that every day when he woke up, he spent an hour and a half with Jesus before he left his house.

"The 1st reading was from the book of Wisdom, and it was at a time when most people did not believe in the resurrection from the dead. But we are a people of hope and believe that we do not die but are transformed into a new life.

"And our second reading from the Book of Revelation describes this new life in that there will be a new heaven and a new earth, and a holy city come down from the heavens that God will dwell in. In this new dwelling every tear will be wiped away and there will be no more pain or suffering.

"The Catholic burial Mass sums up our faith in Christ. As Michael's body entered the church, has casket was sprinkled with holy water as a reminder of his baptism. As the casket approached the altar, the crucifix was a reminder of the need to suffer, but not without hope as the casket was placed in front of the Paschal Candle, a sign of the resurrected Christ. We mourn the loss of Michael, but we need to rejoice and to celebrate the peace and the comfort he has finally achieved.

"As a final word, Michael was in the first graduating class from Seton Catholic Central High School that started together as freshmen. Their nickname was the Saints. We thought about it last night and thought it might be nice to include "When the Saints go Marching In" in our song selection. But it was too late to make the change. I would try to sing it for you, but I am afraid it would clear out the church. Oh, when the saints go marching in, oh when the saints go marching in, I want to be there in that number when the saints go marching in."

***

After Communion Cucci sang "Ave Maria" in his beautiful, powerful voice, which had entertained Mike and the Irregulars in their younger days.

Next it was time for Chris's eulogy.

He started with the words, "Love, Love, and Love"—which captured Mike's incredible love for God and everyone he met. It was a real tear-jerker and an incredible tribute.

Vinnie left the funeral in tears. He immediately jumped on a plane to help friends in another state who were struggling with depression. Mike's inspiration led Vinnie and his family to intervene for these loved ones and was a catalyst for their remarkable turnabout.

A short time later, Julie would be inspired by Mike to undertake a similar intervention with a friend with an addiction issue. It was successful.

After the funeral luncheon Flint and Wayne went down to the old Patterson Creek Bridge. As they looked near the bottom of bridge, they found the letters they had hoped to see that were engraved so long ago, "IRNA"—the Irregulars of Norton Avenue.

Mike's burial took place a few days after the funeral at Riverhurst Cemetery in Endwell, about a block away from where Flint use to live and had so many great memories with Mike.

I looked out to Main Street, where Mike had walked hundreds and hundreds of times, and said, "Mike owned these streets. He walked these streets and prayed so much."

While I wish Mike could have been healed in this life, my brother Rob reminded us that sometimes healing doesn't come on this side of heaven.

It was time for me to put my entire heart into finishing our work and winning the campaign in the incredible race we were still in the midst of.

I returned to Mike's grave shortly after his burial to pray for victory in our effort.

Amazingly, my opponent, Congressman Hinchey, wrote me a personal note of condolence after Mike died. I had learned that Hinchey's own brother died in a car accident when he was young.

My family and I were convinced we were going to win. Mike had died, but we were certain he was going to help guide us to victory.

We had a ton of incredible volunteers, signs everywhere, and all the momentum as hundreds of thousands of dollars in campaign ads poured in for both sides.

We also heard from the Hinchey camp that he thought he was going to lose. He reportedly couldn't sleep and went to church for the first time in a long time.

On Election Day, Diana and I went to vote at the polling place at the Church of the Holy Family, right by our house. I spoke to the news media afterward and asked all of our supporters to come out to vote.

When we got home, there was a huge garter snake right in front of our front porch. This gave me a bad feeling that did not subside.

After the polls closed, we gathered at the Holiday Inn in Binghamton to watch Election Night returns. I wanted so badly to win for Mom and Dad. I felt that I had let them down by letting Mike die and hoped to bring them joy by getting elected to Congress.

The early returns came in from Hinchey's home county—Ulster. Our numbers were very good—close enough to win the race overall.

Unfortunately, early returns also came in from Ithaca, home of Cornell University, and a bastion of liberalism. We were getting absolutely crushed and were in danger of not even getting 20 percent of the vote in this part of the district.

Numbers from Broome, our home county, were coming in late but very strong. Would a huge victory in Broome be enough to offset Ithaca?

I sat in a hotel room with Diana, Mom, and Dad, our campaign staff, and a few top campaign supporters and close friends.

Broome numbers coming in so strongly for us made the race very close, but they would not be enough.

I was just heartbroken looking at Mom and Dad as the results came in. I had failed in my mission to keep Mike alive and now in the congressional race.

Overall, the situation seemed devastating—losing a race we thought we had and, more importantly, losing Mike.

I went to Mike's grave a few days later with a major request: I was seeking forgiveness for forcing Mike into treatment and all the suffering that ensued.

As I prayed before Mike's grave, I was overwhelmed with a tremendous sense of peace and grace. I felt that Mike was telling me I was forgiven, and that everything would be alright for me and Diana in our life and future.

There would be more graces and blessings from Mike's life in the days ahead.

Tom Gallagher, or "Gals," Mike's friend from high school who palled around with the Irregulars, learned of Mike's death and dedication to

Catholic Relief Services. Tom had become a leading writer in national Catholic circles.

Tom called a family friend of his from Binghamton named Bill Canny who was a graduate of the old Catholic Central High School and an executive at CRS.

This got the ball rolling, as CRS contacted the *Catholic Sun*, the Syracuse Diocese's newspaper. A reporter named Janika Barnes contacted our family and did a beautiful front-page article on Mike's life, entitled, "His Life is a Lesson," which I will reprint at the end of this chapter.

Bill Canny also came to visit my parents to pay condolences on behalf of CRS, which Mike loved so much and did so much to support.

The meeting was in Mom and Dad's living room, and it was deeply moving. It was surreal to think that a CRS executive was in their home, and that he was so kind.

One of the many hard jobs after Mike's death fell on Dad's shoulders. He had to write the girls Mike had met at the Westchester County eating disorder clinic who had become his pen pals. They loved Mike so much, and it must have been very hard for them to get the letters about Mike's death from Dad, and so hard for Dad to write the letters.

Thankfully, Diana's pregnancy continued in the months following Mike's passing. As soon as we knew we were having a boy, we decided to name him after Mike.

Diana was in labor on May 28, 2011. After nearly twenty-four hours of labor, baby Michael was born.

When I looked up and saw the clock on the wall, it was 5:07 p.m.

Seven months had passed since Mike had passed away. Mike had called Chris around 5:00 p.m. the day he died to say that he was not feeling well. When Chris arrived at 5:15 p.m., Mike had passed away. Did Mike pass away at exactly 5:07 p.m.?

It was amazing. As with the births of our other two children, we were overwhelmed by God's grace. We felt Mike's presence in an incredible way at this special moment.

We thought a lot about Mike during the birth of our next son, Martin, in January of 2013, because his due date was near Mike's January 9 birthdate.

Our son Martin was born on January 16 after a very difficult labor that led to an emergency C-section. We are confident Mike's prayers were with us on that day as well.

Chris and Rob both had dreams about Mike that he was in a better place.

In one dream Chris felt that Mike was actually in his bedroom speaking to him. Mike said, "One, One, and One."

Chris believes Mike was talking about the Trinity.

In another dream Chris saw Mike, young and restored—like the healthy-looking, young football player he had once been. Mike was traveling around the world to Ireland and Africa.

***

A short time after Mike passed, Chris was at a crisis team meeting at Johnson City High School, where he worked. Father Corey Van Kuren—Mike's longtime pastor at St. Paul's Church—came to the meeting to lend support for the students.

When he saw Chris, Father Corey said, "I am so sorry about your brother. He was a saint."

Around the same time Chris ran into Father Hobbes, Mike's longtime confessor and spiritual advisor. Father Hobbes had already told my father he was humbled to hear the confession of a Saint.

Father Hobbes told Chris that Mike inspired him to pray more and to be a better priest.

Flint has had some incredible stories about Mike since his passing. Whenever he needed Mike, he would go to the cemetery to talk to Mike at his grave.

A short while after Mike's death, Flint had exhausted all his housing options, and it appeared that he and his son Justin would have to be homeless—at least for a short while. After asking for Mike's support through prayer, Flint unexpectedly ran into a landlord who just happened to be walking on the street and had an affordable apartment.

My dad hypothesized that Mike knew Flint had come so far from his often ill-tempered youth and his rough break-up with his wife, and that he had gotten his life together. Mike didn't want to die, but he knew Flint would be alright without him.

When I told Flint the story, he believed what my dad had said and got upset. He said, "I wish I hadn't pulled my life together. I wish I was still messed up, so Mike couldn't have left me!"

I have written already about the amazing process of Dad uncovering Mike's journals, Dad's prayer and discernment, and the publication of *Conversations with Jesus: How an Alcoholic and Anorexic Found Deep Joy in Chris*, followed by *The Passionate Love of Jesus As Experienced by a Sinner*.

Both have brought great joy and inspiration to our family and many others.

A local AA leader read the first book. He said he had lost his faith, and reading Mike's journals caused him to regain it.

AA honored Mike posthumously at the beginning of a meeting they invited my dad to attend.

I will conclude this chapter with *Catholic Sun* article on Mike. The article was published on January 25, 2011—the Catholic feast of the Conversion of St. Paul. Once Paul saw that great light of Christ on the road to Damascus, nothing was ever the same. Nothing could replace his newfound joy.

Like that great saint, Mike was afflicted with "a thorn in his flesh," but he was made stronger by it in weakness.

And like that great saint, Mike had so many gifts, talents, and passions. By surrendering his life to God, he accomplished many extraordinary things.

Amazingly as I reached this point in my first draft of the book, I realized the date was January 25, 2021—ten years to the day the article was published.

HIS LIFE IS A LESSON

By Jennika Baines—Tuesday January 25, 2011
Sun Associate Editor

He lived in a one-bedroom apartment in Binghamton. He had no car, few clothes, but many friends. And when he died on Oct. 19, 2010, Michael Phillips was one of Catholic Relief Service's longest large-gift contributors.

On a social worker's salary, Phillips had slowly and steadily donated a total of approximately $250,000 to the charity.

Jim Lund, vice president for charitable giving at Catholic Relief Services (CRS), said that due to donor confidentiality he was not able to say the exact figure that Michael donated during his lifetime.

"But it was in the six figures," he said. "For a substance abuse counselor, it's a substantial amount of his income."

Michael didn't designate his donation for any particular area of CRS's work, Lund said. "He gave the money to care for, in his own words, the hungry in the world."

Michael's father, Deacon George Phillips, helped Michael with his monthly budgeting and his taxes. He said there was one year when Michael made around $34,000 and donated $17,000 to CRS.

"So, you take the taxes out of that and you see what he had to live on," he said.

Few who knew and loved Michael had any idea the amount of money he had donated over the years. But none were surprised. Michael was very clearly someone special.

At four- or five-years old Michael asked his parents if he could stay with his newly-widowed grandmother so she wouldn't be lonely. A few years later he talked some of his pals into volunteering to rake leaves for elderly neighbors.

As a student at Seton Catholic High School, Michael belonged to a group on the outer fringes that called themselves "The Irregulars." They were the misfits: the eccentric personalities, the new kids in school, kids that were too shy or too round to fit in elsewhere. And Michael was always finding new friends to invite into the group.

"He was a friend to the friendless," said Chris Phillips, one of Michael's three brothers.

Julie McWright grew up next door to Michael and knew all about the Irregulars. "We all came from different places of need and he seemed to know where we all were," she said.

"He loved being Catholic and he lived for Jesus. He suffered without ever complaining because all he did was love Jesus more than I could ever understand," McWright said. "Through his example of love I felt like a piece of Jesus was here on earth. That's the kind of friend I was blessed with my entire life."

She remembers Michael crying with her over high school disappointments and praying for her through illnesses of her own and in her family. The two remained close even when she married and moved to another state.

"I'll tell you right now that I was his best friend," McWright said, "but I guess some other people might probably say that, too."

One of those people is Jim Flint.

The two met in high school after Flint had transferred at the start of his junior year. It was the first day of football practice. Flint didn't have cleats and had to wear high-top sneakers in his old high school's colors. "Everyone called me a big, spoiled brat and pretty much knocked me flat on my back all during practice," Flint said.

"Afterward, Michael came up and introduced himself and we became friends. We were best friends from that day for the rest of my life."

Michael helped Flint manage his temper and allowed him to be the best version of himself without placing any expectations on his friend. "When you had a bad day, the phone would ring or someone would be at the door and it would be Michael. He just had that ability to know when people needed someone," Flint said.

Flint and Michael would walk to Mass or around the neighborhood and Michael would stop in to check on elderly or sick neighbors. He would take out their trash, walk their dog or check that they had been taking their medication. “In this day and age, most people don’t even know their neighbors,” Flint said.

When Flint was married with small children and a new house, Michael knew his friend was struggling for money. At Thanksgiving, he would come by with a card with $400 in it for Christmas presents for the children. “He would insist I take it, or he said he wouldn’t come by anymore,” Flint said.

“He was probably the most kind and generous person I have ever met,” Flint said. “I will never in my entire life meet another person like Michael Phillips again.”

Michael spent two years of discernment at the Franciscan seminary in Holyoke, Mass., but he found that his vocation lay elsewhere. He began working at Covenant House in New York City.

There, Michael counseled teenage girls who were pregnant, runaways, or trying to escape a life of prostitution. After two years, Michael returned home to work as a case worker for the Salvation Army in Binghamton.

He went on to earn a degree at Binghamton University and began working as an alcohol substance abuse counselor for Broome County Mental Health Forensic Unit. He worked with mentally ill and addicted people in the criminal justice system.

It was a job he told his father that he wasn’t sure he could handle. “He was in with all these big tough guys, but he just had a way with them,” Deacon George said. “He said, ‘I just prayed that I could love them as much as Jesus loved them.’”

In 2002, Michael was honored as Counselor of the Year.

“I’d walk with him on the streets of Binghamton and quite often some former client of his would come up and say, ‘Hi, Mike, I’ve been clean for so many years now,’” said Michael’s brother George K. Phillips. “He cared for people that no one else did.”

George said he also saw how passers-by would mock his brother for the cross he drew on the back of his clothing and for his frail body. From his 20s onward, Michael struggled with anorexia. At his healthiest, he weighed only around 120 pounds. At his sickest, his weight would plummet closer to 80 pounds. He was in and out of hospitals and treatment-centers.

But the mockery of others and the illness he struggled with only served to deepen Michael's faith. He lived in an apartment that cost him about $200 a month in rent. The furnishings were sparse, but he had a prayer bench where he would spend the first hour and a half of every day.

"He had a real relationship with Christ. He lived it daily and it wasn't fake," his brother Chris said. "He always felt you were blessed to have faith."

Michael taught his brothers how to pray to Jesus throughout the day and even encouraged them to pray for those who had been unkind to him.

His brother Robert said Michael also had a striking ability to listen.

"He was in the present moment and he was totally there listening and just empathizing and hearing you out," Robert said. "You'd talk to him and his sole focus was on affirming you and making sure you were heard and understood. I think I've never had someone listen to me the way he did in my whole life."

When he was well enough, Michael would meet with his father after the noon Mass on Sunday and walk the seven miles from Binghamton to Endwell. This was at a time when Deacon George had just retired.

"Life was changing a lot for me. I didn't know what direction I was going in," he said. Michael became his father's spiritual director and encouraged him in his journey through the diaconate.

When Michael could no longer walk that distance, they would walk shorter distances.

Eventually, he could only make it a few houses down the road. On Saturdays he would walk across the street to spend some time sitting with a widow who enjoyed the company. "Some people might say he was odd, the way he didn't have new clothes or buy things," his brother George said. "He used to say did he not get it or did the rest of us not get it. You know, 'Wait a minute, there are kids who are starving here, and this is what we're doing with our money?'"

Michael moved from his parents' house back to his own apartment in the months before he died. One night in October, Deacon George had stopped by Michael's apartment to help him with his groceries. Michael was too weak to put away the boxes and bottles, so Deacon George was putting them away for him.

"When I went to leave, he looked at me and he said, 'Dad, I love you.' And it was something that he normally said, but it was the only thing he said," Deacon George said. "I think he knew."

Deacon George called Chris to say that he should check on his brother, he didn't look good.

When Chris arrived in Michael's apartment, he found him kneeling on his prayer bench. He had died from heart failure due to his anorexia.

The night after he died, Chris and Deacon George were carrying out boxes of items from Michael's apartment to donate to Catholic Charities when a woman came up to them.

"You don't know me," she said, "but Michael changed my life."

She explained that she was a neighbor of Michael's and that she had struggled for many years with an addiction to crack cocaine. Michael would walk by her house on his way home from work and say hello to her and her daughters. After a while, he would stop and sit on the porch with them to chat. Then the chats turned to talks. One day, he brought the woman a rosary.

This, she said, was the beginning of her recovery.

The woman brought a rosary of her own that she hoped to put in Michael's casket. The one that Michael had given her, she said, she would keep with her the rest of her days.

XX.

A MIRACLE AND CONTINUING MIKE'S MISSION

I CAN'T TELL YOU HOW MANY people referenced the "His Life Is a Lesson" article to me through the years.

Time and time again when I've introduced myself, people often link me to my father, Deacon Phillips, and then say, "I still remember that article on your brother. It was amazing. What an incredible person!"

A number of people close to Mike have passed away since his death. These include the widows Mike ministered to; Julie's mom, Mrs. Trasolini, whom Mike prayed for so much; the majority of our beloved aunts and uncles from our Hornell roots; and three beloved cousins: Martha Lyon, Greg Phillips, and Jimmy Brosseau, whom Mike was so close to.

Julie's mom's death was emotional for us all in that it came only a little over a year after Mike's passing on an amazingly similar beautiful fall day.

At the funeral home, when I reached Julie in the receiving line at her Mother's wake, she was overcome by emotion and said, "Your brother Mike is holding me up right now."

Two Irregulars—Danny Cucci and Steve Legge—have also passed.

In January of 2013 our family received news that Dan Cucci was not doing well and was fighting for his life in the hospital.

With one of their own down, the Irregulars sprang into action. Flint, Vinnie, and Chris went to visit Cucci.

Cucci's mom told the boys, "Danny will pull through for me. He won't let me down."

Cucci's health problems were just too severe, and he passed away in January of 2013.

All I can think about was Mike and the night of the DWI. Mike made the wrong decision that night because he didn't want to let Cucci's mom down, out of love for his friend.

I finished my first draft of this book and went to a Sunday evening Mass at St. Patrick's Church in Binghamton.

I was surprised to learn that the date, January 31, was the anniversary of Cucci's passing, and the Mass was offered for Cucci.

On July 2, 2016, Mom passed away. Her heart gave out after a surgery to treat the excruciating pain she was having from osteoporosis and broken bones.

Like Mike, whose bones were severely weakened by his eating disorder, Mom's bones were cracking just by coughing due to her osteoporosis.

I had the honor of giving Mom's eulogy.

The theme of my talk about her life was centered around the lesson she had told Mike, which he had repeated to me.

I told the congregation, "I can still picture Mike beaming around the kitchen table, saying Mom taught him that the purpose of life was to know, love, and serve God, to find some happiness in this life and eternal life in the next.

These were the words that nuns taught Mom at St. Ann's School so many years ago. And these were the words that made Mom and Mike saints.

Mom came to know God through her own suffering and perseverance and to share God's love with everyone she knew.

The Binghamton Press found her Mom's life interesting because she did so much service and decided to feature her for their special column, "A Life Remembered."

The title of the article was "The Little General Put Faith and Family First." It was a moving tribute to my mom and the joy she brought into this world despite her hardships.

Mike knew Mom never got the recognition she deserved. He would have been proud—or might I say he was proud looking down from heaven?

I read the article about Mom to my AP US history class, and they gave Mom a rousing ovation for a life well lived.

We have missed having Mike and now Mom raising our three boys, but we know they are looking out for us during good times and bad.

Mike and Mom would have been so proud of Diana when she dressed Martin up in the greatest Halloween costume ever—"The Little Pope." Martin was the spitting image of the actual pope on that memorable day.

In 2022 our sons Martin and Michael's teams both won championship games at Maine-Endwell Little League on different levels on the same night in extraordinary fashion—with Martin scoring the winning run after we had been down ten runs. I thought about Mike watching me on those lazy summer afternoons playing for American Legion Post 80.

George—who loved his Uncle Mike so much when he was little—has been a fantastic soccer star. In a game last season against our archrival, Chenango Valley, George scored a walk-off overtime goal in dramatic fashion while playing with cracked ribs.

I was really nervous that night because of George's ribs and wore Mike's old green Saints football jacket with the cross on it to help me feel Mike's presence.

After the game, Flint embraced George in the parking lot. All I could think was that this was the place where Flint and Mike met so many years before, after their first football practice together.

I'm confident Mike continues to pray for our three boys as well as Rob, Flint, and Julie's children and the many family and cousins from his Hornell days he loved so very much.

As I worked on publishing this book, Dad raised a powerful question about Mike's extraordinary life:

Should an investigation be opened up in the Catholic Church into Mike's life for sainthood?

Mike's became such a holy, Christ-centered, and sanctified man through his life of suffering and love. I have no doubt he is a saint.

It is very humbling to think of my brother as a saint, but I know he was.

I consulted with several priests and Mike's old friend, Tom Gallagher, who had worked on Mother Teresa's process for sainthood.

Could Mike—with his eating disorder—still be declared a saint?

Tom explained to me that many great saints in history were "off," or may have suffered from mental illness by today's standards.

For each person—even those with mental illness—there still needs to be a path to holiness. Mike followed this path with his whole heart.

This gave me confidence to move forward.

I set out on a journey to speak with as many people I could about Mike's life, and I asked them the following question, "Did Mike live a life of heroic virtue, and do you believe this life should be investigated by the Catholic Church for possible sainthood?"

The response was an overwhelming and an enthusiastic yes.

My conversations with those who knew Mike—many of whom I had already interviewed for the book—were humbling and deeply moving.

But there were amazing new stories and insights as well. Diane Hiller—Mrs. Fertig's daughter—gave a beautiful testimony about Mike's tremendous outreach during her son Ryan's battle with cancer.

Mike got several religious medals blessed and gave them to Ryan, whom he prayed so much for. Thankfully, Ryan made a full recovery.

Every year in my classes, I talk to my students about Mike's life on the anniversary of his death.

In 2021, two of my fifth grade students—Bridget Hayes and Elsa Siegers—wrote unexpected, beautiful letters of sympathy to me about Mike after I told his story. Both of these young girls, in their own way and with sincere hearts, beautifully professed that Mike was a saint.

In all, I prepared fifty-five letters and documents for the Diocese of Syracuse, headed by Bishop Douglas Lucia, to review.

They included Mike's writings, testimonials from his obituary, his award as Broome County Drug Counselor of the Year, his being honored posthumously by Alcoholics Anonymous, and many other letters and stories that demonstrated Mike's life of heroic virtue.

I felt like an attorney making the case on behalf of my client. I was confident that I was bringing together a slam-dunk case about an amazing Christian man who continues to inspire so many.

Our cousin Patty Phillips brought forth the most amazing story of all. In the early 2000s she was a single mom with a three-year-old son named Christopher.

Since Christopher's birth she had had chronic hip pain. Doctors had said it was related to inflammation during pregnancy, but they could find no cure.

Mike visited Patty at her home in Syracuse with my brother Chris. They prayed with Patty, and Mike laid his hands on Patty's hip in a few moments of intense prayer.

Nothing seemed to happen at that moment. Mike and Chris returned to Binghamton.

That night Patty was putting her son Christopher to bed. She complained that the pain in her hip was agonizing.

Christopher said to her, "Mom, that man prayed with you. You have to believe."

Patty closed her eyes and imagined Mike praying on her. She immersed herself fully into the moment and believed that through Mike's intercessory prayers she could be healed. That moment, the pain stopped and never returned.

Patty is adamant that her healing came through Mike's prayers and is ready to present her case to the Catholic Church.

She strongly believes—as Father Corey Van Kuren wrote so beautifully in his foreword to this book—that two incredibly strong spirits existed in

Mike at the same time: the spirit of the horrible eating disorder and the spirit of the Holy Spirit and Jesus that miraculously healed her.

I absolutely believe that what happened to our cousin Patty through Mike's prayers and the power of God was a miracle. And I am hopeful that more are to come.

With Patty's amazing story and so many other powerful testimonies gathered, I knew I had done everything I could to bring together incredible aspects of Mike's life of heroic virtue, and I presented our documents to the Diocese of Syracuse for review.

In May of 2024 I had the honor of meeting Joe Hein during a talk at the Vestal Library. Hein was Mike's program director at the Salvation Army, and he had written so beautifully about him in the comment section of his obituary, which I have already shared.

In what was for me a transcendental moment, Hein glowingly spoke about my brother. He said he never met someone who was so Christlike toward the young people he worked with and his co-workers.

Hein explained that he was also a Protestant minister and that he had talked about Mike many times through the years in his sermons, citing him as an extraordinary servant of God.

A few years before Mike passed away, Hein said he happened to be driving near Mike's neighborhood in the middle of the night.

He saw Mike with his old jacket and homemade cross on the back, and he knew exactly what was happening: Mike was going to see someone in need.

I can picture Mike walking briskly with his green Saints football jacket with the cross on the back, thinking and praying how he could help save one someone who was on the brink.

Like the Good Shepherd who left the flock to find that one lost sheep, Mike was out in the middle of the night to reach that one soul.

The decisions made by others at critical moments shape all of our lives.

Aunt Gert's decision to take my mom and her sisters in after her own mother left her brought Mom to Hornell, where she would meet Dad.

Mom's decision to ask Dad to the dance in junior high school set the stage for their fifty-six-year marriage.

Dad's decision on the train that night to leave a secure job working for the Erie Railroad for the uncertainty of college at Alfred eventually led him to move to Endicott for his job with IBM.

Mom and Dad's decision to put their whole lives into the Church and continually sacrifice for others opened the door for Mike to develop his own incredible life of faith and charity.

Henry and Mary Trasolini's decision to buy a house on Norton Avenue resulted in Julie and Mike's amazing friendship.

Sister Michelle's car accident led her to lack the energy to run a traditional class and instead do meditations that transformed Mike's relationship with Jesus.

The fight Jim Flint got into in the hallway at Union Endicott and his parents' decision to send him to Seton resulted in his and Mike's incredible friendship, the creation of the Irregulars, and so much more.

Father Bruce Ritter's talk at Seton Catholic Central caused Mike to want to work at Covenant House and join the Franciscans.

On top of these decisions by others and important moments, there were the thousands upon thousands of Mike's own free-will decisions that shaped his life.

There were some poor decisions, especially during his Irregular Days, but many, many more good ones, until virtually every single decision and every second of his life was focused on his love for Jesus and his life as a Christian.

Mike kept no money for himself, had very few clothes, which were mostly worn and old, and had no car. He never traveled outside the Northeast, except for his trip to Kansas with Flint and a childhood car drive to vacation in Florida with Mom, Dad, Rob, and Chris. He never flew on an airplane. He didn't have a car, cell phone, or computer.

As Paul wrote in 2 Corinthians 12—the passage about the thorn in his side, which meant so much to Mike, "When I am weak, I am strong. My power is made perfect in weakness."

In so many ways Mike was so incredibly weak. His weight was 100 pounds or less for twenty years. He suffered the physical, mental, and emotional anguish of anorexia.

And yet he was so strong—stronger than any of us could have ever imagined.

Few have loved their family, friends, clients, work, and faith more.

Few have prayed and called on the name of Jesus more.

Few have had a greater passion and sympathy for the unborn, the world's poor, and the salvation of souls.

Few have detached themselves more from things of this world to sanctify their own souls.

And when he was at his worst moments and suffering during hospitalization, he still ministered to and was such a joyful spirit for both the nurses who served him and the girls at the eating disorder clinic. They loved him so much.

One might say he wasn't successful in overcoming his eating disorder and living a long life.

But the abuse and the eating disorder it caused—that great thorn in his side and great suffering—made everything else possible, as Mike allowed God to work through him in his great brokenness.

As Garth Brooks wrote in his beautiful song, "The Dance," "I could have missed the pain, but I'da had to miss the dance."

The pain in Mike's life was so awful, but the dance was more beautiful and extraordinary than you could ever imagine.

I hope I have done justice in bringing together the incredible story of his life.

Julie said something profound to me: that Mike actually found great joy in his suffering. He became so close to Jesus. He was in solidarity with the world's poor and so many other suffering people.

The pain led to this amazing life for others in which he accomplished so much more in forty-eight years than almost anyone could accomplish in a much longer lifetime.

The goal—and really the only goal that matters—is to make it to heaven.

His *Conversations with Jesus*, spiritual writings, donations to CRS, friendship with the Irregulars, and his outreach to prostitutes and homeless kids on the streets of New York, kids separated from their parents at the group home, drug addicts in jail, widows, and the hungry in the world in Africa were all truly part of a life of heroic virtue.

I still believe one of the most amazing parts of Mike's life was that no one maximized his time more. Virtually every single minute of every single day, Mike was either ministering to another person or praying.

Happiness came for Mike through Jesus—not material things, fame, wealth, or worldly pleasures.

My brother Mike Phillips was the happiest and most successful person I ever met. There was sorrow mixed into his life with his eating disorder and abuse. But the joy and happiness that radiated from him during so much of his time on earth and that he got from loving God and others is just beyond words.

Mom was correct about her son's happiness—what she focused on the moment he died. She said, "He was a happy person." Mom had sent him on the path to know, love, and serve God—a path he embraced like few others.

Chris was also correct. Fundamentally, Mike's formula was simple: Love, Love, and Love.

It has been so exhilarating writing about my brother's amazing life. I have journeyed back to walk in his footsteps—the footsteps of a spiritual giant the guys at the jail called "Big Mike." I have felt the great love of Christ that was the core of Mike's life, that transformed him and touched so many other lives.

Fundamentally, Mike was a saintly man with a deep, deep personal relationship with Jesus, a man Jesus empowered to be a spiritual warrior and great champion for the least of these.

Mike would discount all of this praise. He would say it was simply Christ working through him.

All who were blessed to know him saw a glimpse of Christ's suffering through Mike, and we saw Christ's great love through Mike as well.

I believe the great joy our friends and loved ones feel from Mike's life is the power of the Resurrection of Jesus now seen in Mike's life after death.

The thorn in Mike's side is long gone now.

That great Apostle Paul, who talked about the thorn in his side, also told us that nothing would separate us from the love of God, not even death.

The pain, suffering, and sadness Mike felt on earth have been fully replaced by God's grace and glory.

Dad closed his eulogy for Mike with that great song from high school: "Oh when the saints go marching in…how I want to be in that number… when the saints go marching in."

I am fully confident that Mike is in "that number"—with the saints in heaven, now and forever.

I believe Mike did have conversations Jesus.

It may not have been a voice from heaven, but it was at least a profound experience of prayer.

The angel said to the women at Jesus's tomb, "Why do you look for the living among the dead?"

Mike's spirit is fully alive and stronger than ever. I know he is now with the Communion of Saints—marching and praising God.

He lives on through his *Conversations with Jesus*, his writings, and the many lives he touched.

Now you know Mike's remarkable story. Thank you for taking time to read this book.

Mike's mission is now your mission and my mission.

It's pretty simple, really.

It is the message the nuns taught my mom at St. Ann's School so many years ago, the one she shared with Mike.

To know love and serve God.

Mike did it better than anyone I have ever met.

***

If you have been inspired by reading this book, please consider helping us with our mission.

We need your help distributing books. We are donating books to people who might be inspired by Mike's life, including those in jail and prison, those struggling with addiction issues, and those struggling with eating disorders.

You can donate on our website: www.HisGraceisEnough.org

Donations can be mailed to:

His Grace is Enough

PO Box 24

Endicott, NY 13761

Also we would love to hear stories about how Mike and his book have impacted your life.

Please email us at: testimony@hisgraceisenough.org.

Finally, our cousin Patty is certain Mike's prayers led to her miraculous healing.

We are sure Mike is looking to help out with more miracles. Feel free to use our prayer below.

Remember what Patty's three-year-old son, Christopher, said: "Mom, that man prayed with you. You have to believe."

Prayer Requesting the Intercession of Mike Phillips

> Mike Phillips, you dedicated your life to Matthew 25, serving "the least of Jesus's brothers and sisters."
>
> You loved God with your whole heart and soul, and you saw Jesus in every person you met, including family, extended family, friends, young people in need, those in jail, addicts, those

with eating disorders, widows, the unborn, and the poorest of the poor in the world.

You loved receiving Jesus's unconditional forgiveness in the Sacrament of Confession and Jesus's Body and Blood in the Sacrament of the Eucharist.

When times are difficult, help us to remember that God's yoke is easy and his burden is light if we turn to him as you did.

Help us to love God and others as you did.

Help us to pray the Jesus prayers you prayed so much:

"Lord Jesus Christ—Have Mercy on me a sinner," and "Jesus, I Love You. Save Souls."

In the name of Jesus, I ask you, Mike Phillips, to please pray for the following intention:

You struggled with a thorn in your flesh but kept loving.

Help us to always remember that "His Grace is enough," as you did.

Amen.

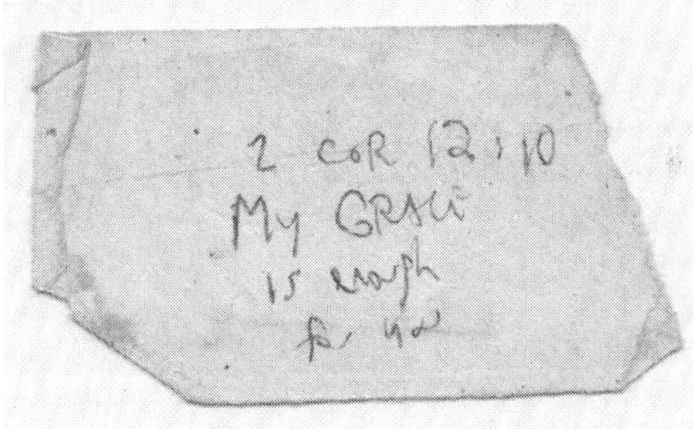

2 Corinthians 12:10: "My Grace is enough for you."
Mike wrote this for me. It described his struggle with his eating disorder and amazing Grace he found. After my wedding ring, it is my most prized possession. Verse 9 actually references, "My Grace is enough," while verse 10, another favorite of Mike's, states, "when I am weak, then I am strong."

ABOUT THE AUTHOR

George Phillips grew up in Upstate New York—14 years younger than his brother Mike. He obtained degrees from Villanova University and the University of Notre Dame and has taught high school, middle school, and community college. His teaching career includes work in inner city schools and a maximum security youth detention facility. George also served as an aide to Congressman Chris Smith, has been a candidate for United States Congress, and has done work for the Jack Kemp Foundation. He continues to reside in Upstate New York with his wife Diana and their three sons George, Michael, and Martin. His brother Mike has and continues to have an incredible impact on his life.